The TAO of MARTHA

Other Titles by *New York Times* Bestselling Author
JEN LANCASTER

Bitter Is the New Black

Bright Lights, Big Ass

Such a Pretty Fat

Pretty in Plaid

My Fair Lazy

If You Were Here

Jeneration X

Here I Go Again

The TAO of MARTHA

My Year of LIVING, or Why I'm Never
Getting All That Glitter Off of the Dog

JEN LANCASTER

 New American Library

New American Library
Published by the Penguin Group
Penguin Group (USA) Inc., 375 Hudson Street,
New York, New York 10014, USA

USA | Canada | UK | Ireland | Australia | New Zealand | India | South Africa | China

Penguin Books Ltd., Registered Offices: 80 Strand, London WC2R 0RL, England
For more information about the Penguin Group visit penguin.com.

First published by New American Library,
a division of Penguin Group (USA) Inc.

First Printing, June 2013

REGISTERED TRADEMARK—MARCA REGISTRADA

LIBRARY OF CONGRESS CATALOGING-IN-PUBLICATION DATA:

Lancaster, Jen, 1967–
The tao of Martha: my year of LIVING; or why I'm never, ever getting all that glitter off of the dog/
Jen Lancaster.
p. cm
ISBN 978-0-451-41763-3
1. Lancaster, Jen, 1967–   2. Authors, American—21st century—Biography. 3. Stewart, Martha—
Influence. 4. United States—Social life and customs—21st century—Humor. I. Title.
PS3612.A54748Z46 2013
814'.6—dc32
[B] 2013002071

Printed in the United States of America
1   3   5   7   9   10   8   6   4   2

Set in Cochin
Designed by Spring Hoteling

PUBLISHER'S NOTE
Penguin is committed to publishing works of quality and integrity. In that spirit, we are proud to offer
this book to our readers; however the story, the experiences, and the words are the author's alone.

While the author has made every effort to provide accurate telephone numbers, Internet addresses,
and other contact information at the time of publication, neither the publisher nor the author assumes
any responsibility for errors, or for changes that occur after publication. Further, publisher does not
have any control over and does not assume any responsibility for author or third-party Web sites or
their content.

For friends, old and new,
and for the divine Miss M (she knows why)

C·O·N·T·E·N·T·S

PROLOGUE 1

1. RESOLVED 9

2. GET IT TOGETHER ALREADY 21

3. LET US NEVER SPEAK OF THIS AGAIN 33

4. THE TAO OF STEAK KNIVES 43

5. THANK YOU, EASTER BUNNY, BAWK BAWK! 57

6. THE NEW GIRL(S) 65

7. MY CAT FROM HELL 77

8. MUCH ADO ABOUT DIRT 87

9. I NEVER PROMISED YOU A ROSE GARDEN 97

10. ZUCCHINI RICH 115

CONTENTS

11. I Never Promised You an Organic Garden, Either 127

12. Baby, You're a Firework 135

13. Put a Bird on It 157

14. The Ambien Diaries 171

15. Banana Grabber 191

16. My Kingdom for a Crock-Pot 203

17. Every Day Is Halloween 221

18. Trick or Treat! 245

19. Living, Zombie Style 255

20. Gobble, Gobble 269

21. Not Semihomemade 281

22. I'm Aware Now, Damn It 293

23. And Then We Came to the End 315

Acknowledgments 333

Life is too complicated not to be orderly.

—Martha Stewart, *Harper's Bazaar*

. . . .

Martha, you're making us all look bad.

—Every Other Woman in America

The TAO of MARTHA

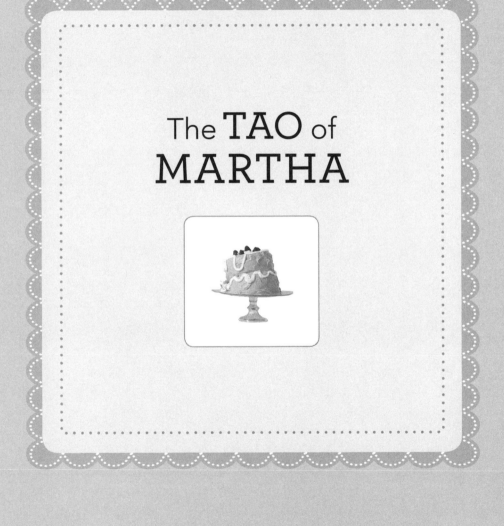

"*You think Martha Stewart shoves her clutter in a gun cabinet?*"

I clamp my lips together, saying nothing in response as my husband, Fletch, points to the pile we just unearthed. He's not smug; rather he's amused, but the difference doesn't much matter.

Despite his having finished his army tour of duty seventeen years ago, Fletch's bearing is still distinctly military. He's practically standing at attention, sporting his fresh short haircut, shiny shoes, heavily starched gingham oxford, and flat-front khakis. I squirm under my meatball-stained workout shirt and yoga pants, with bonus unwashed ponytail.

I'm loath to admit that he's right—I'm sure Martha would have never stuffed her countertop untidiness into the bottom of the kitchen gun cabinet in the first place.

Martha probably doesn't even *have* a kitchen gun cabinet.

Then again, I can't imagine anyone who lives on the grid opting for a kitchen gun cabinet.

The only reason we currently possess this handy fridge-adjacent firearm storage is that it came with the place. The previous owner was a retired naval officer and huge military history buff, so the house once showcased many of his treasures. (We're presently hanging our Christmas stockings on the fireplace hooks that used to hold a cavalry saber.)

He erected a set of glass-front locked gun cabinets. Why he felt the breakfast nook was the best place to display his Enfield musketoons, I can't say.

Maybe he was a Civil War reenactor?

Maybe he was paranoid?

Or maybe he simply enjoyed gazing at his artfully lit and secured vintage weapons stockade over eggs Benedict?

Personally, we moved from our sketchy Chicago neighborhood to the northern burbs specifically so we *didn't* have to eat breakfast fully armed, but who am I to judge?

Plus, the old owner installed a new cedar shake roof and a dual-zone HVAC system, so in no way is the gun cabinet indicative of other instances of poor judgment. Rather, it's just a tiny anomaly and gives the place a bit of character. At some point, I'm going to convert it to a china cabinet, so it's totally fine.

Of course, I've been saying that for more than a year now.

I tell Fletch, "The good news is that I found my recipe."

Seriously? I've been tearing the house apart for three days looking for this one cookbook that contains the best Bolognese sauce recipe on the planet. The reason I couldn't just buy another copy or find a duplicate online is that all my notes are handwritten in the margin. Although the recipe itself is stellar, the tweaks I've figured out along the way are what make it legendary. (The mortadella must have pistachios, okay? *Must.*) We're throwing a post-Christmas, pre–New Year's dinner party on Thursday, and without this recipe, I may as well open a can of SpaghettiOs and call it done.

Fletch gingerly picks through the other items I've unearthed in the cabinet. He waves a handbag at me. "You felt the gun cabinet was the best place to stash this purse?"

I can't help but admire the gorgeous pea-green leather with contrasting chocolate trim. "Show a little respect. That's a Chloe bag. Got it for seventy-five percent off at Nordstrom. You know how hard it is to snag a deal like that? Please. You'd have an easier time finding a unicorn or a professional athlete who hasn't banged a Kardashian. Point is, I've been meaning to have it reconditioned, so I brought it downstairs."

"When? Six months ago?"

I nod and he sighs, moving on to the next item in the pile. He reads a slip of paper. "And your prescription for blood pressure medication?"

I press my hand to my heart. "Huh. That would explain my racing pulse."

He peers down at a couple of orange packets. "What do we have here? Let's see, not one but *two* overdue parking tickets. How old are these? We haven't lived on Altgeld for three years!"

I shrug. "I was busy."

He frowns as he examines a rather important-looking letter from our accountants. "Help me understand why you wouldn't want to, say, store these items in the proper place. Walk me through the process where you said, 'Yes, the gun cabinet is the perfect repository for every random bit of crap to ever pass through our kitchen.'"

In my defense, it's not like Fletch married me for my organizational skills. Hell, when we got together in college almost two decades ago, I didn't even have a dresser, so all my stuff lived in piles along the walls, kind of like a nest. Sure, the chaos and disorder made him twitchy, but let's be honest: I was a lot cute (and a little easy) back then. It's not like I roped him in by pretending to be tidy at first. He knew what he was getting into the first time he ever tripped over a tower of my shoes.

What's important to note is that over the years, I've upped my household game considerably. Seriously, if Martha Stewart herself were to step inside my home right now, she'd give my empty counters and the pristine baseboards two thumbs up. Maybe I haven't quite managed to shower yet today, but it's because I've been busy cleaning. Due to my efforts, the hardwood's shiny, the windows sparkle, and the granite glows. Plus, Martha would never find a mess in my sink, because I can't sleep in a house where the dishes are dirty, even if it means scrubbing lipstick off of champagne glasses at three thirty a.m. while half in the bag.

Because I share my home with a number of pets who have no problem besmirching a Persian rug, I own three vacuum cleaners, not counting the Shop-Vacs, which brings the total to five, half a dozen types of mops, and a professional-grade RugDoctor to address such indiscretions.

Of which there are many.

Yet my dirty little secret is that the place seems immaculate because I shove everything into cabinets, drawers, and closets to keep it looking that way. Today's foray into gun cabinet storage?

So *not* my first rodeo.

The worst of it all is located in my nightstand, which Fletch has dubbed the Drawer of Shame. Again, because I live with fragile creatures predisposed to swallowing anything they can get their paws on, I'm insane about scuttling potentially dangerous items out of sight.

The Drawer of Shame is a big, knotty mess of choking hazards like used dental floss and old hair bands, interspersed with free-range antacids, uncapped, half-chewed lip balms, pretzel wrappers, and eight thousand tubes of whatever was the big new antioxidant eye cream six months ago. Whenever I reach for one item, the whole lot comes out, too.

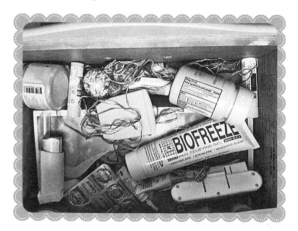

The thing is, all my drawers and closets are disgraceful, much to the hyperorganized Sergeant Fletcher's chagrin. Open the spice cabinet and it rains bottles of oregano, garlic powder, and artisanal salts. Crack the drawer next to the kitchen desk and scores of empty plastic grocery bags will explode as though being shot from a cannon. And my closet? Let's just say it's a testament to single right sneakers, solo socks, and a disproportionately high number of meatball-stained workout tops.

Yet, honestly, I'm fine with the behind-the-scenes chaos, because I've been busy with personal growth.

Okay, that's a lie.

I might be a *tiny* bit lazy when it comes to organizing. But when I consider the process of getting organized, I feel overwhelmed. I *know* that my desk is filled with antique Jolly Ranchers and dead batteries and ten-year-old business cards. I'm holding on to garbage, essentially. I definitely don't have the hoarder mentality, where I can't possibly live without my broken stapler or the gas bill I paid two addresses ago, though. If I could miracle that shit out of existence with one wrinkle of my *Bewitched* nose, I'd be on it in a second. I have zero emotional attachment to crap, and I'm not holding on to things simply because they give me All the Feels.

Rather, there's so much else I'd prefer do with my time, like drive to the city to have lunch with my girlfriends, or shop for antiques, or hang out in the TV room with Fletch and the dogs, who are perpetually draped across our laps. And are you aware of how many good books were published *this year alone*? Plus, I don't want TMZ to go out of business because no one's visiting poor Harvey Levin's site, and if I stopped paying attention to the Real Housewives, they might cease to exist. I can't have that on my conscience; hasn't poor Taylor Armstrong been through enough?

My point is that everything looks superneat and clean, largely because I'm always stashing whatever crap accumulates. Maybe what's beneath the surface is a wreck, but SFW? Having cluttered closets and disorganized drawers is like wearing a ratty bra under an awesome party dress—no one who hasn't pledged lifelong devotion to me in front of

God and the Nevada Gaming Commission is ever going to see it, so it doesn't matter.

Suddenly I remember why I stowed all that junk in the bottom of this particular cabinet in the first place; back in August, my college's alumni magazine came here to take pictures of me because they wanted to showcase what an amazing, accomplished, savvy, and successful professional author I'd become.

(Pretty sure I'm editorializing on Purdue's intent. What's more likely is they opted to feature me, the quintessential eleven-year-plan-only-to-finally-graduate-with-a-C-average student, because they thought that in addition to writing books, I might also write them a check.)

(They were not wrong.)

My point is, I wanted clear countertops in the pictures, so I shoved the pile of important items I'd been housing on the kitchen desk and then promptly forgot any of it ever existed.

So, to answer Fletch's initial question, no, I'm sure Martha Stewart would *not* stuff her clutter into the gun safe. But that's not because I'm Martha-bashing.

Far from it, in fact.

I worship Martha Stewart.

I see her as our nation's overachieving older sister. Like, I might resent her a tiny bit, but mostly I'm in awe of how she makes everything look so damn easy. Whenever something goes awry in my house, we seem to invoke her name, e.g.:

"I wonder if Martha Stewart has to chase her asshole cats off the appetizer buffet?"

"I wonder if Martha Stewart spends four hundred dollars and an entire summer fertilizing a garden, only to end up with two anemic tomatoes and an unholy army of slugs?"

"I wonder if Martha Stewart rights the crooked mirror in her dining room with a wad of chewed Dentyne?"

"I wonder if Martha Stewart's bourbon chocolate pecan pie is both so liquid and so boozy that it's technically a cocktail in and of itself?"

"I wonder if Martha Stewart's guests are greeted at the door with her sweating, crying, and shouting, 'Here's a recipe; get to work or we're never eating Thanksgiving dinner!'"

I live for Martha and her perfect little universe, but outside of cooking, I've yet to find a way to incorporate her processes into mine. I mean to, of course, but . . .

Fletch crosses his arms and leans back against the counter. Gently, he asks, "Can you at least agree that being organized might take less effort than being disorganized?"

To Fletch's credit, he's not one of those guys who'll bitch about his wife's wrongs and never try to right them himself. I see those asshat husbands on shows like *Dr. Phil* all the time. The guys will be all, "My wife doesn't do X, Y, or Z." Then Dr. Phil will ask, "Do you do X, Y, or Z?" which of course he doesn't. That's when Dr. Phil will rain down his homespun hellfire, all, "So we're going to have a donkey barbecue and you're gonna furnish the ass." What's not to love?

Anyway, I figure the key to our eighteen years together is that we don't attack each other. Tease? Yes. Mock? With good-natured relish and love. (Mostly relish.) Criticize? Never. Instead of complaining, Fletch is perpetually coming up with systems to keep everything in line.

The problem is, Fletch is an odd variation of perfectionist, and he's never encountered a project that he can't overcomplicate. Early this year, I asked him to repaint a dresser. Easy-peasy. Just slap some of the extra robin's-egg-blue paint left over from the island cabinet and there we go.

Instead, Fletch reengineered the whole thing, taking the dresser apart stick by stick before beginning a two-month-long reconstruction project that rivaled the Big Dig in scope and complexity. And suddenly my little honey-do turned into his version of Steve Austin, the Six Million Dollar Man. (He had the technology; he could rebuild it.) He kept saying, "This will stand up to a hurricane now!" Pretty much I just wanted it to stand up to the weight of a few perfume bottles, but I had mad respect for his enthusiasm.

At least, after the fact.

This is why when he organizes something, I can't keep it straight. His systems are too complex. I shouldn't require a country-of-origin spreadsheet to know the garlic is housed in the Mediterranean section of the spice rack.

"Absolutely, hundred percent agree," I tell him. "Yet it's the process of *becoming* organized that trips me up. Anyway, we can figure all that out later. Right now, we have a party to prep and I need a clean workspace."

"Got it. What can I do?" He gives me a little clap and rubs his hands together.

I point to the pile.

"Shove all that clutter back in the gun cabinet, please."

O·N·E

RESOLVED

Welcome to Holiday Central!

The candles are lit, the Christmas carols cranked, and the buffet is laden with each of my best dishes—pasta with Bolognese sauce, of course, short-rib ragout, Italian brisket with rosemary horseradish, both Caprese and kale salads, the kind of antipasto platter that would bring Mr. Frank Sinatra himself to his knees, a traditional three-meat lasagna, and a roasted-red-pepper version, because my friend Julia "doesn't like cow."

The desserts I'm serving require their own separate table, stacked high with apple pies from the Elegant Farmer and Blue Owl (an Oprah's "favorite thing"), Kahlúa cake, and ten varieties of homemade Christmas cookies.

The wine's flowing, the guests are mingling, and all the dogs are dancing around in their festive jingle-bell collars wearing perma-grins because ain't no table scrap like a party table scrap 'cause a party table scrap don't stop.

(Ten points for you if you caught *The Office* reference.)

The house itself couldn't be more festive. Each mantel is decked with piles of greenery and lights, and the tree is so big and lush, it takes up a quarter of the living room. Outside is a veritable winter wonderland, with enough LED strings to almost, but not quite, cross the border into *Christmas Vacation* territory. I'm overcome by the miasma of Fraser fir, San Marzano tomatoes, and the spicy cinnamon tang of the rose hips in all the potpourri bowls.

In the dining room, a couple of guests are laughing so hard that the walls practically shake.

This is the perfect holiday dinner party.

And yet all I can think is, *GET OUT, GET OUT, GET OUT OF MY HOUSE.*

Let's take a step back—we have wonderful friends and we love entertaining. We bought this house (gun cabinet notwithstanding) because we knew it would be the ideal place for gatherings both great and small. When we left the city, we moved away from ninety-five percent of our social circle, so every time our peeps actually RSVP yes, we're thrilled to have the opportunity to host them. Plus, tonight's extraspecial, because our buddies Beef-free Julia and Finch are up from Atlanta.

The problem definitely isn't the guest list.

The problem is that my ambitions are greater than my abilities, so in order to get this shindig together, I put in three eighteen-hour days in a row and now I'm freaking exhausted. As I watch dirty plates stack up and wineglasses multiply, I just feel weary. I don't have the energy for this, and that's so not like me.

You see, this has been a rough year. Not in a huge, job-loss, death-in-the-family kind of way. More like in a poor-little-you, *Eat, Pray, Love* fashion, except with a solid marriage and no road trips.

Starting in January, things systematically began to go wrong in a plethora of small, exasperating instances. Death by a thousand cuts.

I experienced professional setbacks and the consequences of business missteps, then a series of minor yet incredibly stupid and slightly debilitating health-related issues. (Did you know your ears are full of tiny crystals and when they slide out of place, they will *mess you up*? Believe it.)

Over the course of this frustrating year, checks didn't arrive when they were supposed to, deals fell through, and this summer we lost power practically every other week, which was an added stressor when I was attempting to meet a book deadline. Seemed like anytime something had the potential to go wrong, Mr. Murphy showed up. He and his damn law can kiss the fattest part of my ass right about now.

In February and March, we had to put down our two oldest cats, and then we lost Gus, Chuck Norris, and Odin to an escape attempt. We eventually rounded up all our stray felines, thank goodness, but it was a rough few days. Gus has especially been a jerk ever since we finally captured him again and brought him back inside, registering his displeasure on the curtains in the family room. He's all, "How ya gonna keep me down on the farm after I've seen Paree?" (Sorry, pal. Ranking mammal making the decisions here.)

I know, *I know* . . . why don't I run around Italy eating all the pizzas and gelato and then the world can feel extrasorry for me when I give myself a tummyache before I go live on the beach? (Perspective . . . perhaps I should get me some.)

Make no mistake: This is first-world bullshit right here. We've been through far worse, and I weathered those events with more grace and dignity. Possibly some swearing, but with much more aplomb.

Back when times were darkest, after we'd both lost our jobs and Fletch was racked with depression, I managed to find little ways to be happy. I had to, for my own sanity. Maybe we'd go for a walk, as much for fresh air as for a respite from the constant call of bill collectors. Yet while we'd stroll our slumtastic neighborhood and fret about our future,

I'd still stop to smell all the just-bloomed lilacs and be instantly cheered. Now I live securely in a lovely community, but instead of rejoicing in my own lilac bushes, I'll grouse about the encroaching buckthorn. That's all wrong.

So many people, including friends, are currently dealing with *real* issues—illness and job loss and problems with their children. I watch the news and my heart aches for those who are truly suffering. I haven't earned the right to throw myself a pity party, and I need to buck the hell up.

What really aggravates me is that Fletch and I have worked so hard over the past ten years and made so many sacrifices to get to this point in our lives. I'm furious with myself for allowing ridiculous little things to have an impact on my happiness.

Is it really a big deal that the customer service agent was rude to me?

Is the world going to end over a minor disappointment?

And why on earth do I give a shit about what some stranger says about me on Facebook?

Didn't I used to have a thicker skin?

Years ago, when some guy called me a fat bitch on the bus, I laughed in his face and then turned the experience into the *New York Times* bestselling memoir *Such a Pretty Fat*. What happened to me? When did I become such a delicate flower? I should, in the words of Clark W. Griswold, be whistling "Zip-a-Dee-Doo-Dah" out of my bunghole every day, but I'm not, because I've allowed little things to throw me offtrack.

Is it because I'm just so stressed over my beautiful pit bull Maisy? After meeting Fletch, this little girl is the best thing that ever happened to me. We adopted her back when I'd lost my corporate job in 2001, and her presence in my life changed everything. I fell so deeply in love with her that I became a writer in order to have the excuse to stay home with her every day. Maisy's in no way perfect herself—she's bossy, she's officious, she's spoiled, she's lazy, she defies authority, and she pouts when she doesn't get exactly what she wants when she wants it.

Pretty much she's *me*.

A couple years ago, she was diagnosed with mast cell tumors, and the oncologist gave her six months to live. Of course, Maisy's ridiculously stubborn, and you can't tell her a damn thing she doesn't want to hear (again, *hello*); ergo she's defied every odd thus far. Her doctor uses her as the best-case scenario to comfort other families with sick dogs. Yet I can't ignore that she's not strong like she was before she got sick. She had her second surgery earlier this month—this time for melanoma—and was so weak afterward that her doctor said we should hold off on new rounds of chemotherapy.

Yet the good news is, the mast cell tumors haven't returned. And since we adopted our other pit bull Libby last year, Maisy's spirits have never been higher.

Maisy adores having a mini-me and lives for an audience. She leaps out of bed every morning to roll around and scratch her back, thrilled at the prospect of a new day. And the fact that the biggest downside is that she can't yank so hard on the leash isn't the worst thing in the world. Back in the day, she could pull me over in three seconds flat. My unskinned knees don't miss that.

Yet despite all her positive progress, every time she coughs or sneezes or lingers in bed, I envision the worst-case scenario. I run to the emergency vet like people run to the store.

Because of all of the above, I just want this year to be behind us, and I figured the easiest way to do that would be to ignore the holidays. Back

when we were broke, we routinely skipped Christmas, so it's not like we'd be blazing new territory here.

Fletch was on board with me . . . until a couple of weeks ago, when he realized he wasn't. He decided instead of skipping Christmas, we were going to flip all of 2011 the bird by ending the year in style. And that's what we've done.

Now the lights are up, the presents have been exchanged, and the house is full of food, friends, and fun. It's a hundred percent festive up in here.

I should be on my knees, thanking God for all His blessings.

Yet all I can focus on is how I'm going to be stuck doing dishes until three thirty a.m.

For everyone's sake, I need to improve my attitude in 2012.

"I miss them."

"Me, too."

Fletch and I are sitting in the kitchen, drinking coffee, eating doughnuts, and bemoaning the departure of Julia and Finch. They had to take off at the crack of dawn to get down to Julia's parents' house in St. Louis.

When they arrived earlier this week, my mood was so foul that I almost ruined my own party. But it's patently impossible to not be happy in their presence. Our fine moods last well into the evening, and we're both extrachipper while watching New Year's Eve programming.

No, we didn't go out.

A word about New Year's Eve?

I would rather receive a Pap smear from Captain Hook than venture out on New Year's Eve.

I'd rather time-travel back to junior high and give a speech clad in nothing but a fez in front of the mean girls who used to hassle me on the bus.

(Quick aside? My chief tormentor now gives pedicures in a salon next to the county jail in my old hometown. Sometimes karma looks a lot like OPI's Lincoln Park after Dark.)

There's something that feels so incredibly lonely and self-defeating about all the forced gaiety of New Year's Eve, like if I'm not out there having the very best time, swilling the most champagne, tooting the loudest noisemaker, wearing the most-spangle-laden dress, then I'm somehow failing. It's not that I hate parties and frivolity—eleven years of college is proof positive of that—but I'm enough of a contrarian to balk at the notion of Mandatory Fun. I don't begrudge anyone else their merrymaking, but it's not my bag, baby, at least not on December 31. Let's see: all the amateurs who throw down only once a year, those same amateurs hitting the roads later, and hyperinflated prices for shitty service and watery drinks? Or couch time and Carson Daly?

I choose Carson. All the way.

We watch as Carson interviews people in Times Square about their resolutions. "What do you resolve for 2012?" Fletch asks. He's smirking, because he knows the only thing I loathe as much as NYE is being questioned about my resolutions, particularly by people I don't know. What do I resolve? To find a Starbucks where the baristas are less chatty.

I yell at the screen, "How about this for a resolution, Carson? I resolve to not disclose personal information about my hopes, dreams, and inadequacies on national television."

Look at them all—they're cold and it's loud and they have to pee in Porta Pottis and weirdos are using this as an opportunity to furtively press their junk against the unsuspecting. I simply don't get it. You, right there in the giant plastic 2012 sunglasses? Some pervert just tea-bagged you and you don't even know it.

And you in the sparkly dress? You're going to wake up with a stranger tomorrow morning, having received the gift that keeps on giving. (Herpes.)

How about you there, dressed as Baby New Year? A) You're going to get frostbite, and B) there's no way your wallet's not falling out of your diaper. When you're shivering your way back to the Bronx tonight with nothing but your banner to keep you warm, you'll regret the decisions that led you there.

The square is so crowded that all these dummies can barely lift their arms every time they squeal, "WOO!" at the camera.

As I mock and judge, it occurs to me that I can't recall the last time I spontaneously lifted my arms and shouted, "WOO!"

I wonder if I've done it once in 2011.

Although, as much as I have to say that I hate 2011, this year wasn't entirely worthless. In so many ways, I got my shit together. After living in a state of arrested development for most of my life, I finally buckled down, making a concerted effort to behave like an adult.

Like, I have insurance now.

So much insurance.

Everyone has auto insurance (except for anyone driving around tonight, of course), but I also invested in life insurance, homeowners insurance, a supplemental umbrella policy for what homeowners insurance doesn't cover, flood insurance, mortgage insurance, long-term disability insurance, pet insurance. . . .

I should be the happiest son of a bitch on the planet with all these levels of protection.

And yet here I am.

Welcome to Crankytown, population: me.

I wonder if, in trying so hard to be grown-up, I didn't somehow overshoot my mark. By working diligently to be my most responsible me, did I quash some of my own natural propensity for joy? Is it possible that I've lived through years that were far worse than my current season of Sorority-Girl Problems, and that I never noticed because I was a perpetually grinning adolescent?

This bears further examination.

"It's too bad no one sells happiness insurance," I say.

"Hmm?" Fletch glances over at me with a puzzled expression.

"Think about it: We have every protection known to man, yet I've still had a miserable year. If someone sold happiness insurance, I could fill out a claim and, much like Stella, get my groove back. Otherwise, why would I have paid all those premiums to Big Insurance?"

"Wasn't aware your groove was missing."

Yes. This makes perfect sense.

I continue. "Here's the thing about this year: I've failed at having an attitude of gratitude. I've not come at my life from a place of yes. I've not chosen *me*."

He gives me the whale eye. "You been watching Oprah again?"

I wave him off. "No, no, she went off the air in May. I did like her, though, but I always had some trouble really connecting with her advice. She was all, 'Live your best life!' and 'Chart your vision board!' but there's nothing actionable, you know?"

Fletch pauses Carson and his Conclave of Bad Decisions. "What is this 'vision board' of which you speak?"

I explain. "You're supposed to imagine something you want—like when I wanted to be a writer. To help me visualize my dream, I was supposed to clip out images of what inspired me. Maybe I'd have pasted pictures of Jennifer Weiner and David Sedaris and swimming pools and bookstores in between pom-poms and sparkles."

He's dubious at best. "So it's a craft project."

"No. Well, okay, yes, a little bit, if you factor in the glitter and rubber cement. But I know tons of people who said doing vision boards helped them."

"Yet even without a vision board, you became an author."

I nod. "True dat."

"Never say that again." Even Maisy manages to look disgusted with me. "Let me ask you something: How does sitting around clipping pictures from a magazine advance your goals?"

I scratch Maisy's ears while I consider my answer. Apparently I have pleased her, because she curls her toes and burrows in closer to me, forcing most of my right butt cheek off the couch.

Worth it.

I reply, "Can't say for sure, because I never tried to make one."

He snorts. "Yeah, you know why? Because you were busy actually *trying* to be a writer. You were writing. You were reading. You built a blog audience. You learned your way around nascent social media. You were putting in the effort and not just sticking pictures on oak tag."

"True da— *Ahem*. True enough."

Fletch slips into Professor Fletcher mode, and I suspect he's two seconds away from pulling out a whiteboard. "Okay, you want to be happy. You want 2012 to be a better year. What's your plan? What's going to change? What tangible thing can you do to alter your circumstances?"

"Whoa, slow down! I don't know. I haven't thought about it."

"Maybe you should."

"Oh, yeah? Your year sucked, too. Maybe *you* should think about it," I retort.

"I have and I've made a plan. Happiness guaranteed."

I can't keep the surprise out of my voice. "Really? What are *you* going to do? How are you going to manifest a better year?"

If he's got the inside track on an improved way going forward, then I'm all ears.

"I'm going to grow a beard."

"That's it? That's your home-run swing?"

"Yes. Besides, it's easier than growing a jawline. I decree 2012 to be the Year of the Beard."

I roll my eyes and click play on the DVR, getting back to Carson and the teeming, grinning masses. "Whatever."

Still, a beard's more tangible than a vision board.

So there's that.

T·W·O

GET IT TOGETHER ALREADY

We're but three days into the New Year/new beard and I already dislike both. Greatly. I was kind of hoping for some Carson Daly–induced epiphany on New Year's Eve, but no such luck. The ball dropped, we kissed each other (and the dogs), and that was it. The new year began as inauspiciously as 2011 ended.

We're currently on our fourth visit to the Restoration Hardware outlet store in Wisconsin in pursuit of replacing the funereal drapes that used to hang in our bedroom. Before Thanksgiving, I found a great deal on some discontinued curtains and figured it was high time for a more modern update.

Not only were the old drapes fussy, but they weren't functional; they were made only to frame the window. We had decent Levolor pull-down blinds for privacy and light blocking, but Nibble-y Libby and the Boredom Chews ended what should have been a long life span. Keeping the blinds open had come to require tying a system of Gordian knots, so

most often, the bedroom was dark as a tomb.

Fletch tore down the nonfunctional blinds, only to discover that the sun lights up the bedroom like the map room in the Temple of Doom every day at five forty-five a.m.

I fixed the problem by thumbtacking sheets to the window frame.

Yes, I realize that Martha would shudder at my half-assery. But it was that or rising with the roosters until we found a solution that we liked and that didn't cost as much as a used Honda.

Once we removed the old curtain hardware, I estimated that installing the new rods would take an hour, max. Which it did.

The window-covering situation became complicated only once we determined that we'd hung the rods too low and that the curtains I insisted would match the rug . . . didn't. This development precipitated the second trip to Wisconsin and a fair amount of cursing on both our parts. Then, because we'd punched so many holes in the wall, we had to patch the paint.

The old owners were ridiculously organized, and when we moved in, they essentially gave us a guide to living here. We received binders full of appliance manuals and warranties (what, you thought I was going to say "women"?), as well as a huge phone tree of everyone to call in any household situation, including services we'd never once considered, like exterior window cleaning.

Therefore, what happened next is not their fault.

They left us every scrap of extra material, like tile and carpet and wallpaper, all meticulously labeled and stored neatly. After the rods were finally hung

and the walls patched and sanded, Fletch went downstairs to find the appropriate paint. When he came back up, he was flummoxed.

"I can only find beige paint labeled 'sitting room.' This doesn't mean bedroom, does it? Maybe this is for the TV room upstairs," he said.

We opened the paint and compared. Far as I could tell, it was an exact match.

"Seems a little darker," Fletch said.

I rolled my eyes. "Come on, Fletch—who would use two almost but not quite identical shades of beige in the same house? I promise it's the same. The color will absolutely dry lighter."

Three days later, Fletch and I had to have a little discussion about promises I couldn't keep. The project continued to slide off the rails, but once we hang the last set of curtains we're buying today (because I can't count to eight, apparently), we should be finally, mercifully done.

"I bet it wouldn't take Martha Stewart two months to hang curtains in the bedroom."

Something about Fletch's invoking Martha's name causes a spark of recognition.

"Say that again," I demand.

He smooths his beard and looks apologetic. "Hey, I'm sorry. I don't mean to give you the business."

But I'm not irked; rather, I'm inspired. "No, no, about Martha Stewart—say it again."

"That it wouldn't take her two months to hang curtains?"

"Exactly!"

Fletch shrugs and goes back to sorting through the bin of reject drapes while my idea takes shape.

Okay: Right now, Martha Stewart definitely wouldn't consider the way I live my life a Good Thing. Yet that doesn't stop me from adoring her and respecting her and wanting to subscribe to her newsletter, you know?

I've been obsessed with Martha since I tried her buttercream cupcake frosting recipe. "Transcendent" doesn't properly describe this concoction, and "delicious" is an insult. Her recipe creates something that feels like cashmere and tastes like it was whipped by angels and flavored by God's own vanilla beans. Seriously, it's strip-and-go-naked kind of good.

Although I wasn't a fan of the Martha back when she went to prison, she conducted herself with such grace and dignity that she eventually won me over, and that's when I started buying her magazine and watching her show in earnest.

See, instead of curling up and dying in that situation, she made the best of it.

She made gourmet microwave dinners.

She made friends.

She made *ponchos*, for Christ's sake.

She rose to the occasion, and I can't not get behind that.

Millions of women adore M. Diddy (what the gals in the joint called her), because she can break down even the most difficult tasks into something simple and lovely and doable. I read that she doesn't own a bathrobe, which means when she rolls out of bed, she hops straight into the shower. That boggles my mind. I live in a world where pajamas have been worn to the dinner table . . . on days I wasn't sick.

I realize Martha Stewart isn't everyone's icon, but she *is* mine. I love her because instead of lording her superior skills over everyone and making them feel bad about themselves, she's out there breaking it all down for even the least talented among us. Had I thought to consult her guides, the curtain project truly would have taken two hours and not two months.

This is not to discount the Magic That Is the Oprah. Millions of women are Team Oprah over Team Martha. Actually, I believe there are only two kinds of women in this world: Martha people and Oprah people. That doesn't mean one can't have an affinity for both of them, but my theory is that every chick is more firmly in one camp than the other. The typical Oprah woman is all self-actualized and best-life-y and *Eat, Pray, Love*. The Big O seems like the kind of gal who'd insist we all spend the afternoon wearing jammy pants. And how fun would that be?!

But Martha?

She's not putting up with that nonsense, and that makes me adore her all the more. She'll tell you *what* to eat, *where* to pray, and *who* to love, and I appreciate the guidance.

I mean, I *have* a best friend; I *need* a drill sergeant.

(Related note? Were Martha and Oprah to cage-fight, smart money is on M. Diddy, because you KNOW she's a scrapper.)

On paper, Oprah trumps Martha in terms of fortune and fame and felony convictions. But if the apocalypse my tinfoil-hat-wearing husband (bless his heart) predicts is indeed coming, I have to ask myself: Do I want to follow the lady who encourages me to make dream boards for a better tomorrow, or do I want to listen to the gal who can show me how to butcher my own game hen *right now*?

I'm Team Martha, no questions asked.

After reading and loving *The Happiness Project*, I've been mulling over the idea of taking on my own project, but I don't want to be derivative. Plus, Gretchen Rubin has pursued happiness with such a systematic, analytical, scholarly approach that I could never match what she did, and then I'd be unhappier when I ultimately failed.

Yet if I were to, say, try to live my life like Martha for a year, I suspect I could indeed be happier.

I could possibly feel more like my old self.

And maybe when something truly bad does happen, I'd be better equipped to handle it.

Although I'd never out-Martha Martha, I could definitely emulate her. I could live 2012 by adhering to her dictates from various television and radio shows, books, magazines, and Internet presences. The moniker of Omnimedia isn't an exaggeration; name me a medium and she's on it. I have so much respect for her level of saturation in our society.

I wonder exactly what would happen if I were to follow her advice from A(pple brown Betty) to Z(ip-line-attached Christmas ornaments). Would my life be easier—and Fletch less twitchy—if I used her tricks to get organized?

My guess is yes.

Could my dogs be more satisfied if I fed them what she gives to her French bullies, Sharkey and Francesca, and chow chow, Genghis II?

In terms of personal relationships, might I grow closer to my girlfriends who knit and sew when I finally show some interest in their boring-ass hobbies?

Would I morph from the person who gives guests a recipe and instructs them to start cooking to the hostess who goes ballistic if someone dares wear cream to my White Party?

And would that be the worst thing in the world?

Most important, could I be happier if I were to pattern my life from her recipe?

I plan to find out.

As soon as I finish with these damn curtains.

Since I've decided to live My Year of Martha, I have to set up some parameters, like what I plan to concentrate on and how I'll measure success. My first task is to figure out what makes me happy.

So I ask Fletch.

"Can you tell when I'm happy?"

Fletch is sitting at his desk, going over bills. He swivels around in his chair all Bond-villain-style to address me. "Oh, God, yes. You're an entirely different person when you're in a good mood. You're effusive, you're chatty, and your voice goes up. You whirl around the house like a maniac and you're just, like, delighted at everything. When you're pleased, you clap like a seal. You also spend a good deal of time congratulating yourself."

I flop onto the couch across from him. "Huh. Didn't know that. What do I do when I'm unhappy?"

He strokes his chin and looks up at the ceiling while he thinks. "Your voice is flatter and you get really quiet and withdrawn. You don't sing—badly—while you're cooking. You don't bust out your patented disco dance moves like you do when you're just overcome with joy. You're less social, and you're a lot less likely to leave the house. Also? You argue with strangers."

That doesn't sound right.

"I argue with strangers when I'm happy, too. It's kind of who I am, like with the complaining. I'm often delighted to be able to bitch about something inconsequential. Like, I *live* to grouse about our postman."

He nods. "True enough. But when you complain and you're happy, you don't take the situation personally and you're just trying to be funny. So, how about this—you ruminate more when you're not happy. You don't take a perceived slight and turn it into something positive or a call to action. You fixate. You stew. You have trouble moving past the most minor thing. You're a lot quicker to escalate."

Chuck Norris saunters into the room, jumping over the pile of dogs perpetually in my wake, and settles into my lap. I knead the fur at the back of his thick neck and he purrs appreciatively. "Sounds kind of awful."

"For better or for worse, you know? Last year did a number on you. But don't worry; the beard understands," he says while lovingly rubbing his chin. (I cannot be held responsible if someone shaves him in his sleep.)

As I greatly dislike the description of Unhappy Jen, I'm determined not to let 2012 get the better of me, so I need to nail down this happiness business.

Because I've been so tuned in to what made me unhappy in 2011, I'm at a definite advantage. I simply need to take a look at everything that made me cranky and then do the opposite.

Chaos and disorganization made me unhappy last year. Like, I despise being late, yet I was delayed walking out the door at least a hundred times when I couldn't find my stupid shoes. Much as I want to imagine I'm still all cute and perpetually twenty-two years old, flighty and adorably seat-of-my-pants like I was in college, I have to admit that this haphazard way of life no longer works for me. I don't have my college metabolism; nor do I have my college capacity to thrive in disorder. I need to be deep-down organized, and not just what-looks-good-on-the-surface tidy.

The idea of living a more orderly life is seriously attractive. I suspect that Julia and Finch are so happy because they're organized. They always have a plan. Julia's a pharmaceutical rep and a mom, and if she couldn't manage all those details of both jobs, she'd never have time to take care of herself. Finch is a pilot; if he weren't meticulous and systematic in his checklists, people could die. They're poster children for lives free from chaos, and I'd do well to model myself after them.

I also feel like I spent a lot of time last year being reactive, rather than proactive. Like, the first time the power went off, we were caught completely unaware. We had to run out and buy everything—ice, coolers, flashlights, etc., and I hadn't had the foresight to keep any of my electronics charged. I hated the insecure feeling of not even being able to make a call because our mobile phones were dead and our landlines required electricity to work. (In addition? Not being able to Google to settle a stupid bet on whether Paul Michael Glaser played Starsky or Hutch is torture!) (Duh, he was Starsky.) Since then, we've made sure to be prepared, and that feeling of security is a key component to happiness, at least for me.

I spent so much of 2011 trying to act like an adult, I forgot to have fun. I wasn't silly. I eschewed irreverence. I was too mature for foolishness. Like I said, I don't remember having any hands-in-the-air "WOO!" moments last year. I imagine last year would have gone differently had I simply played more.

I enjoy the process of learning, and I didn't take many opportunities to expand my horizons last year. I spent most of 2009 and part of 2010 working on *My Fair Lazy*, and in it, I tried so many new things, like going to the theater and wine tastings and cooking classes. I kept up many of these activities long after I finished writing the book. I was in perpetual motion for the longest time and I loved it, but somehow I didn't keep the momentum going once we moved in 2011. Although I don't need to be in a classroom, per se, I definitely want to be a student again.

The above point dovetails into my next parameter—there's nothing I enjoy more than leisure time after having been busy. There's no greater feeling than getting to sit down and relax after having plowed through all my to-do items. I'm not sure I accomplished much in 2011; ergo, my downtime didn't feel like a reward.

Having once been broke, and having learned the importance of a cash reserve for unexpected expenses like multiple dog surgeries, I'd like to up our level of fiscal responsibility this year, too. I want to be less wasteful, more mindful. I hate being banged with late fees when I don't get around to paying something on time, even though I actually have the money in my account. That's unacceptable. Plus, I want to be thriftier so that I can afford to be more charitable, because I realize it's not all about me.

Speaking of charity, I spent a whole year volunteering, as I'd hoped to write a book about the experience. Although the memoir didn't pan out, I have such an appreciation for the value of extending myself, my time, and my effort. Being helpful makes me happy, in whatever capacity that may entail, so I definitely want to bring more of that to the party.

In terms of which of Martha's dictates I'll pursue, I need to narrow my focus on a few areas. I can't do everything she suggests, because that would be impossible. Since I've already established my desire for a less chaotic home, I'm definitely embracing the notions of organizing and cleaning, with a dash of decorating thrown in, because I swear there's nothing more soul-satisfying and therapeutic than rearranging a room.

And, of course, I want to make sure the four-legged members of this household are copacetic, so I'll also focus on ways to keep pets as happy and healthy as possible.

A few years ago, I was broiling naked pork chops within an inch of their lives and then slathering them in store-bought, MSG-laden barbecue sauce. Although my culinary skills have come a long way since then, I'd like to continue to evolve as a home chef, so cooking will definitely be a consideration.

I thrive when I'm around people I enjoy, so I'm absolutely going to concentrate on entertaining, with the goal of actually spending time with my guests, rather than just functioning as a glorified caterer.

Until now, I'd forgotten that when I was unemployed, I used to make jewelry and tile mosaics. Both of those activities really took me out of my own head, so I definitely want to add crafting to the mix.

Finally, and because I love a challenge, I want to conquer an X factor, meaning a yet-unnamed category. During the course of this project, I hope to blaze my own path in some activity. I'd like to see if there's some tiny niche that Martha hasn't yet conquered, and if so, I can take that opportunity to enlighten others.

I can't say what my X factor is yet, but like Justice Potter Stewart (relation to Martha? I should find out), I'll know it when I see it.

So take note, 2012—this is how it's going to play out. I'm planning to up my game in every way possible. I'll have a clean house not only on the surface, but deep down, too. Items will no longer tumble down from the farthest recesses when I open my closets. I'll work to make my home prettier and more functional, and I'll revel in the praise when guests notice all the welcoming touches at my frequent gatherings. I'll find better ways to be prepared for whatever life presents next, and I'll cap the year off with a big, festive, handcrafted Christmas.

This is going to be great!

And maybe while I'm at this whole process, I'll discover something entirely new. Perhaps I'll figure out more about who I am, or possibly I'll have some kind of epiphany about the *Living* philosophy. What if there's some greater principle that guides the whole Martha Stewart enterprise and it's waiting for me to uncover it?

Like, a Tao of Martha, if you will.

Regardless of how it happens, ready or not, happiness, here I come.

LET US NEVER SPEAK
OF THIS AGAIN

F ilm.

There are rolls of film in here.

Yet I haven't owned a camera that required film since 2002, which means I've been storing rolls of film in my desk *for almost ten years.* What the hell am I going to do with film? Does anyone even develop film anymore? I may as well try to have my Betamax repaired, or attempt to get the cathode ray tubes replaced in my console television.

Shameful.

And that's only the beginning.

My inaugural Martha project is to clean out my desk drawers. I have a book due in two months, so I figure the best place to start is where I work. Maybe if I can establish a better sense of order, my writing will go more gooder.

See?

See what's happening?

I'm mangling words because I'm currently sitting at a desk full of old film, among so many other patently ridiculous items, the highlights of which include:

- one flea collar, slightly used

- fourteen dead batteries, in various states of oxidation

- a banana hair clip

- nine Sharpies, five uncapped, all dry

- pistachio shells from the nuts I received in my Christmas stocking in 2008

- wineglass shards

- three empty rolls of Scotch tape

- one FURminator (for dog shedding)

- eight unmatched Barbie shoes and two Barbie hats

- the orange City of Chicago violation sticker placed on my fence when my terrible landlord didn't pay the water bill back in 2009

- 7,226 scraps of paper, each containing either random sums or single words like "Sockets!" that have long since lost any semblance of meaning

- an entire handful of petrified pieces of Bazooka gum that I should not ever attempt to put in my mouth again (note to self—call dentist re: loose filling)

- a free-range piece of Silly Putty, studded with something grainy (pistachio salt?)

- an ancient flip phone as well as a charger to the Black-Berry I haven't seen since 2006

- my wedding video as well as the VHS recording of my Supervision 101 class presentation in 1991 (I'm keeping these)

- two screwdrivers, both Phillips-head, one covered in unknown goo

- three sets of cat nail clippers

- my business cards from the company that laid me off in 2001

- an ATM card from when I had a bank account with X.com in the dot-com days

- fifteen Kleenex, in various stages of disrepair

- a note card I passed to my friend Stacey at our friend Sarah Pekkanen's book signing that reads: *Remind me to tell you about the dream I had where I was pregnant and didn't know it until the baby fell out. I was so happy because I realized that was why I was fat! Wait, I guess that's the whole story.*

Under all the junk, I unearth three boxes of my favorite kinds of pens, two bags of the mechanical pencils I really like, a pair of Gucci sunglasses, and $17.31 in loose change.

I also find rock-bottom, because clearly this is what I've hit.

In *Good Things for Organizing*, Martha suggests I create and stick to a simple filing system, reasoning that this will make my boss proud. Well, I'm the boss of me, and proud is not what I'm feeling right now. But maybe I could be.

I take a kitchen trash bag and start filling it with all the crap I've been lugging around from house to house. In the last two places we've lived, we've hired movers, so there's an extra level of shame in knowing I paid people to pack up all this garbage. Were they all, "Maybe they're *sentimental* broken wineglass shards"?

When airplanes crash, the NTSB arranges all the wreck's detritus on the floor of a hangar so investigators can piece together what led to this great tragedy. I do the same with my desk contents, so I can understand not only where I've been, but where I need to go.

After pondering the wreckage, I begin to sort everything into piles. Martha suggests grouping like items together, so that's what I do. My pens are in one stack, my pencils in another, as are my fifteen unopened packs of Post-its. Whoa, where did they come from? I can use those! Hey, look at this—I'm already saving money by having unearthed a lifetime supply of sticky notes.

My desk contents begin to make more sense as I sort through and categorize it all. Some of what I initially thought should be trashed will actually be useful if it's stored in the right place. Like, I can move all the pet supplies downstairs to the drawer Fletch has designated and now I won't be all, "I can't find what we use to clip the cats' nails, so I'll have to pick up yet another one."

Net savings: ten dollars.

Add that to the $17.31 I found in the drawer and I've already covered the cost of the box of color-coded file folders I bought.

What's funny is that the act of cleaning out my desk takes an hour, yet I've been dreading it for so damn many years. How much time have I wasted in fretting about organizing this instead of actually organizing? I kind of don't want to know.

I set up my desk so I can access everything I might need in the course of a workday. I place my pens, pencils, letter opener, and ruler in pretty mugs to the left of my monitor, and I keep a little box with scratch paper, a nicely scented candle, and a paperweight on the other side. My desk is small, so I take some of my book covers and photos with friends and put them under the Plexiglas protector on top of my desk, so it's still decorative, but not cluttered with actual frames.

In my left-hand drawer, I store extra pens, cords, note cards, and cough drops, and I use the top right to house my ample supply of Post-its, binder clips, lip balm, a stapler, and measuring tape, because I'm dyslexic when it comes to guesstimating dimensions and ordering on-line. (Hell, I'm still crab-walking past certain sofas because four feet is wider than I imagined it would be.) The second drawer houses infrequently used items, like extra staples and lightbulbs. And the lowest drawer holds papers, which now live in alphabetically sorted folders, and not just one teeming stack.

At no point am I euphoric while I work on this task, but the idea of opening a drawer and finding what I need is not without merit. Having my desk in order won't change the world, but it will allow me to focus more on the task of writing, especially when I have a deadline in two months.

Hey, it's a start.

I tackle my closet next, organizing footwear and maximizing the space by using those clear shoe boxes that Martha's so hot for. In fact, Martha says that in terms of storage, you need only three things: sturdy shelves, clear plastic bins, and a label maker.

Yet I did struggle with the notion of tossing out all my pretty shoe boxes with their fancy designer labels, largely because I'm shallow. How will the strangers who walk into my closet learn that I own Tory Burch sandals if I don't display her box?

I know, I *know*. Crazytown.

What finally convinced me to change is that shoe boxes aren't consistently sized and I don't have X-ray vision. Now I can actually *see* my shoes and they're in tidy stacks. Right before I hit the closet, I made a note that I needed a casual black shoe with a kitten heel, yet as I dumped out all the old boxes, I found exactly what I needed and end up saving *four times* the amount I paid for storage boxes. Perhaps I could get used to this.

During the closet reorg, I uncover tons of items I no longer wear (read: are too tight), and I'm able to make a nice donation to AMVETS.

Did this cleanup change the world? No.

Did it make it quicker for me to dress in the morning? Yes.

Will what I've given away benefit others? It will.

So not only does this progress make my life a tiny bit easier, but it spurs me on to tackle other projects.

For some reason, whoever built this house hated medicine cabinets, as evidenced by our having none. I find this deeply, profoundly annoying. For the first two months we lived here, I'd walk into the bathroom all, "Where did they keep their aspirin?"

I finally figure out that they must have stored all their toiletries in the weird little enclosure off the master bedroom. Although this closet is as tall as the door in front of it, it's only about nine inches deep, so it's filled with shelves. Frankly, I don't understand why anyone would bother with such a stupid space, but it's on the other side of the shower, so maybe it's for easier access to the pipes? (I'd have asked the old owners, but their attorney handled the closing, which was kind of a bummer. I'd have liked to know more about the gun cabinet, too.)

Anyway, I discover that this little closet is the perfect place to store all my hair-care products, of which there are many.

Many, many.

I'm perpetually buying whatever my stylist pushes on me, yet I'm also perpetually dissatisfied by whoever's cutting my hair, so I'm always switching salons. In turn, this cycle has produced quite the cache of antifrizz items.

Actually, the mini-closet is a great place to shove all assorted bits of personal detritus, and now a whole Sephora spills out every time I open the door.

Because there's no rhyme or reason to how I've been stashing items, I'm always making duplicate purchases.

That ends today.

I decide to pick up cute cloth-covered bins at Target in lieu of the

clear plastic boxes, because I don't need lids for this stuff, and I don't necessarily want to see every single item in here. Actually, I believe the closet will look neater if some of the bottles are obscured, and there's no reason to ignore aesthetics. I'm confident that Martha would approve of this logic.

The closet's crammed with a million different things, so I lay them all out plane-wreck style to assess. Maisy decides to join me in my endeavor, plowing like Godzilla through all the bottles before settling on top of the mountain of pillows on the bed. I give her a quick snuggle and then get back to work. Once I right everything, Libby comes trotting in, upsetting it all again. Realizing that Loki and Gus, Chuck Norris, and Odin (aka the Thundercats) could come through at any minute keeps me from any further tidying efforts. I can right or I can sort; I choose to sort.

I decide to narrate the experience for the dogs.

"Welcome to the Jen Lancaster Show! Today I'm going to demonstrate how to tackle a messy nonmedicine medicine cabinet. As you'll see, I've removed all the items from the closet and laid them out on the floor. This looks like a plane wreck, but really, most of these items can be sorted into one of five categories: hair product, body lotion, perfume, travel size, and makeup."

Libby thumps her tail in appreciation, while Maisy gives me the stink eye. She cares not for my mad emcee skills.

"You'll notice that I have a bottle of Living Proof hair spray, so I should place it in the hair-care bin, right? Wrong! If you look closely at the label, you'll see that it meets the airlines' requirement for carry-on liquid sizes, so we'll sort this into the travel bin."

Even though this is a Martha-based happiness project, I can't resist giving Gretchen Rubin her props by taking a task I hate and have actively avoided and trying to make it more fun; hence the narration.

"And what's this? A sample-size bottle of Jo Malone Wild Bluebell. My favorite! Maisy, where do you think this should be sorted?"

She cocks one skeptical eyebrow at me. I'm disturbing her nap, so I'm pretty sure exactly where she'd like to me to place this bottle.

"That's right, sweetie. Even though this is perfume, it also goes in the travel bin! Why? Because I'm never going to be the asshat in the security line arguing policy with the TSA. Mummy doesn't want to get strip-searched!"

I continue sorting and hosting my show. Libby and Maisy eventually fall asleep, lulled by how soothing my voice is as I give them the blow-by-blow on why Smashbox makes the best eye shadow. Of course, I curse myself when I find six nearly identical pots of said shadow, yet I'm beyond pleased with the end result.

I can't believe I spent so long dreading and avoiding what ended up being kind of—dare I say it?—enjoyable. I'm going to save time by quickly locating what I need in this cabinet, and cash when I'm not always shelling out for duplicates.

I feel a sense of pride in having gotten over this small, yet incredibly frustrating hurdle, like I wrestled a tiny bit of control away from the chaos that seems to follow me.

As I'm going to be pretty busy with my book for the next two months, I won't be tackling any huge organizing projects, but I *am* happy knowing that I can chip away at

various drawers and closets when I'm taking a break from my manuscript. So, unlike with every other book deadline, when I become so hyperfocused that the house falls apart, this time I'll be actively taking steps to keep it together.

Organization is going to lower my own stress level, which will impact all of us—me, the pets, Fletch . . . and the beard.

It's a good thing.

F·O·U·R

THE TAO OF STEAK KNIVES

"You're trying to be Martha Stewart?" Wendy asks, with more than a little skepticism in her voice. "You realize she doesn't hem her curtains with a steak knife, right?"

"Hey! I only did that once in college," I reply, doing my best not to sound defensive.

Okay, so *maybe* I shouldn't have shared that particular story while Wendy was unveiling her seamstress-grade sewing room in her newly remodeled basement. But when I gazed upon the majesty of all those identically labeled jars of sorted buttons and rows of color-coordinated ribbons and crisp patterns hanging neatly on their individual clips, I felt the gravity of my transgressions against sewing, and my words squirted out of me. Wendy's workshop felt like the kind of holy place where I needed to confess my tailor-related sins.

(At least I didn't mention all the times I used a stapler to fix errant pant cuffs. So there's that.)

Also, Wendy's known me since my idea of entertaining revolved around opening jars of Ragú and shoveling piles of laundry, magazines, hair clips, shoes, Diet Coke bottles, and cat toys into a closet, so her misgivings have *some* basis in reality.

Even when I started to improve on all things home-related, I'd make the occasional misstep, like when I threw my first dinner party for the girls a few years ago and I didn't quite master the food-to-cocktails ratio. But come on! I'm sure *other* husbands have also stepped in to take over at the grill when his wife was "so soaked in alcohol that you've turned yourself into a human wick."

Plus, I totally threw away every piece of shrimp and chicken the cats licked that night. It was fine.

Wendy's silent on the other end of the phone, so I press on. "Besides, you have it all wrong. I'm not trying to *be* Martha Stewart, and not just because I don't look good in chambray shirts. See, my goal is to start employing her techniques so I can be a better *me*. I feel like there's a correlation between living a Martha Stewart lifestyle and happiness, so that's the thesis I'm pursuing. When I started this project a couple of months ago, I just figured I'd live like her and see what happened. But now that I've gotten into it, I realize there's more to it—I'm not just trying to live like Martha; I'm trying to discover the Tao of Martha."

"Meaning?"

"Meaning that as I slowly begin to emulate her lifestyle, I'm coming to realize that Martha's way of living is more than just the sum of all her advice. She's more than plastic storage bins and tasty cupcakes and hand-hewn chicken coops. The Tao of Martha is a way of being. Like, it's a bunch of different concepts and ways of doing things—*Living*, if you will—that coalesce into a path. And I believe that path will lead me to being happier. Anyway, Saturday, are you guys in or are you out?"

"I see. So, yeah, we're in, and thanks for asking. The girls will be so excited. But . . . will you need me to bring anything? Possibly my fabric scissors?" Wendy asks.

She's seriously never going to let me live that down.

"See you Saturday, smart-ass."

I make three more hash marks on the pad next to the phone. I have to steady myself when I realize all the hash marks add up to sixteen. Whoa. I really didn't think everyone would say yes, especially to such a last-minute invite.

Looks like I'm hosting a pre-Easter brunch and egg hunt for sixteen in two days.

Normally, this is when I'd bitch-panic, but I've got Saint Martha of Bedford on my side, and I'm filled with a beatific calm. Between Martha's Web site, a stack of back issues of her magazines, and her book *Handmade Holiday Crafts: 225 Inspired Projects for Year-Round Celebrations* (fancy talk for crafting), I feel like I've already got a handle on this. At least in theory.

After reading up on Amy and Adam Forbes's Easter in the April 2011 issue of *Living*, I decide that the kids will decorate Easter baskets while parents sip mimosas sprigged with fresh mint from my garden, during which time I'll stock the buffet table. I'm serving protein-heavy dishes, because I don't want my poor friends to have to drive home with nine children in the throes of Sugar Terrors.

After we eat, everyone will retire to the front lawn, whereupon the children will frolic in the grass, leisurely hunting for the eggs that I will so lovingly have stuffed myself.

Yes.

This is going to be *perfect*.

At least, it had better be if I'm ever going to live down that whole steak-knife thing.

"I'll need to see your ID, ma'am."

I'm here at Target, scanning the conveyor belt, trying to figure out what purchase might require identification. I already stocked up on champagne at the grocery store, so I'm at a bit of a loss. I've picked out a mountain of candy as well as tons of those little plastic eggs, but unless I use all of this to lure unsuspecting children into my panel van, I've committed no discernible crime.

I locate my license and hand it over. "Here you go."

(Anytime I show someone my ID and they aren't all, "You? Why, you can't be in your forties!" I die a little inside.)

(So pretty much every time. Stupid thirty years of avoiding sunscreen.)

"Thank you," the cashier says, handing back my license.

"What am I getting that makes you need this?" I'm not picking fights with strangers, *Fletcher*. I'm just really curious. Is there a limit on how many fun-size Snickers I can buy? Because I don't want to live in that world.

The cashier gestures toward the two-pack of compressed air she's just scanned. "For those."

Huh?

"What do people do illegally with *compressed air*?"

The cashier gives me a weary sigh. "They inhale it."

"Really? But it's twenty bucks! For twenty bucks, people could buy a couple of liters of cheap vodka, cranberry juice, and a bag of chips and throw a party for their whole pledge class! Compressed air is a terrible return on investment. Also, I feel like there's no better high than blowing all the crumbs and cat hair out of a keyboard. And why wouldn't they just pick up ten cans of aerosol whipped cream instead? I noticed they were on sale. Plus, you could serve shortcake before you tweaked."

(Apologies to druggies if I've used the wrong word here.)

The cashier shrugs and continues to ring. Her salary likely doesn't cover having to explain away my existential angst.

For the record, I'm buying compressed air only because I couldn't find an ear syringe. I plan on hollowing out Easter eggs for decoration purposes. Per page eighty-one of the crafting book, the best way to blow out the yolk is with an ear aspirator, which I can't find. I figure if Target doesn't carry them, they no longer exist, because maybe ear aspirating has gone the way of medical leeching.

(Side note? All these years later, Target is still in my holy trinity of places to shop, only I've since replaced Trader Joe's and IKEA with Whole Foods and Williams-Sonoma. Of course, the height of my Target obsession occurred when they briefly carried Origins, Kiehl's, and Clarins products. That was, like, the best six-month period of my life. Except then all the boxes were eventually trussed up in antitheft devices, because people kept stealing them. I bet that's why those lotions and potions aren't there anymore. Too much trouble with all the locks and keys. Store management was probably all, "Yeah, we'll secure cameras, computers, and iPads, but Creme de Corps? No." So disappointing.)

(And thanks for taking away my ability to one-stop shop now, you stupid thieves with your supple skin and tiny pores.)

Anyway, the compressed air comes with that long, narrow straw that, in theory, will be the perfect size for really getting into the shell. This seems like a rather elegant solution, and when it works brilliantly, I plan to share this news with the folks at *Living*, because I'm that kind of magnanimous. Ooh, maybe draining Easter eggs will be my X factor?

I leave Target and head to Michaels, where I hope to find some variation of inexpensive Easter baskets. I make a major score when I discover stacks of pastel plastic buckets with attached shovels outside the front door on sale for a dollar apiece! They're plain, yet they look almost exactly like the ones I saw in Martha's "Last-Minute Easter Ideas" section of the Web site, covered in cute, puffy stickers.

As this place is the Thunderdome for all things cute and puffy, I easily locate loads of Easter-themed stickers. I select a few sleeves of pirate stickers for Wendy's son, who I suspect is attending less because he hopes to hunt for eggs and more because Joanna's daughter Anna is freaking adorable. At the checkout line, I also grab a few packages of these sparkly little daisies, which I plan to spread across the tablecloth to make it extrafestive.

When I arrive home, Fletch offers running commentary on all my purchases as I unload.

"Fifteen pounds of candy? How many kids are coming again?"

"Nine."

Fletch is incredulous. "You bought *fifteen pounds of candy* for nine little kids?"

I frown. "Is that not enough?"

He snickers. "You do candy math like you do drinks math." At the holiday dinner party, I budgeted three bottles of wine per guest, which is apparently two and a half bottles too many, unless Fletch wanted to drive everyone home.

Moving on to the grocery bags, he says, "What's with all the discount eggs? Are you planning on avenging your honor at the Sig Ep house?"

I actually feel bad for purchasing cheap eggs, because I've used only certified-humane products since January. I tried becoming a pescatarian after the New Year, figuring I could use Martha's recipes to learn how to cook fish. Everything was going beautifully until I ate some bad sea bass, and now I can barely even look at anything with fins. So my compromise is buying meat that's pasture-raised and humanely processed whenever possible.

The eggs we normally choose are free-range, and the chickens are raised on a sustainable farm and fed a diet of vegetarian whole grains without hormones or antibiotics. For the price, I wouldn't be surprised if the chickens all have their own iPhones and Pottery Barn bedding, too. In fact, the label shows the farmer hugging his hens, so you know they're spoiled rotten. But at five bucks a dozen, especially when I'm dumping the actual contents down the sink? Sorry, no hugs for you, sweatshop chicken.

"We're decorating eggs tonight," I tell him. "We're going to marble-ize some and do designs on other ones with a wax pencil. Well, actually, I couldn't find a wax pencil, and the craft store kind of creeped me out. Seriously, you've never seen so much glitter in one place outside of a Ke$ha concert. I grabbed crayons instead, because I figure it's the same thing, right? Anyway, I bought discount eggs in case we break a few. The cute bunny centerpiece I ordered on eBay holds twenty-four, and I figure we might lose a few in the process, hence the extra."

"Sounds reasonable. When are we starting?"

"As soon as I finish stuffing these plastic eggs. Shouldn't take me long."

Three hours later, my hands are cramped and gnarled and I kind of never want to smell chocolate again. I'd planned on supplementing some of the eggs with a bunch of dollar bills, but I had only three of them in my purse, and coins seemed kind of chintzy. Plus, I really need the eggs for all the candy, and what are little kids going to do with a handful of singles anyway? Hit a prepubescent strip club? So I placed a single dollar in each of three eggs and figure it's going to be fine.

My pile of stuffed eggs is borderline towering. There are so many of them! Then I begin to wonder if making kids hunt for this many eggs is less "fun" and more of a "violation of stringent child labor laws."

Also?

Candy Math—1.

Jen—0.

"We're boiling these?" Fletch asks, gesturing toward the tower of egg crates in front of him.

"Nope, no need. We're going to hollow them out," I reply. "We're supposed to take a craft knife and poke holes in either end, then stab the contents to break the yolk, blow out the innards, and presto! They're the perfect blank canvas!"

The dogs surround our workspace, because they believe that what we're doing is food-based and, damn it, they want in. Loki and Libby love eggs, but Maisy has always turned up her nose at them. Like eggs offend her delicate sensibilities. How can this be? She's a *dog*; this is actually the kind of shit she'd forage for in the wild. I could see how she wouldn't eat apples or carrots or green beans (three of her favorites), but to snort in disgust every time I offer her a bite of my omelet? I don't get it.

Of course, it's pretty much Maisy's world around here, so it's not unusual to see her wolfing down beautiful dinners of Tiki Dog Kauai Luau with whole prawns while I have canned tomato soup. But if she's happy, I'm happy, so it all works out.

The dogs nudge each other for purchase while I assemble Fletch's supplies, which include a paring knife, a paper clip, and a can of compressed air. He curls his lip at my offerings, because he never trusts me to use the right tools for the job. I mean, yes, I understand he's the kind of man who has seven different kinds of hammers in his workshop, but it's all the way downstairs, and sometimes the heel of a loafer works just as well in driving a nail.

Wordlessly, he steps out of the kitchen and returns with a power drill topped with a long, narrow woodworking bit.

Typical.

"I'm shocked you're not wearing your tool belt," I say.

He shrugs. "I considered it, but I thought you'd laugh at me."

He's got me there.

While I stage my dyeing production line, he works on the maiden egg. He drills the first hole without issue and offers the egg for my approval.

I'm grudgingly impressed. "That worked surprisingly well." I can't believe this isn't something Martha would have suggested herself.

Of course, I'm less impressed three seconds later when the egg cracks on his second attempt.

"No problem," I assure him. "We have plenty to spare."

We blow through a cool dozen before he gets the hang of the drilling. Once he has his first double-holed specimen, he inserts the compressed air tube and sprays.

The egg doesn't *crack* so much as it explodes with a deafening pop, flinging shards and ectoplasm upward of fifteen feet. The previously invested dogs make a beeline for the safety of their beds on the other side of the house, all, "The eggs ain't worth it, man."

"That didn't work," Fletch observes.

"You don't say," I reply, picking pieces of shell out of my hair.

We realize the problem is that he didn't break the yolk first, which sends him on a ten-minute wild-goose chase looking for the right tool, until I can finally convince him to just try the damn paper clip at least once. Reluctantly, he does, and I'm shortly rewarded with my first perfect hollow egg.

Which I promptly shatter when trying to rinse it.

Argh.

We bash through another dozen until we finally have one ready to dip. I mix the dye using vinegar, hot water, and food coloring, and I pointedly ignore Fletch when he remarks that the concoction smells like my loafers when I don't wear socks.

I decide to try plain dye before I get fancy with marbleizing, and after repeated dipping, I craft an egg the exact shade of Tiffany-box blue. Oh, my God! This is beautiful! Now we're cooking!

We continue our process, netting one perfect egg for every six that detonate and splatter across every kitchen surface. I make a note to wipe the whole place down with bleach so that guests don't get salmonella by brushing against the counter.

We continue to adjust our methods in terms of emptying the eggs. First, we each take a crack (pun intended) at trying to blow the raw egg out with our mouths, but I almost black out and Fletch grumbles something about listeria. We find that we have the fewest instances of egg Kristallnacht when we use a turkey baster to force egg out of the bottom hole. In retrospect, I should have checked for an ear syringe at the drugstore, exactly what Martha recommended. Had I done more than skimmed the article, I'd have known.

The good news is that this experience has led me to the first conclusion in my whole theory of the Tao of Martha, that being: There's no benefit to blazing your own path when the perfect trail already exists, dumb ass.

Maybe she wouldn't add the dumb-ass part, even though it's totally appropriate in this situation.

As Fletch surveys the final dozen eggs, he asks, "Are you sure you don't want to hard-boil these?"

I shake my head. "No, I hate the idea of having cooked eggs out on display around the house. You know I'll forget about them and then suddenly the house will be all eau de garbage truck."

Fletch nods. "I used to have to hunt for hard-boiled eggs when I was a kid. What was the point of that? Was I supposed to be, 'Yay! I found them! Egg-salad sandwiches for everyone!' I was seven! I wanted *chocolate*, not bioavailable protein."

We finish the final candidate and end up netting eleven eggs out of six dozen. That is *sixty-one* failures, for those of you keeping track at home, or a fifteen percent success rate. Shameful. I suddenly wish I'd decided to build Martha's vermicompost heap so at least the sweatshop chickens wouldn't have toiled in vain. But when I read the part about how fat red wiggler worms do all the work? No.

I arrange the few good eggs on one side of my fancy centerpiece. It's not perfect, but if you look at it from one side only, it's really lovely.

While we tidy up the kitchen, Fletch offers me the gigantic silver bowl full of egg innards. "Are you going to use this for the frittatas?" Fletch asks.

"No, I thought I'd use the carton of Farmer Phil's eggs in the fridge. They'll taste better, and they aren't full of eggshells and spit."

As Fletch drags out the stepladder to scrub the sunburst of yolks from the ceiling, I stage the buffet table in the dining room. Although I didn't read explicit instructions from Martha on how to present the table (sensing a theme here?), I believe that I'm upholding the spirit of her work in mapping out where each dish will go and readying serving pieces beforehand.

With this brunch, I plan to neatly erase everyone's memory of My First Thanksgiving, as well as that whole steak-knife-curtain thing.

Before I can set out anything, I have to cover the table. My dining room table is an odd shape because it's very, very wide. I've always had trouble finding the proper covering, until one time I accidentally discovered that a recently dry-cleaned duvet cover fit impeccably. So I guess the shape isn't "odd" if you're familiar with the dimensions of a king-size bed.

"Hey, Fletch? Have you seen my table duvet?"

"Check the hall closet."

I do and it's nowhere to be found. The last time we used it was at our holiday party. "It can't still be in the dry-cleaning load, right?" All domestic chores in the past three months have fallen on Fletch's shoulders while I've been on book deadline, so it's not unreasonable to expect him to have handled this. Plus, after our holiday party, Fletch had *one job*, and that was to police the dirty linens.

Ipso facto, my clean table duvet should be here somewhere.

Fletch doesn't answer me. "Right?" I call again.

"There's a slight possibility it may be dirty," he admits.

Now I'm frustrated. I stomp into the laundry room and discover the Bolognese-sauce-and-wine-speckled tablecloth buried under seventeen soiled sweaters, all of them mine. Well, that also explains why I've been forced to wear the same damn hoodie every day. I've said it before and I'll say it again: Worst. Assistant. Ever.

I make do with the tablecloths I have, fashioning a long white one over a short one. I have created the equivalent of a table mullet—business in the front, party in the back—but I don't have a lot of other options. I place these over the strips of protective cloth that I duct-taped together because I could never find the right-size table pad. (Note to self: Look into water-resistant mattress pads.)

Now I'm ready for the fun part—decorating! What Martha does so brilliantly is decorating in a manner that's beautiful, but doesn't come across as too stuffy. There's always an organic element to everything she creates.

Instead of buying big, formal flower arrangements to place on the table, I take a couple of clear glass vases and fill them with cuttings from the apple trees currently blossoming in my backyard. I curse these damn trees three hundred and sixty days a year, as the spindly branches catch my hair and tear at my clothing every time I round the corner to the side of the house. Then they block out the sun all summer before depositing hundreds of small, infested apples that bob merrily atop the surface of the pool at the end of the season. But for five days a year, the branches droop with the weight of hundreds of pink-tinged blooms, filling the entire yard with the heady scent of apple blossom. So they live. For now.

As soon as I place the branch-laden vases on the table, the Thundercats slink out from their basement lair to investigate. I have to hook a spray bottle of water to my belt loop, and I blast the little bastards every time they hop up on the table.

Martha keeps a healthy supply of bunny-related items on hand, and suggests to her readers that they stock up when items go on sale after Easter. Fortunately, I'm delighted to have gotten ahead of this trend years ago, and my guest room is filled with my massive collection of ceramic and cast-iron rabbits.

Fletch, of course, thinks this room is creepy. He claims that all the rabbits' cold, dead eyes stare into his soul.

Fletch may be right, but I don't care.

I haul my collection down the stairs and artistically arrange all the rabbits with my right hand while blasting cats with my left. Then I place bowls of jelly beans in my pink poinsettia Depression-glass pieces and sprinkle the whole thing with the tiny pastel daisies I picked up at the craft store. There's not an inch of the table that isn't color-blocked, flower-topped, or lapine. (*Watership Down*, bitches!)

As I step back to survey my handiwork, I'm pleased. "Hey! Come in here and tell me what you think!" I shout. Fletch has finished scouring ceiling yolks and started on the dishes.

He takes in the table and the sparkly eggs hanging from the chandelier and the garland that he crafted from dozens of adorable fabric carrots. "Looks like Easter threw up in here."

Which means I totally nailed it.

THANK YOU,
EASTER BUNNY,
BAWK, BAWK!

I'm up at dawn to get the food together. I approach the dining room on the way to the kitchen and I'm compelled to stop to admire my handiwork. This is my first full-fledged, soup-to-nuts, Stewart-style project, and I could not be more pleased with how everything is going, eggsplosion notwithstanding.

In terms of gauging personal happiness, this particular project has checked a number of boxes for me. The preparations have forced me to be out and about, instead of hibernating in front of the television. I've greatly enjoyed the creative aspects of the project, while still maintaining a sense of frugality. When everyone comes and has a great time, there's a huge potential for praise, and I've met my deadlines and learned new, better ways of approaching certain tasks.

I definitely feel happy today, and Maisy has picked up on my excellent mood. She's been trotting all around the yard for the past few days and showing the kind of energy I haven't seen since last summer. In fact, she keeps swiping pillows off the couch and running away with them, which is something she does only when A) she feels well, and B) she is seeking attention. We call this the Naughty Run, because she chugs away with the purloined item in her teeth, looking over her shoulder the entire time to make sure we're paying attention.

Hands down, the Naughty Run is my favorite thing in the entire world, and my heart is lighter knowing that she's in a good place right now. So, for a second, I don't feel the crushing anxiety of what may come. I can unclench, at least for today.

I smile and nod my head as I survey the dining room, recognizing that this is a good day indeed.

Of course, that's exactly when I notice that one of the vases has been knocked over and the entire tablecloth is saturated.

Argh!

This is what happens when I let down my guard.

Not only is everything wet, but the Day-Glo-yellow Post-it notes I used as place markers have bled onto the white cloth, as have all the scattered pastel daisies. I appear to have attempted a Wavy Gravy–style tie-dye at a recent love-in. Damn it! Even my festive, color-coordinated bowls of jelly beans have fused into singular sticky clumps.

That's when Chuck Norris, chief feline instigator and vase toppler, hops onto the table to demand breakfast.

For years I've considered myself a "cat person."

Today, I am reconsidering that designation.

I round up the asshole cats and put them in the basement with their breakfast. I'd planned on getting them out of the way for the brunch anyway, but now I'm doing so a few hours early. They shan't be missed.

At this point, Fletch ambles out of the bedroom and suggests I just replace the tablecloth with another one, and I strongly consider locking him in the basement, too. Instead, I set him up with a hair dryer, and he tackles the most egregiously wet spots. Looks like we'll be able to live with the results, but I'm pretty sure I just conceded a few happiness points.

To try to make myself feel better, I Google "Martha Stewart holiday disaster" to see if she's ever shared any true tales of her day going horribly awry. I find plenty of homemaking nightmares, like cooking the plastic giblet bag inside the turkey, dropping tidal waves of caramel sauce, and setting the better part of the kitchen on fire. Of course, these stories come from others attempting to run the show Martha-style, and not Martha herself.

Then I'm struck with the notion that this wouldn't have been a disaster for Martha, because she'd have plenty of freshly pressed tablecloths on hand. She'd clean up the spill, lay down a pristine new cloth, and never give it another thought. She wouldn't ruminate, she wouldn't dwell, she wouldn't agonize, and she wouldn't plot her husband's early demise. This leads me to a new revelation in her Tao:

Wipe it up *and* suck it up. You're fine; it's fixed; move on.

So that's what I do, and my pleasant mood returns.

Joanna, her girls, and her sister-in-law Karen arrive early to help, and I put them to work on Martha's green bean–ham-and-cheese frittata and asparagus-Gruyère tart, respectively. I set out the ingredients for the Menning Mimosas and stock the lime-green beverage tub with a variety of berry-flavored LaCroix waters.

In starting this project, I tried to look at what Martha does from a macro point of view. What I've learned is that every aspect of her events makes sense. Her entertaining advice reminds me of a movie set— everything you see in a film must serve the purpose of advancing the story. Normally, if I knew I had children coming over, I'd buy ten million different soft drinks and juice boxes because I wasn't sure of their favorites.

Now that I've dipped my toe into Martha's world, I realize that an assortment of pretty, pink-canned, sugar-free sparkling waters makes much more sense than loading the kids up with nine million flavors of soda, because today's really about the egg hunt. There's no need to gild the lily, as it were, with a bunch of extraneous choices. In serving a set beverage menu, I can give the impression of having gone to more effort in planning than if I ran around buying everything. Less has truly become more.

As the kids arrive, they're beyond delighted with the bucket-decorating station I've arranged in the kitchen. They're close enough to the action for us to keep our eyes on them, but they're so involved with their projects that they don't mind having to wait to eat. Plus, this gives the parents time to sip their Menning Mimosas and visit with other grown-ups.

While all this is going on, Fletch, otherwise known as the Easter bunny, hides the eggs, going so far as to wear floppy ears. I love that he's getting into the spirit, too.

Brunch is ready, and I tell the kids they have five minutes to finish their buckets. I walk the length of the table, admiring everyone's handiwork, but I can't quite get past all the artistry that's gone into Wendy's youngest daughter's bucket. Even though she's only seven, she's applied her stickers with such style and panache that I'm blown away.

"My God, Wendy—did you see what Trixie did?" Her bucket is resplendently eclectic, with her name perfectly bracketed by equidistant spirals of bunnies, tulips, and crossed swords from the pirate sticker collection.

Wendy nods. "She's amazing, right? That one's going to pay to put me in the *good* home someday."

The kids load up on Greek yogurt, fresh berries, and organic bacon, but they also dive into the frittata and asparagus tart. Yay for kids with adventurous palates! They eat well, but quickly, as they're ready for the big dance.

Fletch positions himself on the front walk so he can capture everyone's faces as they realize the bounty of candy waiting to be found. I think my final count, before I developed arthritis and had to stop, was about four hundred eggs. With eight kids—Wendy's son couldn't make it—I estimated they'd find two eggs per minute and that the hunt would last up to half an hour. I assumed they'd ooh and aah over each treasure and lovingly place their prizes in their buckets before moving on to search for the next location.

Yeah.

Way off on that.

The kids explode from the house like angry lions released from a cage. Their rabbit ears flop in the warm spring sun, their brows beetled with concentration and a thin sheen of sweat. They pounce on each pastel orb with the lawless abandon of Viking raiders, or options traders deep in the commodity market pits.

Don't get me wrong; these are fine, fine children. I adore each and every one of them. I love how polite they are, always sending me hand-written thank-you notes after a day at the pool. They're sweet and gentle, and I appreciate the way they respect my home and gingerly pet my jackass cats. Yet I've never before pitted them against one another *Mad Max*–style, so I guess I can't be surprised by their intensity level.

When the first kid finds a dollar, all hell breaks loose, and my lovely spring garden party turns into game six of the 1996 Detroit Red Wings/Colorado Avalanche series. The kids are dragging one another to the boards and kneeing their competitors in the heads. I'm pretty sure I see a tooth fly by.

"But it's just a dollar," I comment, as parents do their best to referee the melee. "Why are they going ape shit over a buck? I mean, they're *children*. What else could they possibly want to buy other than candy?"

Becca starts, "You're kidding, right? Nintendo games, LEGOs, American Girl dolls—" But she has to tag out to keep one of her kids from high-sticking.

Wendy manages to say, "They want Barbies and craft projects and smartphones and e-readers and iPads," before she has to warn one of her girls about the penalty box.

Joanna tells me, "Anna wants clothes, stuff to decorate her room, makeup, and nail polish. She likes to deposit money in her savings account, too."

"I really had no idea," I tell them. "All I wanted as a kid was candy. Had I known, I'd have emptied out my big change jar."

With all the exertion from slam-dancing in the Easter mosh pit, one of the kids has an asthma attack, and the others, sensing his weakness, throw off their gloves so they can really fight.

And by the way?

The egg hunt lasts all of four minutes.

Candy Math—2.

Jen—0.

When the hunt is complete, all the kids return to my front steps to inspect their booty, while their parents dress their open wounds. And that is when I learn a very important lesson about what happens when the sun beats down on little pastel terrariums filled with treats possessing a very low melting point.

Also, judging from the husks of empty plastic shells and shiny wrappers at the edge of the wood line, squirrels have an affinity for miniature Reese's Peanut Butter Cups.

I make note of that for next year.

Fortunately, I had the foresight to create additional bags of Easter treats for the kids so they have something to munch on while the contents of their found eggs solidify. The final candy weight count is about nineteen pounds. That should keep them in chocolate until my Halloween party.

As everyone has plans for later in the day, the party winds down after the hunt, and the house is empty and clean again by two p.m. Fletch and I retire to the TV room with a bottle of champagne and a carton of juice.

"For me, the best part wasn't watching the kids. All the parents were so happy!" Fletch tells me as he hands me my glass. "Wendy was thrilled, because she says now she doesn't have to do this before church tomorrow."

"If I can pull off more events like this, I may just get her to forget the whole steak-knife thing." I raise my glass and clink with Fletch's. "Well, at least until she tries to teach me to sew."

Despite the mishaps (Chuck Norris and Egg Assassin, I'm looking at you), I'm proud to have provided a fun day and the kind of happy memory that those kids will carry all the way to adulthood.

I'm less proud that a couple of the kids will also carry the scars.

Apparently, postparty, not one but TWO children had to go to the ER for Easter-related emergencies. One was for the asthma attack and the other was when one of the girls was so hopped up on chocolate that she thought she could fly and instead bashed into a coffee table. Stitches were involved.

Candy Math—3.

Jen—0.

Still, I delight in the fact that someday my friends' grandkids will reap the benefit of what their children experienced today. And today, more than ever, I truly believe that I'll be a happier person by discovering the Tao of Martha.

Well played, Martha.

Well played.

THE NEW GIRL(S)

"I can't believe you're leaving me alone with them."

He grasps my arm for comfort and lets out a ragged breath.

I lift his hand and kiss the back of it, in hopes of comforting him with pure reason and rational thought. "I have to go on book tour, Fletch; it's part of my job. You can do this."

"But I'm afraid to be with them."

"Don't be afraid; you'll manage them fine."

Even though many would be terrified to step into my house because of the two pit bulls and massive black shepherd, that's not what currently has Fletch's pulse racing. These dogs are safe as kittens . . . unless you're a ham sandwich. Nor does he fear taking care of Maisy by himself, as she's doing so well right now. We just opened the pool and she happily christened it with the first lap of the season.

Maisy has bursts of energy that would be the envy of any dog, let alone one who's ten years old and has had almost three years of chemotherapy,

only to be hit with a second kind of cancer. When Maisy had her melanoma surgery, Fletch was all, "Congratulations, the dog beat you to skin cancer." Now she's supposed to wear a sun shirt on both ends when she's outside, which will be the cutest thing ever.

Point? The dogs aren't the issue. What Fletch is afraid of is the ten collective pounds of fury known as the New Girls.

"What do you want for your birthday?" Fletch had asked me last year.

"To adopt a black cat," I replied.

Fletch didn't even hesitate with his answer. "Never going to happen. What else is on your list?"

I crossed my arms and scowled. "Nothing. All I want is a cat."

And that was true. My sole desire was to rescue a new kitty to add to our current menagerie, because I'd heard so many sad stories about family pets being abandoned in the economic downturn. We had time, space, and love to spare, so what was the big, hairy deal?

When my birthday finally arrived in November of 2011, I was spent. Not because of the pets, although we'd just rolled off of yet another stressful surgery for Maisy. She was fine, but I was exhausted, because I'd spent two months locked in my office working on *Jeneration X*. I was pale and haggard, in desperate need of a cut and color, a mani-pedi, a spray tan, and forty units of cosmetic fillers, stat. I didn't feel like going out or having a party, because I looked like my own personal portrait of Dorian Gray. I didn't even want any presents. My only desire entailed a quiet dinner featuring a filet with goat cheese and a balsamic vinegar reduction, followed by cake and the opportunity to catch up on a month of TiVo'ed fall television premieres.

Small dreams, people. Small dreams.

Fletch was in charge of dinner, which, coincidentally, you don't have to be Martha to prepare. The filet requires a salt, pepper, and garlic rubdown, but the trick is to warm the meat to ninety-five degrees in the oven before pan-searing it. Doing so dries off the outside, which means the entire inside stays pink, yet allows the perimeter to form the most gorgeous char crust.

(Wait, I learned this trick from watching Martha. Oh, well.)

While the filet rests under a tent of tinfoil, top with a layer of goat cheese, which should be crisped until it's golden. I normally pop the whole thing under the broiler for thirty seconds, or I use my little crème brûlée torch if I've remembered to refill the butane. Goes without saying, of course, that I almost never remember to refill the butane. But, really, who keeps excess butane on hand? What am I, a welder?

(Related note? Fletch wanted to buy a full-size blowtorch for our future brûlées, but as I don't want to see our home reduced to a pile of smoking rubble, I put down my foot on this one.)

Anyway, back to my First Choice in Last Suppers—so, goat cheese on a filet is fine, but the step that turns the meal into magic is the balsamic vinegar reduction. The sweetness of the sauce contrasted with the creamy sourness of the cheese is nothing short of transcendent. Plus, the sauce is so easy to make, a helper monkey could do it.

I take four parts of high-quality balsamic and mix it with one part sugar. Placing the mix in a saucepan on low, I cook it down for twenty to thirty minutes. The key is constant whisking as it reduces, which would be especially easy for a monkey, as he could also stir with his tail.

Once the sauce is thick and syrupy, the bittersweet tang is the perfect complement for anything from roasted vegetables to ice cream.

Most recipes don't mention this, but it's important to understand the downside of making this miraculous elixir: reducing vinegar makes your house smell like feet.

For a week.

Also, without constant whisking, the sauce will overcook and then your house will smell like *burned* feet.

For a week.

Martha would say that this is the opposite of a good thing, particularly because that stench gets in the walls.

As Fletch cooked that fateful November day, I wandered in and out of the kitchen, one wary eye on the reduction. He promised me he was on top of it and continued to shoo me away.

I was down the hall watching something *Real Housewife*-based when I caught a whiff of the familiar trace of burned vinegar foot. In the time it took Fletch to pick out the wine, the sauce overheated and was ruined.

As we sat down to my unsauced steak, I felt an unbearable, yet completely unwarranted sense of sadness. My issue wasn't the dinner. Fletch tried, and I love him for making the effort.

Rather, there's something about finishing a book that leaves me feeling depressed. You'd think I'd be all celebratory and overjoyed to have the deadline off my back, but that's never the case. When I turn in my manuscript, the *absence* of having that pressure feels like a loss. That's why when people complete a marathon, they run past the finish line. The human body can't handle the drop from one hundred to zero. For me, it's always jarring to go from that which consumes my life to nothing with the sending of one e-mail attachment. Without a mental cooldown period, I'm left feeling like I have the worst case of PMS ever.

And it's because of this that I started to cry while eating my stupid balsamic-free filet.

"Are you okay?" Fletch asked, voice full of concern.

"I'm fine," I promised, sniffling into my napkin.

"Clearly you aren't."

"I just . . . I just . . . I just wanted my balsamic. That's all I wanted for my birthday. I just wanted my stupid sauce." And then I began to sob in earnest, not because I was sad, but because the book—and really the whole awful year—had been so stressful.

Fletch moved next to me and patted my hair. "Jen, I'm so sorry. I stopped stirring for a second; I swear. I can make more."

"No, I'm just tired," I wailed. "That's it. I'm fine. I'm just tired."

"What would make you feel better?"

"Nothing."

"Do you want to go out to dinner?"

"NOOO! I can't go out in public; I'm hideous."

"Do you want your cake now instead?"

"No."

"Do you want me to watch your stupid housewife show with you?"

"No. You'll just make fun of it and then I'll be even sadder."

"True." Then Fletch squared his shoulders and took some deep breaths, like he was wrestling with something internally. "Do . . . you want to go to the shelter tomorrow and pick out a new cat?"

I sat up straight and narrowed my gaze. "Do not toy with me right now. I'm in no mood for toying."

He looked right into my eyes. "I'm not toying with you. I'm serious. I'm giving in. You win. So, do you want to adopt a new cat tomorrow for your birthday?"

My tears stopped and I began to collect myself, suddenly forgetting all my monkey dreams. "I would love that. Thank you."

"Good." Then he gave me a big kiss and went back to his seat.

I began eating my filet with renewed vigor.

After a few seconds I said, "Hey, Fletch?"

He smiled at me. "Yeah?"

"We should adopt two."

Here's something Martha never tells you: Don't go to an animal shelter and ask for the two hardest-to-adopt cats they have.

Because you'll get the two hardest-to-adopt cats they have.

I'm not sure why I believed that I'd somehow be rewarded by requesting the cats most in need of a good home. Maybe I thought all the volunteers would be so moved by my compassion and bonhomie that they'd, in fact, point me to the two most awesome felines.

When we arrived at the shelter, we sat down with a volunteer and began to complete adoption forms. She'd handed me a clipboard with a stack of paper, and after I finished the first page, I turned to what I thought was the second.

"Are there more pages?" I asked, gesturing to the stack. "This is just the first sheet over and over."

"No, no," she assured me, "this is it."

Huh. Turns out it's way easier to get a shelter cat than a rescue-group pit bull. Libby's adoption required six double-sided pages of essay questions, three character witnesses, and affidavits from Maisy's oncologist, surgeon, hydrotherapist, and primary-care vet.

One would think that *employing* a canine oncologist, surgeon, hydrotherapist, and regular vet would exempt us from the home visits and interviews, but no. We had to run the whole gamut. At the shelter, we had to promise only that we wouldn't use our new kitties as clay-pigeon substitutes when shooting skeet, like, if at all possible.

While we waited to meet candidates, my attention was drawn to the huge glass wall at the end of the hall. Easily what were three hundred cats peaceably coexisted in a maze of indoor/outdoor rooms filled with a million toys, scratching posts, and multilevel beams. An entire feline kingdom lounged, waiting to meet us.

Fletch nudged me and pointed. "It's like looking into your future."

"Not funny," I replied.

"But not untrue," he countered.

I scowled in return.

My first clue that things were about to go horribly awry should have been when the volunteer pulled two cats out of a small cage they shared, and not the big kitty commune. But at no point did it occur to me that maybe there was a reason that these two particular cats had to be kept separate from the three hundred others.

The volunteer handed me a bite-size tortoiseshell cat with green eyes that took up almost half her face. Fletch took her plump counterpart, a gray Siamese mix with slightly crossed eyes of cobalt blue and the pink nose of a bunny. "What's their story?" I asked.

"Someone adopted them from us and had them for a year. Then they had to move, so they brought them back here. They've been with us for . . ." She checked their file. "Oh, dear. They've been here for two and a half years."

Oh, my God. These poor little babies had a home and then were forced to live in a cage again? That's awful!

"But why hasn't anyone taken them? They're beautiful!" I exclaimed, hugging the little one to my chest. The cat gazed up at me with huge liquid eyes straight out of a horrible velvet painting. She leaned into me and purred.

She shrugged. "I'm not sure. But it's really hard to adopt out a pair. We're about to break them up to see if that helps."

Um, not on my watch.

"We'll take them!" I exclaimed.

The volunteer said, "We have other pairs. Maybe you should meet some of them before you make a decision."

"Have any of them been here longer?"

"No."

"Then, SOLD!"

"Whoa, hold on. We need to see how they are with dogs," Fletch reasoned.

We waited and held the girls while the shelter workers brought a variety of dogs through to test the cats' temperaments. Fletch's cat stretched out on his lap, content as could be, and mine snuggled up into my neck.

I melted.

"They're totally fine and they're totally ours!" And with that, we paid the adoption fee, bundled the cats into their carrying cases, and brought them home to their new family, at no point realizing these sweet, docile cats had pulled a con on us worthy of Wall Street.

Because of their coloring, I named them after my all-time favorite characters: Patsy and Edina from *Absolutely Fabulous*. In the past, I found that cat naming is really prophetic. Our first cat, Maggie, had the most twee moniker I could think of back in the day, and she turned out to be just as dainty and delicate as her name dictated. Tucker was thus christened for a really fun, friendly college bartender (who's still our buddy today), and Jordan for the crabby ice princess in the movie *Cocktail*. Point is, I firmly believe that your name goes a long way in determining your personality.

So I should have known better than to saddle the girls with the names of the two most cantankerous, pugnacious, backbitingly vicious vodka-soaked assholes on the planet.

Should have, anyway.

Not long after bringing the new girls home, we discovered that they had an adorable little party trick.

"Jesus!" Fletch shouted.

"What happened?"

"The little one took a chunk out of me!" Fletch barked, looking up at me over the side of the bed and clutching the meaty part of his hand. We'd been trying to coax the cats into their carrier for a vet appointment for a solid ten minutes at that point.

"Her name is Eddy, and she was just saying hello," I

argued unconvincingly. "You know, like those T-shirts that say, 'Sharks hug with their mouths.' She was hugging you with her teeth, being friendly."

He shot me a dark look. "My *friends* don't bite me."

"Oh, stop being so melodramatic. She weighs four pounds. How hard could she bite?"

"*This* hard." He waved his bloody hand at me before getting up to the bathroom for heavy washing and disinfecting.

As it turned out, Fletch wasn't the only one who wasn't in love with the new girls.

Aside from me, *no one* likes Patsy and Edina to this day, which is exactly why Fletch is afraid to be alone with them. The dogs are okay around them, but they aren't buddies like they are with the Thundercats. Libby and Gus chase each other all day, and Odin and Chuck are perpetually using Maisy and Loki as their big canine mattresses.

Anytime a dog comes too close, Eddy does her best Mike Tyson impersonation, smacking the dogs' muzzles with eight hundred lightning-fast uppercuts before scampering up the bookcase to hiss, while a shell-shocked Libby or Maisy looks at me as if to say, all Will Ferrell–style, "Am I taking crazy pills?"

(Loki doesn't get involved. He's like Murtaugh in *Lethal Weapon*, walking around, shaking his head, and grumbling, "I am too old for this shit." He steers clear of the girls and sees them only at night, when we go to bed.)

Patsy and Eddy presently live in the connecting bedrooms on the first floor, where they've been for the past six months. That's right, *six months*. Our attempts to mainstream them into the rest of the pack have been unsuccessful, much like one could consider the final flight of the *Hindenburg* unsuccessful.

Having done my research, I was aware that introducing new cats to the household could be a challenge. And yet, in the past twenty-plus years, I had successfully integrated nine different cats, two pit bulls, and a shepherd into my household without a single incident. We've babysat friends' dogs, spent holidays with my family's pets, and had tons of quality time with Tracey and her pup, Maxie. With all these creatures in and out of the house, there's never been a nip, not a scratch, not a fur out of place.

True, we did spend two months fully integrating the Thundercats, but only because they were so tiny and frail and feral. Every night we'd take turns holding one of the kittens while we watched TV, and as they grew, they slowly learned to trust, and eventually love, all the creatures under our roof. When they were finally big enough to go free-range, they did so in a house full of friends.

I'd done a ton of research, and I read that I needed to isolate Patsy and Eddy for the first week or so, allowing them to become familiar with the scents of the other cats under the door. Then we were to put up baby gates so they could make eye contact for another week. Our instructions were to ferry toys and blankets between the two sets of cats so that when we finally opened the gates, all would be fine.

Sometimes the Internet is wrong.

No one warned me that even when you do everything right, cats don't always get the memo on how they're supposed to behave. When I brought the two groups together for the first time, I didn't anticipate the whirlwind of fur and hate and what sounded like a thousand sheep being slaughtered. The girls turned into two small Tasmanian devils, and their violent reactions triggered whatever was still feral inside the boys.

It was ugly.

Fletch attempted to break up the fight by grabbing Eddy, since she's the worst of the lot, and she turned her anger on him. He began shrieking that she'd slashed him so hard that she'd struck an artery and he was gushing blood.

Turns out she'd just peed on him, a fact in which he took little comfort.

(This may be when he started to dislike her.)

Also, being around the boys gives Eddy a condition our vet calls "irritable colitis," but which is more commonly known in this house as "terror shit."

Did I mention things aren't going well?

To complicate matters, Patsy's and Eddy's fear and anger are putting the Thundercats on edge and they've started to act out. They've been digging trenches in the carpet outside the girls' door, and they're peeing on everything, everywhere.

Taking the girls back to the shelter isn't an option; I could never live with myself. I made a commitment to care for these cats and I will honor it. (I don't want to have to put "or die trying" in here, but it should be inferred.)

In their defense, it's not that Patsy and Eddy can't be sweet; they can and they are. Every night while Fletch reads, they both climb on his back and perch on his shoulder, after giving him a minimassage. Also, they're very friendly with people and are happy to consent to the vet's exam. It's just that they despise the Thundercats with every fiber of their beings. I can't say that I blame Eddy, seeing how Gus slashed her back leg down to the muscle when they first met, requiring forty stitches. As for Patsy, she's less outwardly aggressive, instead preferring to eat her feelings. She looks like a gray football with legs.

Our vet has assured us that the process takes time and that we're doing the right thing. There are solutions she can offer, such as Prozac and declawing, but surgery seems like a cruel and unusual punishment for the cats, as giving them pills would be for us. So we pledge to keep doing what we're doing . . . no matter how much of Fletch's blood it spills.

In retrospect, I bet he wishes he'd kept a closer eye on that balsamic.

I give Fletch a big squeeze and I tell him, "Everything will be fine with the cats. You can do this."

I say this with such confidence that I almost believe myself. Almost.

SEVEN

My Cat from Hell

The first week of the book tour is under my belt. Fletch managed the whole menagerie nicely and I'm proud of him. See? That wasn't so bad after all.

I leave for the second leg of the tour starting in Seattle tomorrow afternoon, which means I repack my suitcase today. I'm so anal that I never leave anything for the last minute when I'm on the road.

Although learning how to travel efficiently isn't a skill I gleaned from Martha, I'm sure she'd applaud my uncharacteristic level of organization. I keep a permanent checklist, and I have doubles of everything I use on a daily basis. From eyeglasses to color-care shampoo to lash primer, I keep one set permanently packed in my carry-on.

In attempting to discover and embrace the Tao of Martha, I realize that the way I travel neatly illustrates a cornerstone of her philosophy: Never, ever scramble.

By maintaining a strict packing list, a predetermined set of mix-and-match outfits, and duplicate personal items, I've removed the whole element of chaos during travel. Traveling light prevents luggage loss or a missed call time because I'm stuck at a slow baggage claim. Mindful packing means I never have to expend the mental energy wondering where I can pick up tampons or a Band-Aid or my special leave-in conditioner on the mean streets of Nashville. Being organized means I can funnel my energy into my events and into remembering to not drop an f-bomb on morning television. Never scrambling is what stands between me and an FCC fine.

As I meticulously assemble items from my list, Maisy observes glumly from her bed. Very little in this life makes her unhappy, save for seeing my suitcase. As I sort, fold, and then roll each item into a zippy Eagle Creek travel packet, she glowers and grunts. Were she able to write me a strongly worded letter on the subject of my leaving, she absolutely would. Many exclamation points would be used.

Every time she huffs, puffs, and groans, I lean down to give her a kiss on her wide snout, and she rewards me by sighing contentedly and curling her toes. If someone could harness the power of my love for this dog, I swear I could singlehandedly end our nation's dependence on foreign oil. As it is, Maisy has such an issue with my leaving that I've shaved a dozen dates off of my tour schedule over the years, winnowing my travels from twenty-plus days a year to a more manageable ten.

Each time I walk over to kiss Maisy, Patsy and Edina deposit themselves on top of my clean laundry.

Clearly Fletch made no integration headway while I was gone last week.

Thus far, no amount of baby-gate conditioning has helped in bringing the Palestinian Thundercats and Israeli New Girls together, and it's been nothing but scud missiles and dirty bombs up in here. At this point, Fletch and I have decided to allow them to live separate lives until I'm finished with all my summer book business.

The whole "two households" foolishness has become a running joke with most of my friends, save for Gina. She had to keep her cats (Bailey and Phoebe) apart, until she lost Phoebe last winter to kidney disease. For five years, one cat lived on the first floor and the other on the second. I used to think that situation sounded a bit crazy, until I found myself living the exact same way.

(I should note here that Bailey's related to the Thundercats, as they look and behave exactly the same and they're all from the same alley in Gina's neighborhood. Coincidence?)

I allow the girls to hang out on top of my stuff—rationalizing that no reader would recognize me if I weren't covered in pet fur—while I head down the hall to pick up my bras. When I arrived home yesterday morning, I stepped in from the garage and immediately began to unpack my suitcase. I laundered my bras first so that I could leave them out overnight to dry, and now they're ready to pack. I retrieve the two nude, one white, and one black (coordinated with the opacity of all my tops in mind) from the closet doorknob next to the dryer.

After a few more Maisy makeout sessions, I finish packing. Once I double-check my list, I'm satisfied that all is as it should be, and I wheel my suitcase to the hallway.

I'm in the Admirals Club at the airport when I first smell something both awful and familiar. I peer up over my book to see who might be traveling internationally, because I figure that's the origin of the stink. (Relax; I'm not xenophobic. I'm only talking about the result of a human body being stuck in a metal tube for many hours between showers, regardless of nation of origin.) However, I'm alone in the cell-phone-free portion of the lounge.

I sniff deeply and I suddenly realize why the odor is so familiar—it's cat pee.

Specifically, *my* cat's pee.

Which means the smell is coming from me.

DAMN IT.

Then I remember how on Saturday, Gus was loitering around my bras hanging on the doorknob. While I petted him, he turned his back to them and did this thing I call "happy tail," where the cat makes little dancing motions with his paws while his tail vibrates. Generally I see this behavior in relation to moments of sheer delight, like when I'm opening a wet food can or carving a chicken, but once in a great while, the cats do so while peeing.

So, rather than making happy tail because he was thrilled to see me after a week, Gus was instead whizzing all over my undergarments *and I didn't even realize it*. And I'm wearing the black bra, which was at the back of the pile, so there's an excellent chance his stream polluted all the bras in front of it.

DAMN IT, AGAIN.

I douse myself in Jo Malone sample, which doesn't mask the scent of urine so much as enhance it, bringing out all the notes of skunk, ammonia, and public urinal. So now my seatmate is going to spend the entire flight trying to determine if I've been traveling internationally.

This is why I can't have nice things.

When I arrive in Seattle, my fears are confirmed: Gus has, in fact, nailed all my foundation garments. I deploy my travel-size packet of Tide and launder all my bras in the sink.

Then I spend the entire week apologizing to readers for smelling like pee when they hug me, because save for an exorcist, nothing is going to remove that stench completely.

We really have to fix this cat situation.

What would Martha do?

Turns out I don't specifically figure out what Martha would do, largely because Martha gets all her cats from the same breeder and they appear to come presocialized. (I suspect you do not sell Martha a feral cat.) Also, I'm sure she's never ruined a sauce; ergo she'd never have found herself in this situation in the first place.

I'm on my own in piecing together her various guidelines in order to come up with a workable solution, because every single member of this household will be happier once we're integrated.

The first set of pet-related tips I can find comes from her Bible-size *Homekeeping Handbook*. I love this book, not only for the information it contains, but also because it's thick enough for me to prop my iPad on when I Face Time with my friend Karyn so I don't look all double-chin-y.

(Non-Martha pro tip? Never, ever let anyone photograph you from underneath—make the photographer stand on a chair for the most flattering angle.)

I attempt to make the solution she recommends, which combines tepid water, a clean cloth, and dishwashing soap, but that just angries up the profound stink of Chuck's, Gus's, and Odin's displeasure. Her next suggestion is to use an enzymatic product such as Nature's Miracle, and that does work in driving cats away from the area they soiled. But instead of being deterred completely, they simply pee on different spots.

Honestly, it doesn't help that my rugs and carpets have been around for cats in kidney failure previously. No matter how much Nature's Miracle I squirt, some of that odor lingers from pets no longer of this mortal coil. I've no choice but to switch to DEF(ecate)CON 2, which includes having the floors and carpets professionally cleaned.

Afterward, the stink rises to the surface, and I pity anyone who tries to do push-ups in my house. Martha says if none of this works, consider replacing all the carpet and the hardwood, which is an attractive but extreme option, as wasting money is the antithesis of what makes me happy. There's got to be a way to fix the larger behavioral problems, and quick, because I notice the Thundercats have been trying to tunnel under the door in front of the bedroom in order to try to get at the New Girls.

I make vet appointments for everyone, to double-check that there are no physical issues turning my beloved creatures into hellcats, and it's confirmed that they're just jerks. I'm still not on board with medicating them, so we try everyone on a new diet, and I invest in all kinds of pheromone dispensers—via collar, diffuser, and spray. These are supposed to make everyone calm and copacetic. My house is so rife with ectohormones that I'm surprised every cat in the neighborhood isn't swarming us.

I invest in these plastic sheaths to put over the cats' nails so that Gus can't attempt to filet Eddy when I put them together. Then I buy really great toys, like the Cat Dancer, that will keep everyone occupied when I do test runs of them together in the same room. And I pick up a kilo of catnip. I work on introducing everyone through concurrent play and their version of weed. Come on! It's a party! Everyone be cool, okay?

Nothing works.

I finally break down and put Eddy on kitty Prozac. The doctor said it will be a month before the meds fully take effect, if at all. So there's a possibility that this warfare will go on indefinitely. Argh, seriously? Don't I have enough to worry about right now with poor little Maisy?

I have to fix this.

I find some cat behaviorists online and am deeply dismayed to learn that the fees *begin* at $125 per e-mail consultation. I'm sorry . . . what? Now, I realize that the cats have cost me at least ten times that in damages, but I can't bring myself to write that kind of check for such a firstworld problem.

Kittens are free, indeed.

I also try to get Jackson Galaxy's *My Cat from Hell* show to work with us, but Fletch refuses to help me make a video. Something about our dignity being at stake? Pfft, like that wasn't gone *long ago.*

I have all of the above systems in place when I suddenly receive a dozen e-mails telling me to check out the link about Martha biting her cats.

Beg pardon?

As it turns out, Martha had just brought two new baby Persians into her house and lets her new cats know she's the boss by nibbling on their little faces.

I swear I'm not making this up.

The Internet pretty much lost its collective mind with Martha jokes, but this woman did not become a billionaire mogul by doling out bad advice. If Martha does it, then this shit must work.

I immediately rush up to my office, where the cats have since been relocated, and I pick up Eddy. I gently give her a nip on her wee cheek and I wait for a sign of recognition that I'm her true leader. She gives me a look as if to say, "I'd advise you against doing it again, bitch," so I figure the fault is mine and I didn't nip her hard enough.

I bite harder, this time on the top of her head. She cocks her head, flattens her ears, and gives me a tiny bite back.

We're communicating here! She gets it!

And then I give her another nip for good measure.

Eddy pulls full back from me and looks up, blinking her trusting green eyes. A true understanding passes between us.

Yes! We have liftoff! I've broken through to her!

Then, with the quickness of a cobra and the ferocity of a lion, she somehow unhinges her jaw and latches onto my nose like the refugees clung to the last chopper out of Saigon during Operation Frequent Wind.

But something happens as I try to shake her from my face. Other than bleeding, I mean.

My tolerance level and capacity for foolishness vanish faster than you can say "cat scratch fever." Here I've been babying these little assholes for months. I've catered to their every whim and tried so valiantly to understand their needs that I've forgotten mine.

I worked hard for these rugs and these floors. I deserve to lay my head on a pillow that's not damp with liquid displeasure, and I'm sick of all my shirts smelling like a litter box. I want to ride in the car with the windows down because I enjoy a breeze, and not just because I want the stench to dissipate.

This ends now.

I am the alpha cat, and every feline in this house needs to recognize that fact.

With a bottle of cat pheromones in one hand and a squirt gun in the other, I open the doors to my office and watch the Thundercats come pouring in. As Chuck and Gus attempt to pounce, I douse them with a solid stream of water, which, from their reaction, you'd assume was battery acid.

Each subsequent time they attempt to mount an attack, I spray them. Eddy and Patsy aren't immune, either. Whenever they give the boys the evil eye, they get a thorough spraying, too.

I spend the next week patrolling the house, squirting whenever needed. I keep a Rubbermaid thirty-two-ounce spray bottle looped through my yoga pants, as well as one in the kitchen, on my desk, in Fletch's office, and in the TV room, and every time a cat growls in warning, everyone gets wet. I find myself calling, "Who's got a hurting for a squirting? No one? That's what I thought!"

Yes, indeed, cats, there's a new sheriff in town.

And she's finished with your nonsense.

I'd like to say that all the cats are BFFs now and spend their days braiding one another's tails. That's not the case. You can't have that much animosity for that long and then all of a sudden become one another's bosom buddy. The girls primarily hang out upstairs, while the boys prefer the first floor and basement. They don't mix.

The thing is, they *do* coexist. They can walk by one another without feeling compelled to attempt an assassination. Their level of tension has dropped, so everyone else feels less tense, too. I'm overjoyed every time I see opposing forces sitting on the same couch. They may be on opposite ends, but they're there together.

Personally, I'm overjoyed to check this task off my list. And there's peace in my kingdom now, finally, because I grasped what Martha's known all along: Take control or be controlled. Your call.

And to think that if Fletch hadn't burned the balsamic, I'd have missed out on one of the most powerful lessons I've learned thus far.

Hurrah for the ineffectual home cook!

Much Ado About Dirt

Secret gardener confession: I hate soil.

Okay, that's not quite true. I love soil that's all rich and pH-balanced, composed of the perfect blend of peat and perlite, with built-in slow-release fertilizer, and tiny little beads that help maintain moisture balance. So, pretty much I like my soil prebagged and placed in my car by the nice kids at Pasquesi's nursery. What's in the actual ground is what throws me. I guess I just hate real dirt.

Container gardens have always been my preference because of the dirt situation. I buy my big, happy bags of Miracle-Gro, and when I reach into it, at no point do I encounter bands of clay or rocks or petrified doody. There are no pesky roots to hack through, and I never have to fling my trowel and run away screaming upon discovering that I've cut an earthworm in half in my gardening zeal.

So, even though I have a solid half acre of yard to garden, my efforts are primarily concentrated on the little baskets hanging off my fence, as well as planters spread across the patio.

I've been trying to do in-ground gardening for almost a decade, with an overwhelming lack of success. One year when I lived on Altgeld Street in the city, I spent weeks planting and tending, doing an admirable job lining the small path between the fence and walkway with all sorts of flowering greenery. This undertaking was successful because I'd dumped many cubic feet of fine bagged dirt on top of the pathetic topsoil, and the tiny yard was really beginning to take shape. But then a cottonwood tree from down the block dumped almost five inches of fluffy seedpods on my fledgling garden, immediately followed by torrential rains. Then I spent the rest of the summer weeding tiny cottonwood trees out of my plot and scattering neighborhood rats with hose spray. I sort of lost my enthusiasm after that.

Or how about last year? I attempted to fill a raised stone garden bed with an artful arrangement of perennial wildflowers and prairie grasses. The thing about wildflowers and prairie grasses is *they grow wild*; they germinate so quickly and spread so widely that people are always cutting them back and trying to contain them. I figured, "How hard could a wildflower garden be?"

As always, these are famous last words.

When we moved in, it was far too late in the season to do anything with the planter bed, so I spent all winter researching what might work there. My hope was that the 2011 wildflower and grass garden would be a lovely contrast to the roses. As my friend Laurie's husband, Mike, services my roses, the perimeter of the house always looks amazing.

I have more than fifty varieties of bushes. In the early summer, when they're all on their second bloom cycle, the fragrance is so intense that the air *tastes* like roses.

Before I had roses, I never knew that their scents varied. I kind of figured they were all rose-scented, yet fragrances can vary from fruit to vanilla to clover. For example, the floribunda by the back door are redolent of cinnamon and spice, while my Elle hybrid teas are more citrusy. My favorite variety is the robust red Mr. Lincoln, which em-

bodies a real traditional damask scent. And yet some of the most breathtakingly beautiful buds in my garden don't even have any fragrance at all. I figure this is the same reason that God gives supermodels boring personalities; you can't be a Victoria's Secret runway model *and* a brilliant conversationalist.

At least, that's what I tell myself.

Anyway, roses are notoriously difficult, so much so that I almost didn't want to buy this house. Fortunately, our Realtor is friends with Mike and Laurie. She explained how, for the price of a bouquet, Mike would continue to service our roses, thus neatly eliminating all my objections. An added bonus is that Mike's married to Laurie and now she and I are great friends.

So, Laurie and I are at our weekly Starbucks gathering and we're discussing my stupid, failed wildflower garden, one of the many small aggravations that was the year 2011.

"How did they not grow?" I ask. "That's like having rabbits that won't multiply, or groupies who won't make out with roadies to get closer to the band. Like, does not compute."

"Maybe it's the soil. Did you test it?" Laurie asks.

I blink in triplicate in response.

She continues. "You may have an acidity imbalance, or if there's too much clay, you could have a drainage issue. Maybe you don't have enough earthworms."

I think back to all the worm vivisections I accidentally performed when planting last year. "No, we're lousy with worms."

I sip my latte and remember a conversation I had with Angie last year. She'd had similar problems with her garden, so she checked to see what Martha recommended. The advice somehow culminated in Angie killing parasites by baking cookie sheets full of dirt in the oven.

"Ever smelled an oven full of hot dirt?" Angie demanded. "No? Then be thankful. Don't let Martha hoodwink you into cooking your topsoil. Stick to containers."

Yet the whole point of the year of Martha is to get out of my comfort zone, so I really can't keep doing what I'd been doing. I don't want another year of 2011 results. What if my future happiness hinges on my efforts in the garden?

Laurie offers, "I can come over and check out your dirt to see what you need."

I have to smile. "I really never thought the quality of my dirt would be important to me, but here we are. Please, yes, come over!"

"Why don't we go after we finish our coffee?"

"Thank you; that would be great, mostly because I don't know what to do with the bed. It's all . . . Well, you'll see." I'm having trouble describing the wasteland of stunted greens and wan, listless sprouts.

Soon we're in my yard inspecting the few pathetic shoots that reappeared this spring, aided by three enthusiastic dogs that keep plowing into us while we're bent over the soil.

I point to the back corner of the garden. "I don't get it. These were supposed to be sunflowers over here! They're practically a weed! You see them all over the sides of highways, and guys have to come out on riding lawn mowers because they grow so tall they obstruct drivers' vision!"

With an expert eye, Laurie assesses the garden placement. "Do these trees cast a shadow?" she asks, pointing to the wood line ten feet back.

A moment ago, the dogs raced circles around us. Now Maisy and Libby are wrestling, while Loki stands a few feet away and barks with much enthusiasm. I love watching Maisy tussle—one, because it means she feels well, and two, because of her fighting position. Instead of standing her ground, she lies on her back and wriggles around, pushing back Libby's advances with four kicking legs. She still has such abdominal strength that she can spin in a 360-degree circle like a breakdancer without ever losing contact with the grass. Fortunately, Laurie's a dog person, too, so the racket they're causing doesn't faze her in the least.

"They're showing off for you," I explain, pointing at the scrum of dogs that've just discovered a tennis ball. "But the shade? Not until late afternoon. This plot gets southeast sun all day, starting at daybreak."

Laurie scans her mental checklist. "What about water?"

I wish the problem were just water—but that's not an issue. "The sprinklers hit the corners, and I have a hose on the side of the house that I drag over. I keep the soil moist, but never saturated." Laurie nods encouragingly. "What really pisses me off is that I spent so much money on these damn plants. How do grasses *not grow*? We cut the lawn every week because it's so hardy. I wish it would grow slower. But the stuff I paid fifteen dollars per container for? Nothing!"

Laurie bends down and pulls off a green, leafy branch and then smells it. "Your mint is coming in beautifully, though."

At this moment, Libby and Maisy rocket through the bed, stomping directly on the mint, which immediately snaps back into place.

"Yeah." I snort. "That's the one plant I didn't want here. Fletch yanked it all out last year but it keeps coming back."

"Mint is the STD of the plant world," Laurie says. "Once it takes hold, it's almost impossible to eliminate completely."

"Tell me about it."

"So what *are* you going to do with the planter? Vegetables?"

I laugh bitterly. "Didn't I tell you? Fletch kept a corner of the plot for tomatoes, and they grew almost as well as the wildflowers. You know, there's a book called *The $64 Tomato*. Pfft, we got that beat.

"After the fact, I learned that Fletch was fertilizing his tomatoes every day. He's since banned himself from trying again."

"Oh, dear."

"I know, right? And at the time I was all, 'Why do we keep buying tomato fertilizer?' Live and learn. Anyway, we're planting a big organic garden on the other side once we have those trees cut down," I tell her, pointing to the area on the east end of the yard. There's a scrubby old pine tree that's about to go, even though I do enjoy watching Loki use the lower branches to scratch his ass. The first time we spied him backing butt-first into the pointy needles, we figured it was a fluke. But the next hundred? Not so much.

Laurie grabs the spade leaning against the side of the house and plunges it into the planter's soil. She turns over a couple of shovelsful and bends down to run her hand through the earth. She decrees, "This is perfect. This soil is truly perfect." Then she demonstrates how well it drains by filling the hole with water.

Maisy thunders over and demands a drink before we shut off the water. She snaps and snorts and ends up wearing more than she ingests. Libby takes off, because she wants nothing to do with the hose. I keep telling Fletch we've got to teach her to swim, and he keeps saying we should be thankful for the one dog that isn't always dampening clean sheets during clandestine bed naps.

"You're kidding!" I exclaim. I really didn't expect to hear my dirt was decent. "That's great news. I thought I'd have to replace it all."

Still, that doesn't explain why the wildflowers didn't take, but whatever. New year, new chance to try again.

"Have you considered a cutting garden over here?"

"I don't really know what that is," I admit.

Laurie explains how a lot of their clients keep a separate spot for cutting outside of the view of their main rose gardens, which makes perfect sense. I'm perpetually snipping off all the best blooms and spiriting them away inside, leaving big, gaping holes in the bushes by the pool.

Having a cutting garden would neatly eliminate the problem of scalped bushes. Plus, I'd feel like a pseudo-royal announcing to Fletch that I was off to the cutting garden, and he shan't expect me for tea. This is a capital idea!

I'm all excited, but then I have to stop myself. "Oh, wait—if I have a rose cutting garden, then I'll be cheating. I'd really need to tend to the flowers myself to stay true to the project."

"Then take care of them yourself. I can have Mike and his guys plant them, but you could be responsible for their maintenance," Laurie reasons.

I consider this. "You don't think that by having my own little plot and working with my own tools, I'd look like a little kid pushing one of those bubble vacuum cleaners, running after their mommy who's actually using a Hoover?"

Laurie swivels her head around to take in the wall of trees and blackthorn on the periphery of the yard. "Who's going to see you?"

This? Right here? Is why Laurie is awesome.

"Excellent point. Okay, let's do this." I'm excited—I'll have bonus roses, and I'll actively be learning from Martha as I review her tips for growing roses. This is great! This is progress! This is going to happen.

Laurie taps herself a note on her iPhone. "Okay, I'll get you a list to choose from. My suggestion is we mix heavy bloomers and highly fragranced roses for the best variety. Maybe group them by color, too, for the most drama."

"Excellent! What should I do?" In my head, I'm already shopping for floppy British gardening hats and open wicker baskets in which to place my snipped roses, because the notion of a cutting garden has suddenly turned me into Lisa Vanderpump of the Beverly Hills *Real Housewives*. Yes! Look at me! Life *is* all rosé and diamonds and hanging out with Camille Grammer! Of course, I'll have to buy lower-cut bras so I can leave my shirt open to midbreastbone, and I'll need to find men with Rod Stewart haircuts attractive. Also, I must meet and befriend Camille Grammer, but I can make this work if—

" . . . and you'll need to prepare the bed."

"I'm sorry; I zoned for a second thinking about the ex–Mrs. Frasier Crane. Long story. Anyway, what'd you say?"

"Clean it out. Yank everything up and transfer any plant you think might come back and you want to save. Then till down six inches and break up any root-balls."

"Whoa, wait, I can't just dump new dirt on top?"

"No need. What you have is perfect. But you will have to get rid of all the superfluous bits so you can start fresh."

Yeah.

That's pretty much the story of my life.

Only with more earthworm killing.

I Never Promised You
a Rose Garden

A string of idyllic late-May days pass, all in the low seventies with practically nonexistent humidity. Do I work on clearing the planter bed on those days? Of course not. As is my way, I wait until the last possible moment to address the task, at a time when the sun is fifteen feet overhead and so blazing hot that it's turning my shovel into molten metal. As I work, I find myself practically blinded because of all the sweat pouring into my eyes.

What I really don't understand is how these pathetic little shoots have such deep and strong roots. I curse each and every coneflower and butterfly bush as I huff and yank and hurl masses of dirty tendrils into the woods.

Thanks for being a dick, lavender hyssop!

I thought you were cool, bergamot!

How about I give YOU a black eye, Susan?

I'm especially angry when I recall exactly how much I paid for each plant, too.

Maybe I should have just put twenty dollars in the toilet instead, purple lovegrass!

As satisfying as it is to hurl these feckless specimens, I find I have to put Maisy and Libby inside, because each time I successfully chuck a recalcitrant root-ball into the woods, one of my ever-helpful best friends retrieves it.

Argh.

The last time I worked this hard outdoors was when I was a volunteer gardener for the city of Chicago back in 2010. What seemed like an excellent idea on paper went totally sideways in execution. I'd signed up to help an underprivileged neighborhood tend their community plot. The neighborhood association needed volunteers, because no one who lived there actually wanted to help, which should have been my first clue that this was a bad idea.

Ninety percent of my volunteer gardening time was spent picking up empty beer bottles, cigarette butts, and Doritos wrappers, although I did crack up the day I retrieved and reconstructed a whole handful of report card shards from the basil plants. One C, three Ds and an F? Yeah, I'd hide those grades from my parents, too, kid.

The most glorious part of the entire community garden was the chain-link fence separating the garden from the alley. What would have been a sad vista of a downscale Chicago alley was made incredibly beautiful by all the morning glories. The spectacular vines and flowers hid the fence and obscured the view with a mass of greens so dense and thick that the chain link looked like a huge bush that spanned from one side of the triple lot to the other.

Imagine my disappointment when the volunteer coordinator asked me to tear down all the morning glories. Apparently since they were a native plant not specifically cultivated by the garden's designer, they had to go. I didn't agree, but it wasn't my place to argue. (But, oh, how I wanted to!)

So I found myself ripping out some of the most lush, densest flora I'd ever seen, on a ninety-five-degree day in the middle of the city of Chicago. Sweat was running down the crack of my ass and pooling in my ears as I grappled with twined vines that had no intention of going down without a fight. I tried to comfort myself by pretending I was President Bush clearing brush at the ranch, and that helped for a while.

Of course, the most interesting part of the day was when I stumbled over a homeless guy sleeping under a particularly leafy outcropping of moonflowers. I'm not sure which of us screamed louder. I wasn't expecting to find a person in the bushes, much as he wasn't expecting to be stepped on by a fat chick wearing Crocs.

Others came running to find out the source of all the hollering. One of the male volunteers demanded that the homeless man leave, but as he was in the middle of having the world's longest pee, his exodus took longer than expected. While the volunteer shouted, the homeless guy kind of spun around and there was a bit of a backsplash situation, dovetailing nicely into another round of screaming.

This was the exact moment that I ended my tenure as a volunteer gardener.

Two points to make here: I'm as hot now as I was that day, and I can't believe none of my stupid morning glories grew last year.

While I attempt to pry out a particularly stubborn root system, Loki comes over to water a corner of the planter bed, which I notice only when a few drops of overspray hit me in the back of the leg. And that's when I realize I've hacked yet another earthworm in half.

God help these roses if they don't thrive here.

The roses have landed!

Or been planted. Same diff.

Because the roses in my cutting garden are brand-new, they don't require as much maintenance as the other bushes, with all their dense canes and old wood. The roses Laurie selected are incredible, and I'm madly in love with how she placed them—they're in groups of reds, whites, pinks, and oranges, all arranged by gradient of color. I keep telling her all *Analyze This*-style, "You, you're very good."

Laurie suggested it would be best if Mike's team sprayed the roses for me, because I don't have access to the same kind of treatments used by professionals.

(I suspect Laurie fears my making potions I found on the Internet and accidentally exploding my garage.)

(I suspect Laurie is right.)

Although I'm doing light pruning per Martha's dictates in her book *Gardening 101*, my main priority is managing the Japanese beetles.

By "managing" I mean killing those bastards dead in their tracks.

Although I'm neither Buddhist nor Taoist, I'm predisposed to respect all forms of life. Whenever possible, I opt to discourage pests, rather than destroy. I'm perpetually lifting spiders onto squares of cardboard and squiring them out the door. When we lived in the city, I'd control unwanted visitors (of the four-legged variety) with ultrasonic rodent repellent. The four months I spent as a pescatarian were among my best days, not only because I felt healthier, but because I felt good about not contributing to the factory-farmed animals' cycle of suffering. And if I ever had to hunt my own food? I'd go full-on vegetarian faster than you can say "Tofurky."

However, my compassion does not extend to Japanese beetles. These shiny little demons serve no purpose other than to feast on my roses. They're so destructive precisely because they have no natural predators in the Midwest . . . save for me.

I started off using various beetle sprays, but they aren't terribly effectual. I mean, they'll kill whatever bug they hit, but there's no residual effect. I can spray now and eradicate all the bugs on the bushes, but pesticide does nothing to stop the ones that fly in an hour later.

Laurie was so sick of seeing coppery-green swarms on her buds that she cut all her bushes down to six inches, as they feed on petals and not leaves. Their reign of terror is only about two months, and by cutting back her roses now in June, she'll have spectacular blooms in early fall.

I, however, am not about to be bested by a bug.

After listening to an archived portion of Martha's radio show, I learned that the most effective way to off the bugs is to knock them into a jar of soapy water, so I started to do that.

At first, I'd walk around the roses all tentatively, wearing gloves and batting the beetles into the foamy mixture with the tips of my pruning shears. But at this point? I'm flicking them onto the ground with my fingers and then smashing them with my foot. I hate my sense of satisfaction when I hear them crunch beneath the sole of my gardening clog. I wonder if there's not something intrinsically wrong with the rush of happiness I feel with every bug I eradicate.

The last time Laurie and I met for coffee, I noticed she had a small black dot on her cheek, which I assumed was mascara. Nope. Apparently it was a bit of beetle that had splattered when she crushed them between her fingers. I'm not the only cold-blooded one when it comes to the Japanese Menace.

I try to do my killing and subsequent watering first thing in the morning, so the plants are protected all day. I learned long ago that midday watering, especially when it's really hot, can burn plants. Because I pretty much just rolled out of bed, I'm wearing a short nightgown and a pair of cutoff sweats. I look like an idiot, and I'm thankful for the thick tree growth between me and my neighbors.

Today's a bad, bad day for the roses. I've never seen the beetles so clustered. There's one fledgling blossom that's so infested that none of the coral petals are even visible. All I can see is a writhing mass of coppery-green, and something primal in me takes over. With one deft movement, I snip off the entire cane and stomp the bejesus out of it while telling the beetles, "I'm not afraid to destroy something beautiful if it means you die as well."

This is simultaneously the most badass and sociopathic thing I've ever said.

I'm in the middle of my ministrations when I hear what sounds like a truck backing up. I'm curious as to what's happening, so I cut through the woods for a peek, careful that the driver doesn't see me or my pajamas. I pick my way through the brush while I'm assaulted by a million tiny branches. I'm hidden behind a line of buckthorn when I can finally see who's here.

Oh, yay! The city's fixing our sidewalk!

Last week there was a knock at our door, and it was a guy from the streets department telling me they'd soon be repairing the sidewalk in front of our house. Last summer, a tree root had caused the edge of a square of sidewalk to rise up about an inch, meaning every time I walked to the mailbox, I'd trip over the uneven spot. However, sidewalks are city property, so there wasn't anything we could do about it, right? Besides, this little blip was nothing compared to the sidewalks on Altgeld, where the cracks were big enough to swallow a Labrador. One inch? Pfft. May as well be one millimeter. My solution has been to simply ignore the blip . . . and make Fletch bring in the mail.

However, because I moved to an area with high property taxes and low crime, a sidewalk blip is a call to action. Someone complained about the blip, so the city immediately dispatched a work order. When the streets guy told us this, I wasn't sure whether to be pleased or insulted. "Oh, you don't like my sidewalk? Yeah? WELL, MAYBE I DON'T LIKE YOUR FACE."

That night, the little blip made me think about the massive blips in the old neighborhood, and I fell down the Google rabbit hole (again). I wound up reading an article about Altgeld Street. The story involved one of my neighbors, whom I specifically remember because she sneered at us for being renters, like somehow we brought down her property value. Yeah, *we* were the problem, with our neatly clipped lawn and sparkling windows, and not the expressway that was literally across the street, or the gang members who used our block as a highway-adjacent drug drop.

Anyway, according to the *Chicago Tribune*, this neighbor has spent the past six years fighting IDOT (the Illinois Department of Transportation) because of the vacant lot across from our row of houses. The lot was meant to be a buffer between homes and the Kennedy Expressway, but what it turned into was an enormous garbage dump full of dirty diapers, hypodermic needles, and old futons, in addition to being a haven for the homeless. The neighbor has been apoplectic over IDOT's lack of responsiveness.

Listen, this sucks and I'm sorry, lady. Don't forget, I lived there, too. I suffered as well.

But the thing is, this area was a trash repository long before she bought her place or I rented mine, and will likely be that way long after she moves away. Does she think she was the first one to drag a city garbage bin down the street, picking up beer bottles and empty Whopper wrappers?

Sorry, honey, not even close.

We'd originally hoped to buy that little row house, but we eventually moved instead, because there was no stemming that tide. The neighborhood was broken and no amount of effort would restore it.

What I realized in living there coincides with my struggle with the Japanese beetles and, truly, sums up another principle in Martha's Tao: Choose your battles—fight those you can win and avoid those you can't.

With diligence and a jar of sudsy water, I can conquer these stupid bugs. But I could never have stopped the onslaught of expressway trash blowing onto my tiny Altgeld lawn, so I eventually left. I am now grateful to live in a town that cares enough to fix minuscule problems before I lose a tooth when picking up the mail.

All is well and I am happy.

I wend my way back through the woods to the cutting garden. Note to self: Next time I want a walk in the woods, for whatever reason, I need to wear actual pants and not loosey-goosey cutoffs. I felt a weird little pinch a few minutes ago from where I do believe a small branch tried to get fresh with me.

I give all the plants a healthy watering, starting with the cutting garden. I like to keep the pressure high, because a steady pinpoint stream knocks off the beetles I missed on my jar mission.

I move on to the hanging baskets on the fences and I give all the pots on the patio a thorough hosing, too. I use the hand that's not holding the hose to try to adjust my underwear—I must have taken too large a stride while walking through the woods, because I've given myself a bit of a wedgie.

Stupid old ratty underwear.

Here's one of the ways that my situational, yet oddly pathological

cheapness manifests it-
self. Whereas I'm a per-
petual check grabber
when it comes to meals
out with friends, and
a new designer purse
still makes my heart
sing (and wallet open),
I can almost never pull
the trigger on the most

basic of purchases, like pajamas, socks, or underwear.

I love seeing how long I can go without having to pay for anything
new. I'm always all, "But I just bought a new pair of underpants four
years ago!" On any given day, I'm walking around in the saddest, most
rump-sprung, spray-tan-stained skivvies in the entire universe. I may
upgrade to business class when possible, yet I still have to inspect
each pair of socks for holes before I travel so I'm not embarrassed in
front of the TSA. Fletch says folding my laundry gives him second-
hand shame, and he'll occasionally sneak the most offensive items into
the trash. He actually got a little shouty when he discovered I was
wearing a workout shirt whose left-side seam was comprised entirely
of safety pins.

I readjust my sweat-shorts again with my left hand. The elastic on
these smallclothes must be busted, because I'm seriously uncomfortable.
I hustle to finish my watering and I head directly to the shower. I'm due
for lunch with the girls in the city in an hour and a half, and I wasted too
much time standing in the woods spying on the streets crew. Better make
this quick.

I run the shower to warm it and I step out of the offending underwear. Huh. This pair isn't so bad. They're neither worn so thin as to be
pornographic, nor are the holes egregious. Shoot, the elastic hasn't even

begun to separate from the leg holes! These are practically my Sunday best!

I wriggle under the warm water, still bothered by the odd pinching, so I lather up the washcloth and begin to scrub, and then . . . ow.

What is that?

Is that *something*?

I glance down.

Wait, no.

No.

Nooooo.

That is all wrong.

That's a . . .

. . . OH, SWEET JESUS IN HEAVEN, I'M GOING TO DIE!

"I have been violated."

Three pairs of eyes at the community table at Lula's cut over to me because that's the last thing anyone expected me to reply when asked, "What's been going on?"

"Is this about the sidewalk?" Tracey asks.

"Is someone on the Internet wrong again?" Stacey adds.

"Oh, no," I exclaim. "The sidewalk is great. I'm *glad* people complained about it. The new sidewalk is outstanding. I'm *all about* the sidewalk. I'm talking about violation."

"Do you need to spell it to tell us?" Gina inquires before taking a sip of her iced tea–lemonade.

We're interrupted by our regular waiter before I can continue. Gina and I ask for our usual breakfast burritos, only she always gets hers without avocado. Our waiter, bless his heart, tells us about his avocado allergy *every single time.* There's not much guaranteed in this world, save for the tides rising, the sun setting, and a skinny-jeans-clad hipster in Logan Square sharing stories of guacamole-based gastric distress.

Once our orders are placed, Stacey leans in and says, "Define 'violation.' You tweeted that you were violated when the girl at LaGuardia was wearing acid-washed jeans and a sports bra. That kind of violated?"

"No, not aesthetic violation. This is serious. I'm talking about *personal* violation. My person was violated." I shudder before parsing out each syllable. "Vi-yo-lay-shun. I was . . . I was . . ."

I have to take a deep breath before I can continue. The horror of what happened is almost too much for me to contemplate and I have to steady myself.

"I was . . . accosted by an arachnid."

I wait for them to gasp and clutch their chests, simultaneously reaching for my hand while daubing away their tears with a napkin.

"Yeah, I don't know what that means," Stacey replies.

I huff, "I'm touched by your compassion. Truly. Maybe you should work a suicide crisis hotline, because clearly you are gifted."

Stacey goes, "Uh-huh. Still don't know what that means."

I try to compose myself. "Okay, there I was, minding my own business in my cutoff sweats, which are great to wear for gardening because they're loose and breezy and my downstairs lady-theater doesn't get sweaty."

"Kudos on finding a way to be descriptive without actually saying v-a-g-i-n-a," Tracey tells me.

I grit my teeth. "FYI? I hate you all. Anyway, some tick sensed an opportunity and took it. One minute I was smiting Japanese beetles, and the next, this mothersucking tick scurried up my open leg hole and into my flappy underpants and then embedded himself directly in my . . . my . . . West Virginia. I was tick-raped."

I pause so that they may take a moment to soothe me.

They do not soothe me.

However, they do cry.

"*Stop laughing at me, you assholes!* Have you nothing productive to say about this?"

Tracey is the first to compose herself. "I thought ticks were arthropods, not arachnids."

"You are wrong; I looked it up," I curtly reply.

"We get covered in ticks at the farm whenever we walk in the woods," Stacey tells me. "Never had one in my pants, but I did have one in my bra not long ago."

I hiss, "It's not the same. Your tick got to second; mine hit a home run."

Gina pats my hand. "I hope you don't get West Nile."

I can feel myself scowling. "Well, shit, I never even thought about that. I'd be all, 'I went on a happiness project and all I got was this lousy autoimmune disease.'"

Tracey helpfully adds, "I'm sure that won't happen."

"You think?" I ask, hopeful that she's right.

"Yeah." She nods. "You're probably more likely to get Lyme disease."

"Oh!" Stacey crows. "Like Irene on *The Real World: Seattle!*"

Gina's face registers a flash of recognition. "Remember when Stephen slapped Irene when she said he was gay? He's gay now, by the way."

I bang my hand on the table. "Let me just say this—one of you motherfuckers is buying my burrito today."

"I think it's my turn," Stacey volunteers.

"So, wait," Tracey says, "you were killing beetles when this happened? You think all the bugs in your yard are in cahoots? Maybe this was insect-world payback, like when there's a gang shooting."

Our meals come and Stacey adds, "Makes sense he headed for your underwear. Ticks do go for warm, moist places, you know."

Then I almost can't each my lunch, what with my hands clapped over my ears and all.

As I chew my burrito and glower at my friends, I make myself two promises:

A) That somehow I'm weaseling out of paying for lunch next time, too, and, B) that I need to buy new underwear, like, today.

Six pairs of Jockey for Her French-cut hipsters have just arrived. Look at them, all fresh and nice and opaque! I try on a pair and they're snug in all the right ways. Nothing's sneaking past these leg holes; I can assure you of that. And they don't hang down in the back like a saggy diaper that leaks! This must be how Kate Middleton felt the day she received Diana's engagement ring!

Although I can't credit Martha or her Tao with this particular win, I'm substantially happier than when I had nothing but raggedy drawers, so it still counts.

I shall celebrate this major accomplishment by executing more beetles . . . in comfort *and* safety.

"Mike's worried about your cutting garden."

"Why, what's wrong with it?" I ask. Laurie and I are at

our weekly coffee date. "I feel like I'm doing everything right. I'm even dipping my shears in alcohol between bushes so I don't cross-contaminate them, just like Martha says."

I've gone so far as to research rose hybridization and have plans to mate the Mr. Lincoln variety with the abundant blooming Betty White this spring. The process involves pistils, pollen sacs, male and female parts, and, let's be honest, likely a bit of giggling on my part, but I'm serious about taking my roses to the next level.

Laurie is not convinced. "Maybe I should check on them anyway. You free after coffee?"

"Absolutely! Come over! I want you to see the hydrangea bushes I planted."

When Laurie was here a few weeks ago, she helped me to visualize what Martha's always talking about—sometimes less is more. I had so many different things happening in my containers that they were more distracting than attractive. Laurie taught me the concept of giving the eye a focal point in the garden, and since then, I've concentrated more on using my plants to tell a color story, and less on HERE'S EVERY-THING I HAVE EVER PLANTED IN MY LIFETIME. LOOK AT IT, LOOK AT IT, LOOK AT IT! I've been delighted with the results.

In planting the row of hydrangeas in calming greens and whites, I even got over my fear of having to put plants directly in the earth.

Okay, so maybe I had Fletch plant them, but I wasn't anxious by proxy, and that's almost as good.

The dogs have joined us outside, but it's so hot that Libby's lying under a tree while Loki takes a few laps in the pool. I admire that dog's ability to regulate his own temperature. I'm less fond of his desire to spray us with pool water as he shakes off, but that's kind of who he is. Maisy's stationed on one of the lounge chairs, because she's as fond of the sun as I am.

Occasionally she'll glance over at us, panting and smiling her enormous pit bull grin. She's happy as a lizard on a hot, flat rock. She thumps her tail in greeting and I blow her a kiss.

Laurie casts a discerning eye on the new growth. "I don't like what's happening with these buds. I see what Mike meant. Look at this little guy—he's listless." She palms a curled brown bud.

"Is it the beetles? Because I've been relentless with them," I tell her. "I have gone Hiroshima all over their asses. I've decimated the beetles' infrastructure and they're not going to rally for thirty years and until they invent a more gas-efficient vehicle. Then they'll eventually rule again due to technology and superior math skills, but I'll probably be dead by then, so it's fine."

"Uh-huh, yeah, the beetles usually go for the more mature flowers. I can't put my finger on what's wrong here, but something doesn't add up. Are you using the drip line all the time?"

I shrug. "Well, yes and no. I mean, I do hose them occasionally, like to knock off the beetles."

"Show me."

"What do you mean?"

"Can you show me how you water them?"

"Uh, okay?" I pick up the hose and blast away. "See? Look at how the beetles fly off when I hit them with the pinpoint of water!"

Laurie claps her hand to her suddenly pale forehead. "Tell me you're kidding."

"What? No, this is how I always water. The water comes out too slow on all the other settings, and if I use the sprinkle option, it takes forever. Plus, if I spray them really hard, the watering job goes a lot faster and then I can get on with my day."

"Jen, you can't spray the roses on that setting."

I'm genuinely puzzled.

"Really? But I thought a powerful stream would make them stronger, like the plants have to toughen up because they're being worked so hard." I lift my arms up to shoulder level and make biceps to illustrate my point.

As soon as these words fly out of my mouth, I realize exactly how stupid they sound when spoken aloud.

"No, no! You're making them weaker! They can't stand up to that kind of water pressure! They simply cower because they have such skinny little necks. Is that how you sprayed your wildflower garden, too?"

Mutely, I nod.

"Well, now you know. Stop it. Stop watering this way. Never do it again, okay? Also, I'm going to call Mike now and let him know we figured out what was going wrong."

While Laurie places her call, I sit down next to Maisy. All I can do is laugh at myself—I honestly, truly thought I was doing what was best for my roses, and in so many complicated ways, I was. Yet the basics? Well, perhaps I could have used a refresher course first.

Still, it took Martha almost twenty years to build up her rose garden in East Hampton, so I'm not going to let this setback discourage me. In fact, I want to expand the cutting garden next year and incorporate bushes from David Austin Roses, which were featured on Martha's television show in 2011. But this time, I'll seek more of Laurie's advice *before* I proceed, instead of after. I guess that's why Martha's always so willing to bring experts on to explain the complicated bits. She's already mastered the piece of the Tao that I'm just now realizing: There's value in doing it yourself; there's more value in learning to do it yourself from someone who's been there before you.

So I'm going to take everything I learned from this experience and channel it into what's next—planting an organic vegetable garden.

Look out, earthworms. I'm a-coming for you.

ZUCCHINI RICH

Now that I have a handle on the roses, my thoughts turn to vegetables.

Specifically, one vegetable.

All I want is some zucchini.

Everyone says to me, "You don't want to plant zucchini—you'll have too much."

Okay, A) there's no such thing as too much zucchini, and B) mind your damn business.

Besides, the idea of an overabundance of zucchini is like saying, "Stop working so hard or you'll have way too much money!" Or, "If you keep dieting and exercising like that, you'll wind up with the ass you had at sixteen!"

Trust me: These are the problems I want.

If my desire is to be lousy with zucchini, that's my choice. I want it to cover my countertops and fill my crisper drawers. I want to stick excess zucchini in the fruit bowl because that's the only place left to put it. I want it to *rain* zucchini up in here; do you understand me?

I love zucchini. I love everything about zucchini. I love saying the word "zucchini." Zucchini, zucchini, zucchini! Even the individual syllables are charming! You can't not be happy around such a big, green, comical-sounding foodstuff. Zucchini's hilarious *and* delicious!

Plus, zucchini's my absolute favorite vegetable, so tales of zucchini the size of baseball bats and in amounts enough to fill a bathtub are anything but a deterrent. Every time I pick one of my zucchini from my organic garden, I'm going to be all, "Ha! Saved two dollars! Ha! Saved two more dollars! Ha! I don't care if the world monetary system collapses, because I will be rich with the only (tasty) green currency that counts!"

I keep hearing, "Oh, you won't know what to do with all your zucchini," but I beg to differ. I'm all about zucchini bread, zucchini muffins, grilled zucchini, sautéed zucchini, baked zucchini, and stuffed zucchini.

In anticipation of my bountiful harvest, I've already bookmarked Martha's recipes for zucchini lasagna, zucchini frittata, zucchini salad, and sweet zucchini cupcakes, followed by zucchini fries, zucchini gratin, and zucchini risotto. I want it roasted; I want it curried; I want it tossed with corn and orzo. I want it steamed and skewered and stuffed in a sandwich. I want to open my freezer this winter and see nothing but frozen zucchini-based dishes, so when everyone else is supping sadly on their third-world zucchini, flown in on ice-cap-melting, polar-bear-killing jets, I'll still be enjoying good ol' patriotic zucchini made right here in 'merica.

I want to build a food pyramid entirely out of zucchini.

I want to cut myself and bleed zucchini and then patch myself up with a bandage made of zucchini.

I want to be the Bubba Gump of zucchini.

(Also, to everyone who's warned me of the ills of zucchini and explained how you had so much you couldn't even give it all away? I never saw a single slice of it, so please know I hate you a little right now.)

So, clearly I'm Team Zucchini, yet there are a couple of obstacles standing between me and All Zucchini, All the Time. Before I can plant my badass organic garden, we have to make room for it.

Presently, there are a few trees in our yard that are the bane of my existence, particularly this one huge ash on the side of the house by the kitchen. Every time it storms, I think, "Well, it was a nice roof while it lasted." Although I'd love a skylight in there someday, I'd prefer *we* install one, rather than Mother Nature.

Bob the Arborist is here today to assess the ash tree in relation to my future zucchini garden.

"Well, from the angle of the sun, I'd say you can find a way to keep the tree without sacrificing light," Bob the Arborist tells us. We've already decided to lose a couple of scrubby pines and one weird tree that causes the birds to shart pink goo all over my patio chairs when its berries are in bloom. The trees are all dying and I won't miss them.

"But the ash keeps dropping massive branches every time it rains. Plus, the limbs look moldy," I tell him. In my head, I call this tree an ash-hole.

"What you see is the early stages of an emerald ash borer infestation. It's soon enough to catch and treat, though. We can save it."

"That's good news, right?" Fletch asks. I cut him some side-eye. Oh, honey, that is *not* good news. The minute an expert tells me something can be saved is the minute my wallet cries for mercy. I brace myself for his estimate. I've learned the rule of thumb in suburbia pricing is to come up with what I think is a fair price and then add a zero to it. We had a chimney repair guy in here who told us he could do everything for the very reasonable cost of . . . fifteen *thousand* dollars. I wasn't even mad; I just burst out laughing. Heck, it's a year later and his bid is still funny. Do I have "SUCKER" tattooed on my face? Did he believe that the Internet doesn't exist and I didn't Google that shit before he got here? Listen, Chimney Dude, unless Channing Tatum himself is going to reline the flues, then no, thanks. I'll stick to burning candles in the fireplace for now.

(Side note: Fletch mocks me for my constant Channing Tatum obsession, but the man has a pit bull named Lulu whom he taught to do the *Dirty Dancing* move where Baby flies into Patrick Swayze's arms at the end. What do you want from me? Channing's calling plays directly from my psyche! I'm not made of stone, you know!)

"Bottom line, how much would it cost to save the ash-hat?" I ask.

"I'm sorry?" Bob the Arborist asks.

"The ash—how much will treatment cost?"

Bob the Arborist launches into a five-minute explanation about various steps and inoculations, and every thirty seconds, I can hear a cash register *ca-ching* in my head.

". . . so over five years, you're looking at about seven," he finishes.

"Seven what? Seven hundred?" Fletch queries.

Fletch doesn't believe my add-a-zero theory, yet it gets him every time.

"No, seven thousand."

Fletch looks as though he's been punched in the gut. Aw, it's adorable that he thinks for one second that I'm going to fork over seven freaking thousand dollars to resuscitate a tree I actively despise.

"And how much to chop it down?" I ask.

Bob the Arborist is aghast. "But it's a great tree! Given the size and spread, it's at least one hundred years old. Surely you'll want to save it."

I snort. "Um, no. For seven thousand dollars over five years, that tree would have to drive me to work. How much to cut it down, grind the roots, and haul it away?"

Grudgingly, Bob the Arborist consults his clipboard. "Four hundred dollars."

"Sold!"

I'm sure in Cantitoe Corners, Martha's Bedford home, she'd do whatever she had to do in order to save her old-growth trees. In fact, the estate's insignia is that of a bushy sycamore. But one of us is a billionaire and the other had to be violated in order to invest in a few pairs of underpants without holes, so there you go.

(Later this year, during Hurricane Sandy, Martha will lose power and outbuildings' roofs when massive old trees begin to tumble all over the property. Although I'm sorry for her loss and I sympathize with the inconvenience, I have to reiterate my point that sometimes trees are assholes.)

As a nod to Martha, when the ash does come down the next week, I take a section and turn it into a plant stand, sort of like what she had Dane Buell (the arborist) of SavATree do when he turned her fallen sycamores into gigantic tabletops.

And now that ol' Ashtree Wilkes is gone, I sort of miss him—like to the point of anthropomorphizing him—but I'm definitely not feeling seven thousand dollars' worth of melancholy.

At least, not until I'm zucchini-rich.

At the very beginning of the summer, Laurie brought me with her to the private gardens of this wealthy North Shore industrialist. She had to deliver one tiny pink rosebush and thought I'd get a kick out of seeing what nine acres of manicured lakefront garden might look like. If by "kick," she meant "life-altering experience," then yes, I got a kick out of it.

I've never before witnessed so much beauty in one spot. On those grounds, even the ordinary was made extraordinary. Like, I buy little pots of pretty pink and purple fuchsias every year. They're annuals, so they die when it gets cold and the plant never grows larger than the standard-size pots I keep them in. Yet that place boasted multiple greenhouses, so the basketball-size fuchsias at my house are as big as Christmas trees there. Maybe you see that kind of thing in the tropics, but definitely not in Lake County, Illinois. Or, I have a couple of fledgling hydrangea bushes; they had a solid wall of them. I have sixty rosebushes; they possessed thousands that are well established enough to enclose an area the size of a soccer field.

Each part of the garden is considered a "room," and every room was designed by a world-renowned horticulturalist. What amazed me so much weren't the parts like three open acres of crosshatched bent grass, ringed with one hundred different types of exotic plants, all symmetrically placed to the point that the owner/landscape architects knew they needed one tiny pink bush, even though those sections blew my mind.

(In those rooms, every tree was sculpted—all were square, round, or rectangular, like it's Willy Wonka's arboretum.)

What got me was how even the smallest bits were painstakingly detailed. I spied a tiny patch outside the living room window comprised of various thyme varietals and arranged in such a way that the colors formed an argyle plaid. Spectacular!

The best part of the gardens was the simplest; on the side of one of the gardeners' offices lay a vegetable garden, but it was so artfully arranged that it was just as beautiful as the knot garden room (. . . and the English rose room . . . and the French avenue of side-by-side square trees and pea gravel room . . . and the Japanese room . . . and the conservatory . . . seriously, the place just went on and on and on). I loved how instead of the tomatoes being staked with cages or a couple of strips of plywood, the vines climbed on antique topiaries. Vegetable sections were defined and divided by clusters of zinnias and dahlias and were interspersed with interesting bits of statuary. (And did they grow zucchini? You bet your ass they did!)

What I took from this experience was to incorporate beauty into my own vegetable plot, though clearly on a much smaller scale. Originally, the plan was to construct a simple raised bed via Martha's *Gardening 101* instructions. Fletch and I would create big boxes from plain pressure-treated pine and we'd do three or four of them side by side, none of them so large that we couldn't access all the plants without stepping inside. Yet here's the thing—the boxes we planned to build aren't pretty. I realize that's a silly complaint, but the boxes would be in full view of the pool and the porch and the patio, and I want them to look nice.

So we're waiting on a quote from Rich the Landscaper for planting boxes made out of the more attractive pressure-treated cedar landscape timbers, like I saw in the big garden on the lake. (I'm dreading the extra zero, naturally.)

We're halfway through June at this point and I'm growing more and more anxious about the status of the project. I meant to get started in May, but the trees weren't down yet. Plus, I spent three weeks on the road for my book tour, and when I was home on the weekend, I concentrated only on my containers. That doesn't mean I didn't gaze longingly at the vegetables while loading up on geraniums, of course, but I didn't want to invest in zucchini or strawberries or green beans until I had a place to put them. I'd tell the little-bitty zuchs, "Hey, good-lookin', I'll be back to pick you up later!" And then, of course, I experienced the big garden on the lake and I changed my parameters. I figured if a vegetable patch is going to be a permanent part of the yard, it shouldn't be an eyesore.

Because I want to feel like I'm doing something productive out here today (outside of not ruining my roses anymore, I mean), I'm eschewing my usual Miracle-Gro fertilizer in favor of this organic stuff I found at Pasquesi. (Best store ever! They sell plants, potpourri, home decor, Vera Bradley accessories, and pet supplies. Again, it's like someone's torn a page right out of my psyche.)

In *Healthy Home 2008*, Martha explains how organic fertilizer is far superior because it's less likely to dry or burn the soil than its nitrate-based synthetic counterparts. Which sounds great. If I were really being conscientious and environmental, I'd do my own composting, too, but I've already mentioned my issues with earthworms, yes? I may hate them more than snakes. At least snakes aren't slimy. Plus, I know my dogs' limitations enough to understand that there's no structure full of decomposing garbage strong enough to keep them out.

Because I'm someone capable of eventually learning a lesson, I'm wearing slim-fit capri pants over my bathing suit instead of cutoff sweats, and I've yanked all my hair back in a do-rag. The dogs had been milling around, but they saw a squirrel on the other end of the yard and lost their minds so hard I had to put them inside. Maisy's a bit tired anyway, so she won't mind the chance to rest.

I must admit I'm enjoying the rare solitude out here. This is nice, really Zen in so many ways. I like feeling one with nature, without benefit of iPod. I'm simply listening to the breeze ruffling the leaves and the birds chirping. This may well be happiness's sound track. I feel both calm and at peace. I suspect this is why Martha's so comfortable with the outdoors—it's a real chance to clear one's head.

I grab a big purple bucket and begin filling it with water. (Even the sound of the flowing water is soothing!) The instructions on this stuff are pretty similar to that of Miracle-Gro, meaning I dump the contents into the bucket, give it a little swirl with my forearm, and then pour an appropriate amount into each container. I always appreciated Miracle-Gro because I can monitor exactly how much I've put in by how blue the water becomes.

I shake up the bottle of enviro-friendly solution and I squirt it into my bucket, and, much to my surprise, the contents are not blue.

The contents are more . . . what happens after you accidentally drink the water in Tijuana.

Ugh, this is disgusting.

I break off a stick from a buckthorn bush, because there's no way in hell I'm sticking an arm in here. As I stir, the first waves of smell hit me and I'm again reminded of Montezuma's revenge. GROSS. What *is* this stuff?

That's when I read the label and discover that I'm fertilizing with bat guano and earthworm droppings. So . . . this is a delightful cocktail of liquid bat and worm shit.

I'd like to barf now, please. Yet I'm committed to at least trying this concoction, so off to my containers I go, breathing entirely through my mouth.

I pour the first batch onto my geraniums, and I swear, if they could sneer, they would. They're all, "I'm sorry. Where's our lovely azure Miracle juice? Have we committed some kind of heinous offense against you that precipitates your dousing us in diarrhea?" A slight breeze blows, and if I didn't know better, I'd say the petunias were shaking with disgust.

As I pour, some of the putrid liquid splashes onto my feet and seeps into the holes of my Crocs. With the same kind of caution one might use when handling a grenade, I set down my pail of *agua diablo* and I scurry over to give my feet a Silkwood shower with the hose.

As the process continues, and despite my best efforts at being cautious, I continue to contaminate myself with bat and earthworm droppings. I thought I'd been through the worst of it when a bit splashed onto my shoulder, but that was nothing compared to when a droplet flew into my eye.

AHH!

I'm going to go blind from eye ringworm, and you know what? *That* will not help me be happier. I've had a whale of a time killing beetles and picking roses and listening to the wind ruffle the leaves, but this? This does not move the needle on the old joy-ometer. What this portion of organic gardening has inspired right now is the opposite of happy. I am feeling downright churlish. What would make me happy is to kick this big bucket o' crapwater across the yard.

I'm not even sure I want zucchini anymore.

Okay, yes, I do, but suddenly I wonder if I might be happier paying two dollars for it at the farmers' market.

However, I blithely remain committed to feeding my plants organic fertilizer, until a bit splashes *in my mouth* and I'm compelled to pitch the remainder of the bottle into the woods at the far end of the yard.

Let us never speak of this again.

Maybe I'll just have a regular garden. I mean, it was all well and good when Aidan Quinn came on Martha's show to discuss organic gardens and talked about honoring the earth, but he said *nothing* about tasting bat shit. I watched the segment twice just to make sure. Also, Martha told

Aidan to use non-pressure-treated lumber to build the planter boxes, so now I'm confused.

After I've showered, I hop on the Internet to figure out what it's not too late to plant. I've already missed my window of opportunity for strawberries, broccoli, peppers, eggplant, tomatoes, and all the leafy veggies, like chard and spinach. That's kind of a bummer. I wanted to have friends over and be all, "Please, enjoy this nutritious salad from my garden, picked fresh this morning," A) because there's nothing like fresh-picked veggies, B) because that seems like such a Martha thing to do, and C) there's a modicum of smugness that comes from being able to create food using nothing but earth and sky. You think Martha's tearing open one of those Dole triple-washed bags for a luncheon? Not bloody likely.

If we're able to set up beds in the next week, I should still have time for beans, beets, carrots, cucumbers, pumpkins, and squashes, which include zucchini.

We're still okay here.

Zucchini bread is going to happen.

I Never Promised You an Organic Garden, Either

Zucchini bread is not going to happen.

The good news is my streak of adding-zero predicting remains intact. The landscapers came back with an estimate of *six thousand dollars* to install four planter beds, and what they proposed wasn't even that pretty. We told them an emphatic no, a hell, no, a do-we-look-stupid no, and decided we'd simply revert to plan A, which was building them ourselves. But then Maisy took a turn for the worse with a bad reaction to new chemo drugs, and we ended up making multiple runs to the emergency vet over the course of a week. By the time we had a minute to get beds together, it was too almost too late in the growing season and our hearts weren't in it anymore.

I probably could have thrown something together, but I've since soured on my former slapdash, good-enough way of conducting myself. The big garden on the lake wasn't built on a foundation of half-assery;

nor should mine be. I can wait until next year to do an organic garden right from the beginning.

This whole process has enlightened me on another Tao concept, which is: Do or do not; there is no halfway.

When we asked Rich the Landscaper for an estimate on the garden, we also requested pricing to plant impatiens and blue salvia along the driveway. There's a currently a couple of little triangles that are nothing but mulch and they make a lackluster entrance to the property. In total, there's about thirty square feet to plant, so given what I know about soil and impatiens pricing, I estimated the cost to be about two hundred dollars. I figured the job was so small that this was one case in which the rule of zero wouldn't apply.

Note to self: The rule of zero *always* applies.

So, Fletch and I are out here again on yet another hundred-degree day, ready to beautify these triangles with sixty dollars' worth of impatiens. Net savings? One thousand nine hundred and forty dollars, or nine hundred and seventy zucchini!

Fletch seems vaguely embarrassed at my outfit—a black-and-blue-striped tank suit worn with bright green track pants, turquoise running shoes, and a white do-rag, but I don't care. I need to be cool and I need to be protected. My slavish devotion to fashion ends at the West Virginia border, if you know what I mean.

"This shouldn't take more than an hour," I tell him. "We're going to line these impatiens up in five rows of ten, dig corresponding holes, and bing-bam-boom, done."

I lay down a towel at the far end of the pyramid to protect my knees while I kneel. I don't have gardener's kneepads, per se, but I do have ones for Rollerblading—they're hot pink. Yet I suspect if I go any more Technicolor Dreamcoat, Fletch will stage a walkout, and I really need his help.

I place my trowel in the earth and pull up a thimbleful of dirt. Hmm.

This area is packed a bit more tightly than what was in the cutting garden. I plunge in again and immediately hit a tree root. I try again and this time manage to move a teaspoon. So I dig and I dig and I dig, and five minutes later I've finally displaced enough earth to insert my impatiens just low enough to cover the roots. Yeah, this is definitely taking a bit longer than expected, by four and a half minutes.

"Is the dirt superpacked on your side?" I ask.

"Check. Hey, I thought you told me this area was ready to plant," Fletch says.

"I thought it was," I reply. "But look, I got these in." I motion toward what I just planted.

"That's way too shallow," he tells me.

"Are you sure? Seems fine to me," I argue.

Then he walks over and blows on the impatiens and they fall down. He steps back and wordlessly places his hands on his hips.

"Okay, maybe it's a little shallow," I admit.

He jumps into my spot and begins to try to dig the hole deeper. After a few minutes, he scoffs, "This is impossible!" then tosses down his trowel, which actually serves to make me feel better. I thought I was just being a big baby.

"I can't work like this—I'm going to run to the Ace and buy a tiller. I'll be back in fifteen minutes." He rushes back to the house to grab his keys and then he's off. I take the opportunity to come inside to give Maisy kisses on her perch in the great room. When she doesn't feel well, she stations herself on the love seat, because it allows the most optimum line of sight into the rest of the house, as well as most of the doors. That way, she can keep track of everyone's comings and goings without having to get up.

I hand-feed Maisy a few bites of pork roast, but she's not as enthusiastic as usual. Normally she'd take off a finger in her zeal, but today she chews politely, as though to humor me. Her bad reaction to the new meds resulted in a lethargic appetite, and I'm a bit challenged to get food into her. So far this week, I've made her a lovely ground-beef-and-rice dish, sautéed chicken tenders, and a pork roast.

However, with patience and diligence, I'm eventually able to get all the pork into her, and only then do I go back outside to meet Fletch. I find him in the same spot, swearing and sweating. The tilling is not going well.

"Maybe we should have Rich's guys plant this area," Fletch says. "They likely understood how untilled this earth was and knew the amount of effort they'd have to put in."

"Yeah, I'm not spending Maisy's emergency fund to plant sixty dollars' worth of impatiens. We can do this." I kneel back on my towel and begin to make a hole. The process is easier this time, slightly, and I manage to get a couple of impatiens in the ground. It's not until I move over a foot that I encounter the massive layer of clay and root. Argh.

"I was afraid it would come to this," he says. Fletch goes back to the garage and returns with some kind of gardening implement. It's two long wooden poles attached to a serrated canister. He lines up his spot and then with all his might, slams the canister part in the ground with a thump and gives it a solid twist, followed by a couple of grunts and a stomp, leaving the perfect-size hole in which to place my impatiens.

"Well, that doesn't look so hard," I say.

"Oh? You want to give it a try, Hercules?" He hands the fence-posting contraption over to me and I attempt to operate it the same way that he does, but I'm able to drive it only about an inch into the ground. "That's what I thought. Okay, I'll make the holes; you plant and backfill them."

We crawl along, thump-twist-grunt-grunt-stomp, thump-twist-grunt-grunt-stomp, and we're still getting only one impatiens in the ground every five minutes. At this rate, we'll be out here for five hundred minutes.

No wonder Fletch no longer believes me when I claim something will take an hour.

We plod on. We're making slow, steady progress and finding our rhythm. Whereas I wouldn't say things are going well, I would say we've found our groove.

That is, until I sit on a nest of red ants, whereupon I'm compelled to whip my pants into traffic. I spend the next ten minutes running around the driveway in my bathing suit and sneakers, screaming and attempting to soothe my inflamed rump with the hose.

I am livid.

"This! This is why I hate dirt! I have lived forty-four years with what, a couple of bee stings and a handful of mosquito bites? But now I am America's Most Wanted when it comes to the insect world. I'm Public Enemy Number One. No, wait—*Pubic* Enemy Number One. Why? What did I ever do to them? I'm nice to bugs! I'm all about the Tao of not killing shit unnecessarily. Yet all they want to do now is *get up in my business*! That's it. I'm done. D-O-N-E. Now I want you to take all the impatiens we've planted thus far and help me stick them in the trash. That's it. No more. We're tossing these out."

"You should probably calm down," Fletch says. "We're almost halfway finished. We can power through this."

"That's easy for you to say; you don't have ants in your fucking pants!"

He gestures toward the road. "Technically your pants are in the street."

"NOT HELPFUL!" I bellow.

Fletch wipes an ocean of sweat away from his brow. "Why don't you go inside and put some Benadryl or calamine lotion on your bites and I'll work on this while you're gone."

"That's one idea," I say. "The other entails sticking every last one of these stupid impatiens in the garbage. Let's explore that option when I get back."

"You really want to put sixty dollars directly in the trash?"

"Most definitely. I've never been surer of anything in my life."

He tries to reason with me. "What would Martha say about your defeatist attitude?"

I shrug. "I don't know. Perhaps we can shove some fire ants in her shorts and find out."

Fletch seems resigned yet determined. "You go get a drink; I'll be here."

I march my scorching case of baboon bottom back to the house, where I wash the affected area and then apply a potion of Benadryl, anti-itch cream, and Neosporin. By the time I'm done hand-feeding Maisy more dinner and rubbing my hindquarters against a doorjamb to quell the itch, Fletch finishes the planting job.

"It's done," he says with great weariness. His demeanor is that of a soldier just returned from a battle full of casualties. He seems changed, lessened, hardened. There's not an inch of his T-shirt that isn't saturated, and he's ringed in filth. And yet he's proud of the job he's done, as well he should be. Right now, he is my hero.

I'd hug him if I didn't think he'd punch me.

I love what he's been able to do with the flowers. The triangles are all bright and festive with coral and peppermint-pink hybrid impatiens. Rich had suggested using New Guinea impatiens, but I hate their big, thick, ugly leaves. These are delicate and ethereal and look much more natural.

"Couldn't have done it better myself," I tell him sincerely.

"You don't say," he drily replies.

"And just think of how much money we saved! Plus, I feel like this fulfills my obligation to create an organic garden. I'll get some environmentally friendly spray to take care of the bugs—I mean, the ones I haven't already stomped into the hereafter—and I can consider this a mission accomplished." I mentally give myself a high five. This isn't where I meant to go, exactly, but I'm certainly glad to have gotten here.

Slowly, Fletch says, "I am hot, I am tired, I am sore, and I am starving. Are we having that pork roast for dinner?" he asks.

Right at this moment, I love him too much to tell him that I already fed his dinner to the dog.

"Absolutely."

Two weeks later I'm busy researching Martha Stewart Crock-Pot meals when there's a knock at the door. I rush down the stairs and standing there in his usual khaki tactical pants and fishing hat is Rich the Landscaper. Despite his occasionally delivering ridiculously expensive and unwanted news, I really like Rich. He gets the pricing from the landscape design team, so the extra zeros are never his fault. He's always willing to help us figure out lower-cost solutions, too. Plus he's very conscientious to swing by to check on the job that his team did. I appreciate his hard work.

"You have downy mold."

"I have what?"

"Out front, you have downy mold. On your impatiens. It's a new disease that came over from Europe and it's killing everyone's impatiens. Not the New Guinea ones, though—they're fine."

"I don't have any New Guineas."

He nods. "That's a shame, because now you have downy mold, which means the leaves on your impatiens are about to fall off and then the plants are going to die. I'll have the guys remove them on Tuesday."

"Whoa, hold up—they've only been in, what, a couple of weeks?

And I use organic spray on them!" We—well, *Fletch*—did not do all that work to lose the damn plants in a damn fortnight!

Rich chortles. "You're not going to find anything organic that can conquer downy mold. It's bad stuff. Gets into the soil and can live there up to seven years. We've got to remove them, and you're going to want to consider planting something different next year, like New Guinea impatiens. They're not impacted. Anyway, just wanted to let you know. See you Tuesday!"

I rush inside to Google "downy mold" and confirm everything Rich just said. I can't do anything but laugh at this point. I'd likely be angrier if the whole situation weren't so damn ironic. Plus, it's not like I lost my whole (heretofore nonexistent) crop of zucchini. I'm not going to let the incident impair my burgeoning happiness. Laughter seems to be the best way to deal right now.

Plus, I have a Fourth of July party to plan and a sweet little doggie who's waiting for a home-cooked meal, so, onward and upward.

But I was right to hate dirt.

You can't deny that.

T·W·E·L·V·E

BABY, YOU'RE A FIREWORK

"How's the little patient? What'd the vet say?"

Our friend Elaine is here for our usual Friday dog-training session. We met Elaine when we adopted Libby from Elaine's rescue group, and since then, we've worked with her every single week. With two pit bulls in the house, we have a responsibility to make sure they're always under control. I mean, we're well aware of how sweet and harmless they are, yet the fact that they even exist intimidates others, so we train for our neighbors' peace of mind. As an added bonus, the dogs love it!

After months off from treatment, Maisy's oncologist suggested we start her on a new course of chemotherapy. She's been doing exceptionally well since her last surgery in February, so she's definitely been strong enough to start again. We were told that eighty percent of all dogs who take this drug thrive on it.

Unfortunately, and for the first time, Maisy's fallen into the twenty percent.

Maisy saw her oncologist earlier this week. The doctor yanked the chemo drug and instead put her on some meds to help her stomach and appetite. We have a follow-up appointment on Monday, and until then, we have to watch her, which I've interpreted as, "Keep her by your side at all times and have panic attacks every time she blinks."

I tell Elaine, "She's okay, but I'm a disaster."

Elaine hugs me and then we get to work.

She asks, "Maisy, do you want to go first?"

Even though my girl's been down, nothing motivates her like a training session. She responds to Elaine's question with a full-on body wag that's so enthusiastic she practically bends in half. She barks and skitters across the hardwood, hitting Elaine almost hard enough to knock her down.

Did I mention that Maisy's a bit of a chunk? She should be in the high fifties in terms of weight, but she's presently in the mid-sixties. At one point, when she was on steroids for her treatment, she was close to eighty pounds. I remember asking Stacey, "Does Maisy look a little fatter?" to which Stacey replied, "Maisy looks like an ottoman." Yet I've always known a time would come when the extra weight would help her, so I've not been too diligent over portion control.

I'm just really hoping that time isn't now.

Maisy's so delighted at the opportunity to train first that she cycles through all of her tricks. When Elaine tells Maisy to sit, she first sits, then lies down, then sits up again, then stands, then lies down, all in the course of about ten seconds, and never once taking her eyes off Elaine. Watching her, you can almost see Maisy's wheels turning as she thinks through every command she knows, offering them up before ever asked for them. We all laugh at Maisy's version of calisthenics, and I decide to interpret this as positive progress.

Although Maisy's tired quickly, she's very pleased with herself as she hops up onto the couch after her turn. She's all, "That's right, bitches. Live and learn."

"Have you been able to distract yourself?" Elaine asks, sensitive to what a wreck I've been.

She begins to work with Libby, who's totally game-face when it comes to training. Libby's such a silly little free spirit, springing around the backyard like a baby goat and trying to engage everyone in play, so it's shocking to witness her level of intensity during our sessions. Libby's long since nailed all the basics, like come, sit, stay, heel, and down, but she's also highly proficient in dog show training commands, like stand, swing, around, give, and take. One would then believe that this would make Libby less of a prankster around the house, and she wouldn't perpetually counter-surf and make mischief, but that's not the case. As Elaine explains it, Libby works when it's time to work and does what she wants during her free time.

Of course, nothing Libby can do now compares to exactly how bad Maisy was as a puppy. She never met a boot she wouldn't chew, and her will was ironclad. If she wanted something, she'd whine, push,

woof, and bully until we finally gave in. When she was very small, we lived in a city loft with a roof deck, so she really had to reach and stretch the time she managed to lock me out on the deck. Another day, we were up on the deck for a party right before gardening season. I'd bought a bunch of bags of potting soil and hadn't yet hauled them upstairs because they were heavy. At

one point, I came down the stairs and looked at the floor—drinks were involved—and briefly wondered, "When did we get black carpeting?"

Also? Pillows used to make her angry.

Very angry.

I don't miss the swath of destruction she used to cut, yet I'd do anything to bring her back to the state where she was vibrant enough to destroy everything I owned.

"Actually, I have," I reply. "I've been trying to get out of my head by planning our Fourth of July party." Never in my life have I been so grateful for a diversion. Every time I open a book or Web page and see Martha's kindly visage presiding over an Independence Day bash, I feel like things are going to be okay. See? Look at all those smiling madras-clad WASPs, surrounded by flag decor, munching away on roasted corn and lobster. Nothing bad happens in Marthaland. They don't even dribble drawn butter on their alligator shirts. All is well.

My original plan entailed making my own decorations, and I wanted

to create the star medallions and gazebo trim in *Martha Stewart's Handmade Holidays Crafts* book. Yet I was so busy trying to interest Maisy in eating that I never quite made it to the fabric store. But then I had the brilliant idea to see if Amazon had any premade Martha-type items and I hit the jackpot! I found banners and bunting and flags and swags!

And . . . then I found oversize novelty Uncle Sam

hats and flag-printed sunglasses, and red, white, and blue tiaras, and tiny rubber duckies dressed like the founding fathers.

At some point during the ordering process, my plans for an elegant, tasteful Fourth of July party went off the rails.

Horribly, horribly off the rails.

This is not going to be an elegant affair; rather, it's going to be a fun party, and frankly, I could use a little joy right about now.

As we watch Loki run through his training paces, Maisy sticks her nose in my armpit and nudges so I have to wrap my arm around her.

Okay, sweet baby, whatever you say.

My friend Angie's leaving for China tomorrow, so we're saying good-bye on the phone today. Even though she lives in Michigan and I see her only twice a year, I'm going to miss her terribly while she's gone, largely because she's never afraid to tell it to me straight.

"You didn't send out real invitations? How do you not send written invitations to a Martha-inspired party?" Angie squawks. I don't need to be on the phone to feel her discontent emanating from three hundred miles away.

"Oh, I suspect the Martha-inspired bit flew out the window the minute I bought the red, white, and blue leis and Statue of Liberty head-bands," I admit. Smart money is on Martha never ordering half of all the Oriental Trading Company's inventory for her Hamptons fete. I bet Martha didn't even pick up stars-and-stripes bandannas for her dogs.

"You're putting all kinds of time and money into this party, right?"

"Yeah, of course. We have something like fifty people coming. I'm buying a ton of food," I reply.

I seem to have gotten her all stirred up. "Do you not get it? The level of effort you're putting into the party should be reflected in the invitation. That's why you never receive an *Evite* to a *wedding*. And you're *buying* food? Caps-lock double-yew-tee-eff? You should be making the food. You should be hand-hewing every burger with the cow you butchered yourself, and stuffing your own casing with your homemade sausage mix."

I haven't told her anything about Maisy's new issues, because I don't want her to worry about me while she's away. "I'm cooking the potato salad myself. The baked beans, too," I argue halfheartedly.

"Well, congratulations. Then that parade you see on TV Wednesday morning will be for you." She sighs heavily. "Are you at least serving a signature cocktail?"

"Yes."

Um, I am *now*.

"Well, thank God for that."

"Ange, I'm beginning to wonder if I'm going to miss you," I tell her.

"And I'm beginning to wonder if I need to stop in Lake Forest on the way to China and kick your ass back into domesticity."

I have to smile. "Fair enough."

After we hang up, I consider what Angie said. Hate to admit it, but I really have lost the whole Martha thread on this party. The party's right in spirit, but will be less so in execution. I realize I don't have to conduct my celebration exactly as *Living* dictates, but that was the point of the project, ergo my year. Founding father rubber duckies are not going to pave the path to the Tao.

I figure the best way to recapture the spirit of the project will be to really immerse myself in Martha's world going forward. I need to live this month exactly as she does hers. Therefore, I'm going to follow her calendar.

I freaking adore Martha's calendar. Featured prominently on both her Web site and her magazine, Martha's calendar contains her "gentle reminders and important dates." Take her June calendar, for example. Some of the entries are really specific, like when she has to pick up her clothes from the dry cleaner on June 4 so that she can pack for Tokyo. Yet many others are less personal, such as how she has to sow seeds for the cutting garden on June 15 or weed the vegetable beds on June 22. So, if I spend July following her calendar, I can't help but fall more in step with All Things Martha.

Tomorrow's July 1, so I'll start then.

July 1
Deadhead Roses and Perennials
Clean East Hampton Pool

Um, not to second-guess you here, Martha, but don't you have people for that?

Hell, *I* have people for that.

When we moved in, there were a few systems in place—Mike the Rose Guy, the landscapers, and the pool cleaners. Since we lacked the necessary equipment to complete any of these chores, and it would cost more to invest in the infrastructure than to keep things as they were, we simply took over their contracts.

The pool guys came every couple of weeks, and I never seemed to be home when they were here. Every time I missed them, I grew more and more curious.

"Hey, Fletch, have you seen the pool cleaners?" I asked after we'd lived here a month. We were sitting on the couch, Fletch watching television, and I was thumbing through the new *Us Weekly*.

He pressed pause and turned to face me. "Yeah. Why do you ask?"

"Well, I've been making jokes about hot pool boys fanning me and feeding me grapes since, like, forever. And now that we actually pay guys to clean our pool, I have to know—are our pool boys cute?"

"Why, do you and the rest of *Cougar Town* want to ogle them?"

"No." He raised an eyebrow at me. "Maybe?"

He laughed. "I told you no good would come of seeing *Twilight*."

I gave him a little shove. "Oh, just answer the question."

"How would I know if they're cute? What's cute?"

"I know it when I see it. What do they look like?" In my head, I pictured either Enrique Inglesias or that adorable surfer kid from TMZ with the big mane of sun-bleached blond hair.

"I can't believe I'm humoring you. Okay, well . . . the guys I've seen are middle-aged and short. Sort of heavy." Then he snapped his fingers as though he remembered a crucial detail. "And the taller one has a gunshot wound on his shoulder. Is that your version of cute? Is that what you were looking for? Should I have some grapes for them to peel next time they're here?"

Anyway, the guys were here on Friday, so the pool's still clean. Yet I'm intent on following Martha's instructions, so I put on my suit and grab a scrub brush, making sure to scour all the pool tiles as well as the surrounding bricks. It's in the high nineties out here today, and the forecast is that it's supposed to be even hotter for the rest of the week, so I'm glad guests will have the option of a swim when they get too hot.

When I'm done, I hit the roses and kill some beetles.

You know what? That was kind of fun.

This calendar thing is going to work out just fine.

July 2
Plan Menu and Table Setting for July 4

Easy-peasy. I've got the table settings down cold. All of my incredibly patriotic shipments have arrived from Amazon, and I've already cooked all the homemade items. Today's largely going to be comprised of a Costco run, after which I'll start arranging beverages in the big cooler on the back porch. The ice will last only about a day and a half, but we'll get more tomorrow afternoon, and that way all the drinks will have a head start on getting cool.

Before we hit Costco, we've got to take Maisy back to the vet for a couple of tests. She's slowly been getting back her appetite. Her energy's still low, but that's likely because it's so damn hot out. We're all listless and draggy. Just stepping out the door leaves us drenched in sweat.

In order to take Maisy without bringing the other dogs along, we have to hide treats Easter-egg style all over the house so that Libby and Loki don't freak out. The delicious-looking marrow bones I bought on yesterday's trip to the store should prove an excellent distraction.

Although Maisy needs a boost getting into the car, we don't think much of it. Her health's been so up and down for the past three years, yet every time she's been ill, she bounces back. We chat about the party all the way to the vet specialty clinic, and I have no inkling there's anything wrong until we're called back to an exam room.

Wait a minute; we're never called back to an exam room.

The vet tech always comes out after testing, gives us an update, and leads us back to a room. Fletch and I exchange worried looks as we're led back to talk to Maisy's oncologist, Dr. Feinmehl.

Without benefit of greeting, Dr. Feinmehl gets straight to the point. "The news isn't good. Maisy's kidney function is less than four percent."

Fletch and I glance at each other. I say, "I'm sorry; I don't follow. I thought her kidneys were okay and the issue was her appetite."

"Her situation has changed, probably because of the vomiting and dehydration. The kidneys have become critical." Dr. Feinmehl glances down at Maisy's file, which is literally three inches thick. "A four percent function is just not compatible with . . . life."

We both nod, intent on hearing whatever it is we need to do when bringing her home.

Her words take a second to settle in.

Not compatible with life?

What??

She continues. "We have to admit her right now, get her on fluids, and try to raise her red blood cell count, because she's severely anemic. I'll need to consult with Dr. Thornhill, who's a nephrologist. I won't know more until he sees her."

"Are you saying she might not make it?" I gasp.

"In all probability," she replies.

Fletch clutches my knee while my hands turn white from my clenched fists. We're in such shock that he can't even find the words to ask questions.

No. No, no.

This isn't how today is supposed to go down. We're supposed to bring Maisy in, get some more antacids, and then take her home before we buy ice at Costco.

I feel numb all over. "I don't understand. She was okay a couple of days ago. She's eating. She's holding her food down. She's playing with her sister. How can you tell me my dog is dying when she was chasing cats earlier?"

Three years ago, when this doctor told me Maisy had six months, I replied, "You don't know Maisy. She'll prove you wrong." But now Dr. Feinmehl says, "Maisy is a very, very determined little girl. She's so stoic that she doesn't show how she's feeling. Looking at her now, she's back there wagging her tail and begging for peanut butter. I'd never know she was dying if I hadn't seen her test results."

That's when Fletch and I both begin to sob. And even tough old Dr. Feinmehl, who's been a drill sergeant/android ever since we met her three years ago, has tears in her eyes. Maisy was her best-case scenario. Maisy was her miracle dog. Maisy was proof to all her clients that their beloved dogs would be okay.

Dr. Feinmehl hands us a box of Kleenex and gently tells us, "Listen, I'll bring her back in here before we admit her so you can see her. And I'll have Dr. Thornhill examine her. I don't want you to get your hopes up, because her situation is grave, but when you're dealing with a dog as exceptional as Maisy, anything is possible."

The two minutes it takes to bring Maisy back to us are the longest of my life. When she comes bounding in, I can't reconcile the news we've just gotten with the happy wiggle-pup standing in front of me.

We both try to hold it together so she isn't upset as we hug her and cover her with kisses.

Fletch stiffens his spine and there's steel in his voice. "This is not over. I'm not saying good-bye. She's coming home with us after all this. This dog is not done living."

I figured that since I've been actively dreading this moment for the past three years, I'd somehow be better equipped to handle it. I've been trying to prepare myself ever since her diagnosis. Yet as we sit on this cold tile floor, holding my precious baby, I can't for one second imagine my life without her.

She's too important.

When our whole world was falling apart after the dot-com crash, and when we lost our car and were about to be kicked out of our apartment, I'd spoon Maisy and know that as long as we had her and each other, everything would be okay. We'd make it.

No matter what, Maisy was always there, ready to snuggle up when it was cold and we'd lost gas service, and happy to lie in a baby pool when it was broiling and we didn't have air-conditioning. When we'd blow a job interview or get threatened by a bill collector, she was right beside us, readily communicating how *she* knew that we were awesome.

This dog has been my touchstone for ten years and a constant source of love, affection, and acceptance. All the important decisions I've made in the past decade have revolved around her, from pursuing a career in writing to where we bought our house, in order to live closer to the vet specialty clinic. And she's my first priority now in terms of the book tour. I still make travel plans based on her health.

The great irony here is that now we're finally living the secure, successful lives we've always imagined, yet I'd give up every single material thing to be huddled on the bed with my healthy, whole little girl.

We eventually have to leave the clinic, and I don't begin to cry again until after Maisy happily trots off with the vet tech. We won't know anything new until after they treat her, and we're instructed to call at seven p.m.

When we arrive home, everything looks exactly the same, even though my entire universe feels altered. I cling to Loki and Libby long enough for them to get a little creeped out, and then I e-mail my friends to let them know what's happening. Their support is immediate and profound.

We spend the next couple of hours pacing around, and at four p.m., the clinic calls us to say that Maisy is stable and responding to fluids. Her levels haven't come up, but they've not dropped.

"What does that mean? Do we come back? What do we do next?" I ask the nurse. Fletch and I are both on speakerphone, as neither of us has the presence of mind to interpret for the other.

"Please try not to worry. We're doing all we can for her, and we'll know more tomorrow."

Fletch is more direct. "She'll have a tomorrow?"

I hold my breath while I wait for an answer.

"I can tell you this: She's resting comfortably right now and she ate a little dinner. We're having trouble getting pills in her, though. She's fighting us."

And at that exact moment, even with all the evidence to the contrary, I have the unshakable faith that Maisy will pull through. No one decides anything for Maisy but Maisy.

After we hang up, we both decide that we can't sit around doing nothing. We debate whether or not to cancel the Fourth of July party, but decide that ultimately we need something to occupy our time, so we head to Costco.

Somehow we end up with two carts full of supplies, but I can't remember a single second of having shopped for any of it.

July 3
Go for a Swim
Visit Local Antiques Stores

You know what, Martha? I've been on your side this whole project, standing behind you, waving your perfectly quilted banner. Whenever I've told someone about this project and they've been all, "Really? Her?" I've defended you.

But today's calendar tasks?

They're smug.

Okay?

They're fucking smug.

Maybe in Stewartsylvania, you have no problem taking a leisurely swim and checking out the Fiestaware for sale in Hamptons antiques shops before fifty madras-clad guests descend on your house tomorrow to not dribble ghee on themselves, but in the real world, there's no goddamned time to sun ourselves or haggle with local merchants. We're fucking busy, okay? We have to feed and entertain fifty people tomorrow. And some of us are pretty goddamned freaked-out over loved ones, so while you whoop it up poolside, I'm going to run around here sticking sparklers in shit, all right?

You know what?

I'm done with your stupid calendar.

Why don't you go ahead and groom your damn miniature donkeys and practice your yoga while I'll be here doing hot-dog math, trying to figure out why buns come in eight-packs while wieners are sold in sixes. How many goddamned packages do I need to buy for the numbers to even up?

Six?

Sixty?

I DON'T KNOW.

I spend my day anger-chopping fruit and shredding lettuce and assembling little sandwiches. On some level, I realize my wrath shouldn't be directed at Martha; she did nothing wrong, particularly since she has no inkling that I even exist.

I just can't stop obsessing over Maisy. She's still holding stable, but her levels aren't doing whatever it is her levels are supposed to do. We check in every couple of hours, and although everyone at the clinic is superhelpful, I don't want to make them crazy with my constant vigilance. There's nothing I want more than to be there to hug her, but Fletch and I agreed it's best if we're not in and out, as we don't want to upset her by leaving without her.

I've never been so happy to have something to do, because at least I can channel all this pent-up energy into something productive. I'm equally glad that we're having this party, because I do want to see all my friends in person. They're been such a source of strength, commiserating, supporting, and whenever possible trying to make me laugh or letting me cry. As soon as I filled Karyn in on what was happening, she took a picture of her Yorkies, Bev and Mary Margaret, with a rosary, telling me they were all praying for Maisy. I've looked at that shot a hundred times since yesterday. Each time it makes me cry.

I'm in the middle of shucking forty ears of corn when the phone rings. Fletch answers and calls me into the room so I can be on speakerphone with him and Dr. Thornhill.

He begins to tell us specifics about Maisy's kidney functions and percentages and medications before he says something about plans for release and home treatment.

"Wait, what?" I ask. "She might actually *come home*? I thought . . . I thought Dr. Feinmehl said that a four percent kidney function wasn't consistent with life."

"That can be true," he replies, "but fortunately no one's told Maisy. I've had dogs who can manage with between three and five percent function, with proper care. It can be done. Maisy's a delightful little girl, isn't she? So happy! This would be a very different scenario if she weren't so ebullient and full of life. The nurses and techs love her."

"They know her pretty well," Fletch says. "She's a frequent flier." We were there for a checkup earlier this summer, and we could actually hear everyone in the back call, "Maisy!" when she walked in, as though she were Norm from *Cheers*.

"Of course, she's not out of the woods by any stretch of the imagination, and she's going to need subcutaneous fluids for a while, but she hasn't given up and neither will I."

We talk further and try to determine a discharge date. As of now, we're hoping she can come home on the fifth, but that will depend on her red blood cell count. If her count isn't satisfactory by then, they'll take the next step, which is a full transfusion.

None of what's about to happen will be inexpensive, and I'm suddenly very, very thankful for all the times I've opted for frugality in the past six months.

New anything simply can't compare to old dog.

Despite the triple-digit temperatures, the party's a rousing success. No one seemed to mind that it was less white-tablecloth and more red-Solo-cup. Actually, the gathering was so informal that everyone was able to really kick back and relax. I loved seeing my friends' kids have such a wonderful time. The best part of a successful party is bringing people together who'd never yet met, like when I found Laurie and Mike having a rollicking conversation with Julia and Finch.

I credit a portion of the party's success with Angie's insisting I create a signature cocktail. I blended coconut Cîroc with pineapple juice

and club soda, and
by the end of the day,
we were pretty much
drinking it right out
of the tap.

Naturally, I made
sure kids stayed out
of it.

Fletch was a total
champ, too. He spent
three hours working
the grill in the blazing hundred-degree sun and never once complained.
It's possible that's because he was swilling Dew Drivers—the white-
trash version of a screwdriver, wherein Mountain Dew is substituted for
orange juice. Regardless, he was nothing short of rock-star.

With the party out of the way and Maisy still not home, this was
normally when I'd ruminate. But I'm so thankful that Julia and Finch are
staying with us until the morning of the sixth. After we see them off tomorrow, we'll pick her up.

"It's funny how you guys always seem to appear just when we need
you most," I tell Julia. "Here we have the shitshow that was 2011, yet you
show up at the end of it to make sure we have fun. And now, the most
stressful time of my life, you're here with Apples to Apples and Catch
Phrase to make sure we're duly distracted. Thank you."

She shrugs. "We're all about good timing."

I spoke with the vets and Maisy is now definitely coming home tomorrow. They had to give her a transfusion and there was an issue, so
now her entire front leg is purple. Her nurse promised this would clear
up in a week, but all I could hear was, "You're going to have your dog at
least another week." Bring on the purple leg.

Julia and I are sitting on the screened back porch, having gotten out of the pool. Looks like we're about to get the first rain of the entire summer. We're eating leftover party fruit; she's topping her watermelon with Splenda and I'm giving mine a couple of shakes of salt.

"How are you feeling about everything?" she asks.

I poke at a watermelon rind with a plastic fork. "Honestly, I'm scared about bringing her home. What if we can't give her what she needs? Her doctor said we have to administer subcutaneous fluids twice a day. We used to do this with our old cat Bones, but he was little and I could hold him. Maisy's not exactly cooperative." Dr. Thornhill told me she kept trying to French-kiss the vet techs when they'd give her fluids.

Julia opens another Splenda and begins to sprinkle right as the wind picks up. All the little crystals go flying out across the tabletop. "Should we go inside?"

I shrug. "Eh, we're okay for now. It's actually nice to feel the temperature drop like this." In five minutes, it's gone from the high nineties out here to the mid-eighties.

"Then what I was about to say was that whatever happens, this is your new normal. As I parent, I've learned that you do whatever it is you need to do. You don't hesitate. You're going to be the same way with Maisy. If you have to hydrate her twice a day, you'll figure out how to build your day around her. You'll make it work and you won't think twice about the process."

I mull this over and realize she's making perfect sense. We'll adapt to anything Maisy needs. Period. I give Julia a squeeze. "Of all the stalkers who walked into my book signings, I'm sure glad it was you."

Four years ago I had a book event in Atlanta and someone asked if anyone had ever stalked me and I'd said no. Then Julia raised her hand and asked if I was interested in having a stalker, as she'd like to volunteer. I replied that I wasn't sure. But the whole nature of her question made me laugh, so I gave her my e-mail address and I told her she was welcome to try. She sent me such funny notes about her job as a pharmaceutical rep that we started to correspond with some frequency. Eventually our pen-pal relationship culminated in our hanging out each time I came to Atlanta, and now here we are.

We're up and ready in the morning when Julia and Finch leave this time, because we're headed to pick up Maisy. I don't know what to expect and I'm so nervous. Will she be the same dog as when she went in? Are we providing hospice for her next few days or might she actually have more life left in her? Will we truly be able to manage the day-to-day of the IV and the meds and getting her to eat?

When we arrive at the clinic, there's another couple picking up their dog. They're ashen-faced and somber as the clerk gently hands them the package of their cherished pet, wrapped in purple velvet with the inscription. "When we meet again on the rainbow bridge."

Fletch and I exchange glances, and at that moment I realize that every single second we have with Maisy from here on out is a gift, whether it's a day, a week, a month, or a year. Whatever it is we have to do, we'll do, and we'll be thankful for the privilege of having done it. I'm not scared anymore, and I don't care when I pay for services rendered, because my beautiful dog is coming home on a leash and not in an urn.

We're brought back to another exam room, but this time it's so we can have a crash course on how to administer meds and fluids. When we're finally reunited with Maisy, it's all I can do not to cry. She's walking a little slowly because of the hematoma all over her leg, but otherwise, she's the same dog who's been by my side for the past ten years.

As we load her up into the car, she gives me a look as if to say, "Well, it's about goddamned time."

Funny, but our new normal seems an awful lot like our old normal.

When we arrive home, she trots into the great room and positions herself on the love seat, allowing all the other pets to come up to her and pay homage. Regal as a queen, she lets the cats sniff around her while

Libby runs circles in excitement and Loki wags his tail hard enough to knock the remote controls off the coffee table.

Maisy's happy to be home; ergo I'm happy.

And in this moment, that's everything.

I'm not mad at Martha anymore.

In fact, I'm ready to hit this project even harder than before. What's so ironic is that I've spent seven months looking for the Tao of Martha, yet I've found something even more powerful.

In many ways, Maisy's illness has been a gift, because it's made me take stock of how much I love her every day when we give her treatment. I hug her while I hold her steady for the IV and I tell her how perfect she is. I always knew this dog had a piece of my heart, but it wasn't until I had to muster up my own strength and determination to keep her alive that I figured out exactly how much.

Like in *The Hitchhiker's Guide to the Galaxy*, I've discovered my own number forty-two through caring for her. I've uncovered my ultimate answer to the ultimate question of how to be happy, and that all boils down to what I've learned from my dog.

I've discovered the Tao of Maisy, which entails three steps:

Be awesome.

Give awesome.

Get awesome.

Maisy started her life Being Awesome. She was rescued by animal control from an abandoned apartment in the projects and brought to Anti-Cruelty, a massive city shelter. Because she was a pit bull, she was automatically slated to be euthanized if no one claimed or adopted her

within a week. And hon-
estly, that would have
been better than the life
she'd have had if she'd
not been found. Maisy
would have been bred,
fought, or used as bait,
possibly all three.

The thing is, Maisy
was special and she knew
it. She paraded herself
around Anti-Cruelty in such a way that one of the clerks called the rescue I
used to volunteer for and said, "This puppy is too awesome to not get a
second shot. Please, please, if you have space, take her."

So Maisy altered the course of the miserable life she was slated for
by Being Awesome.

In turn, she's spent the last ten years being a roly-poly ball of uncon-
ditional love, giving us the full benefit of her awesomeness. Without her,
I'd have never had the push to change my own circumstances. I'd likely
still be working some god-awful sales job. And would I have insisted
Fletch and I get married if we didn't have the impetus of dogs to keep us
together? Who knows?

In turn, our love for her is why she Gets Awesome in return. She's
why we wanted a house with a yard. She's why I decided to double my
workload and write fiction so I could afford a house with a pool, knowing her predilection for swimming.

In so many ways, what Martha Stewart does can be broken down
into the Tao of Maisy, too. Clearly, she's already nailed the Be Awesome
part. You don't become a household name without those credentials. In
teaching everyone the best way to handmake a wreath or needlepoint a
tea towel or cook the perfect vanilla-bean cupcake, she's giving her awe-

some to the masses, which she gets back by way of wealth, power, and recognition.

Those following Martha's way of life are part of the whole cycle, too. For example, when I made my first Thanksgiving dinner, it was because I was at a particularly high point in my life. I'd achieved Being Awesome, so much so that I wanted to share it by hosting a dinner and Giving Awesome. In return, I Got Awesome back from friends who'd enjoyed being a part of the celebration. The Tao of Maisy is whatever the opposite of a vicious circle is, as the more one Bes, Gives, and Gets, the more it perpetuates itself into happiness.

In order for Maisy to receive the maximum amount of awesome between now and the inevitable, I have to give her back awesome, because she deserves it. Her favorite thing in the world is to go for a walk, and honestly, we've not done that so much since we moved here, assuming the acre of fenced yard would be plenty.

For the first time in her life, I don't have to put Maisy on a pinch collar to walk. It's taken two kinds of cancer and kidney failure to instill proper leash manners. What's ironic is that people *still* cross the street to avoid what's surely a vicious pit bull. Argh.

We walk only to the end of the block and back, which would normally take about ten minutes. But Maisy's very much into looking around and taking everything in, so we follow her pace. Sometimes it takes half an hour, and that's just fine.

When I was on my book tour, I found myself running through airports in stupid shoes, and I've since given myself a case of plantar fasciitis. Almost every step I take feels like my heel's pressing down on a knife, but my foot will eventually get better and Maisy will not.

So I hobble along beside her, wincing with every step I take.

Because there's no place I'd rather be.

T·H·I·R·T·E·E·N

Put a Bird on It

"You know, glass is an excellent way to add an inexpensive pop of color to any room."

I'd normally roll my eyes at anyone who ever uttered such a statement, except the person who just said this is *me*.

I'm at HomeGoods shopping for knickknacks, and a woman just commented on the contents of my cart. I'm working on redecorating a room, because I figure I've been on top of cleaning and organizing, as well as gardening, it's too hot for cooking, we just had a party, and pet care now takes up about twenty-five percent of my day.

BTW, a quick word on the things I have to do to get pills into this dog? Last week she wouldn't swallow any meds unless they were wrapped in meat that I prechewed.

I know, *I know.*

Just recently there was a story about how Alicia Silverstone goes all mama-bird and gives her kid prechewed bites. Everyone on the Internet is just appalled, whereas I'm all, "You do you, Cher Horowitz."

I'm feeling particularly effusive because Maisy's had three positive checkups in three weeks. Dr. Thornhill said everything we're doing for her is working and her kidney function is up to six percent! We've even been able to cut back on the fluids we give, so we're down to IVs once a day. She still tires so easily, yet yesterday she rose from her slumber just long enough to steal a bone from Libby. Then she trotted back to her spot on the love seat and went to sleep with it clutched in her paws. Libby didn't have the heart to swipe it back, and I was too busy cheering to help. I love when Naughty Maisy comes out.

Anyway, decorating seems like the most expedient way back into Martha's world. So I'm currently working on the bedroom next to the master. I haven't done much in there since we had the wallpaper stripped after moving in. Hell, I'm still displaying the IKEA prints I bought back in the dot-com era. Although with the eight thousand powder-blue wallpaper bows gone the room's much improved, it still needs an update, because it's boring.

A couple of weeks ago, I had a big book event with my BFF/author Stacey Ballis, Sarah Pekkanen, and Jennifer Weiner. Considering I'd have put Jen's photo on my vision board if I made them, it's so badass to have the opportunity to participate in a signing with her. However, the event wasn't exactly perfect, as we discovered far too late that the venue wasn't air-conditioned. In July. In Chicago. In the third-hottest summer since the weather's been tracked. (We had a great time, despite my having sweated entirely through my bra.)

Point? Jen Weiner's a class act, and she gave each of us a cool little glass plate to commemorate the occasion. I loved mine so much I decided to decorate the room around the color scheme.

I don't want to spend a lot of money in here, so I'm not replacing the perfectly serviceable furniture; nor am I setting fire to the Cookie Monster-blue carpet, despite my overwhelming urge to do so. Instead, I've repurposed two old shelves from Fletch's office and I'm painting them a robin's-egg blue to match the dresser. I also ordered a couple of white shelves that will bracket the daybed.

My plan is to fill the bookcases with little pops of blues and greens, which is why I'm in HomeGoods. I just found the most awesome vase for five dollars and a pretty bowl for seven! This discovery has made me so happy that I've morphed into Helpful Jen, the random customer who takes great delight in giving you her unsolicited opinion and speaking in many exclamation points wherever she shops, e.g., "Try that dressing; it's delicious!!" and, "Those pants are so cute that I insist you buy them right now!!!" I'm greatly annoyed by Helpful Jen, but she comes out only when I'm in a particularly good mood, so I'm going to let her loose until she tries to invite strangers to lunch, and then I'm reeling her back in.

The bulk of what I'm placing on my new shelves is coming from OneKingsLane.com. I found all kinds of cute blue and green items with birds on them. (Fine, *Portlandia*. I've put a bird on it. Happy now?)

I discovered this site while trolling Martha's archives. In April of 2011, she hosted Susan Feldman and Alison Pincus from OKL, and they discussed how they'd built their discount home decor business. Curious to learn more, I visited the site and quickly fell in love, because it's like eBay without the assholes. Items come up for sale in groups and they're available only for seventy-two-hour periods. Plus, when I shop, whatever I get remains in my cart for only ten minutes, so I either have to pick more stuff to extend my time or check out. Once an item's selected, but before it's paid for, it's marked with the stamp "IN ANOTHER MEMBER'S CART." But if it's something I want, and the other customer doesn't act fast enough, I can scoop it up before they can place it in the cart again.

Okay, so maybe I can still be an asshole.

Even though the site occasionally features shops selling old Birkin bags and Chanel jewelry, this is my go-to place to find adorable, affordable knickknacks. In addition, they feature new antique items every day, so once in a while I can satisfy my vintage trophy fix.

The only glitch is that OKL doesn't bill credit cards until the item ships, and mine expired midmonth. So they held everything until I updated my details, and now I'm waiting for a big shipment. In the interim, I found a wall mural of van Gogh's almond branches and applied it behind the daybed like wallpaper. Someday when someone else buys this house, I'm sure they'll mercilessly mock my taste, but I don't care. I'm decorating this for *me*, not for resale value. (I feel a sudden kinship with whoever covered these walls in that hiddy bow wallpaper. I hope it brought that person as much pleasure as my silly mural brings me.)

Anyway, as tempted as Helpful Jen is to trail after the customer who had the bad sense to start a conversation with me, I have to restrain myself. Maisy has another appointment this afternoon and I need to get home for it.

"Six-point-eight!"

The normally reserved Dr. Thornhill shakes both of our hands.

"Maisy's kidney functions are up to six-point-eight percent. Congratulations. You're doing such a good job. She's well hydrated, too, so let's take her fluids down to two hundred and fifty milliliters," he says.

A few weeks ago, we didn't think we'd get past five percent, but she's steadily been climbing. She's even wolfing down her food again and taking her pills without benefit of chewing. Even though we know her health is a tenuous balance, we can celebrate today's victory. Every day that Maisy wakes up happy and rolls around to scratch her back is a good day in my book.

As we drive home, Maisy's in the back attempting to stick her nose out the cracked window. She takes big gulps of air and then blows moist sneezes in our direction. Her little rosebud ears flap in the breeze and she's the very embodiment of joy.

"Who knew that the key to happiness is six percent kidney function?" I say as we round the corner onto Milwaukee Boulevard.

"No, the key to happiness is not watching you chew the dog's food," he replies.

But we both know if it weren't me doing it, it would be him.

Later in the day, I receive further evidence that Maisy's feeling well. How do I know?

Because she just quietly, systematically tore all the batting out of the comforter on the bed in my office.

One minute, she's happily snoozing in the sun next to Libby on the part of the bed with the best outdoor vantage point, and the next, it's snowing stuffing. Maisy's now wreathed in a cottony beard with bonus bits stuck to her eyebrows. As I stare at the carnage, she cocks one be-puffed brow as if to say, "And?"

Normally it's Libby who engages in such shenanigans. Like when Julia and Finch were here over the holidays? We went out to dinner, and upon our return Libby had not only dragged half a dozen bottles out of the wine rack, but had also counter-surfed a can of decaf coffee, which she then pried open and dumped on the living room floor. Clearly her intention was to provide us with postmeal refreshment, as she'd also left a pair of my panty hose on the floor, no doubt because she couldn't reach the coffee filters.

I should absolutely discipline Maisy, but it's pretty much impossible to yell at a dog completely nailing a Santa Claus impersonation. So I rationalize her behavior by telling myself the comforter was old and ugly and due to be replaced anyway. Maisy's knowing look says, "Take the hint." So I log onto PotteryBarn.com and peruse their offerings.

I'm not overly fond of any of the comforters or quilts, but I find a lovely discounted duvet cover. The background's powder blue and there are butterflies and big pink apple blossoms all over it with cranberry accents that match the drapes. Yeah, I could live without the butterflies, but they blend to the point of being nonoffensive. Butterflies are a lot like rainbows: They're phenomenally beautiful in real life, yet no graphic representation can do them justice; ergo, it's best to forgo. Regardless, the overall look is light and cheery and would be perfect in here. Yet I hesitate before clicking the order button, because I *hate* duvet covers. I don't hate them like I hate war, cancer, and Halloween, but they're a close fourth.

I mean, in terms of aesthetics, a duvet cover is ideal. That's not the issue. I appreciate how I can make the surface supersmooth by simply spraying it with a bottle of hot water and engaging in a little oppositional tugging. (This is the sum total of everything I learned working as a hotel maid one summer in Boston, FYI.) Also, duvets offer the flexibility for me to decide how toasty I want the bed—I can opt for a lightweight coverlet inside when it's warm, and something extradowny for the winter. And, as the duvet cover is essentially two sheets sewn together, I can launder it here instead of sending it off to the dry cleaner. Major bonus.

The problem comes in getting the stupid comforter inside the stupid duvet. I've never been able to master this task, to the point that it causes me existential angst. This job should be as easy as sliding a CD into its case or filling an envelope, but no. I always end up sweaty and cursing inside a fabric prison cell, attempting to align all the corners, which I never freaking do. Without fail, ninety percent of the damn thing gets wadded up in the far left corner, and then it's nothing but sheet for the bulk of the cover. No amount of hot, squirted water can smooth it when it's bunched, either.

As I debate, I note Martha's *Homekeeping Handbook* on the corner of my desk. The manual's more than just a prop—it's a definitive guide to cleaning everything in the home. I guarantee there's a section on Duvets for Dummies, so I proceed with the transaction, confident that Martha will show me the way.

"Okay, Maisy, I placed the order," I tell her. "When it comes, maybe you can try to not destroy this one."

Maisy's slow blink in response tells me everything she's thinking.

"I promise nothing."

And I'd expect nothing less.

When my new duvet arrives, I dig a lightweight down comforter out of the TV cabinet in the bedroom. Our house was built back when televisions were still small and square, so in terms of watching the news from bed, the space is useless. But it's the perfect place to store linen, so it's all worked out.

I bring everything up to my office and consult the *Homekeeping* book. "Okay, Martha, baby, lay it on me," I say.

And that's when I discover that Martha has no advice other than using fabric tape. What? Eight hundred pages of text and all she can suggest is *fabric tape*? I don't even know what fabric tape is, let alone understand how to operate it in regard to a duvet.

Damn it! First her July calendar and now this? I can't believe it. This is how I felt the first time I ever saw one of my teachers in the grocery store, all odd and disconcerted.

No, no, this won't do *at all*!

So it looks like I have to figure out how to stuff this damned thing myself.

As I unwrap the packaging, I realize that my singular goal in life is to someday have someone stuff my duvet covers for me. We used to have the house professionally cleaned, but then, once I began the Martha project in earnest, I figured I'd learn enough tips and tricks to maintain the house on my own. Thus far, I have.

I've started to clean wall-to-wall, meaning I begin in one corner of the room and work my way around, tackling everything in my path. For example, when I tidy the kitchen, I initiate the cleaning sequence at the counter where the mail accumulates. I sort and put all those items away, then spray the granite, before moving clockwise to wipe the wall of cabinets. I proceed around to the island for more disinfecting and organizing, finally finishing with the breakfast area. This way I move with a purpose and I don't have to rearrange items to wipe under them. Before I had a system, I'd be distracted by all the different components, but by proceeding in a linear fashion, I can hit everything without getting sidetracked.

In retrospect, my chambermaid job would have been far easier if I'd read Martha back then, but I was a lot more interested in meeting hot guys from Tufts. Oh, well.

The point is, my house has stayed orderly even though I'm doing everything myself.

I suspect this is largely because I've lowered my own standards in regard to cleanliness.

Whatever.

Anyway, I spread the duvet across the bed, and immediately wet dogs burst into my office to dance all over it. I see they've been swimming, like, thirty seconds ago. Maisy's still really just wading into the pool to get a drink, but wet is wet.

I shoo them out, shutting my office door behind them. Maisy keeps snorting under the door while Loki nudges the doorknob. I hear Libby take off after a cat, because she has the attention span of a hummingbird.

I lay out the duvet again and position the opening at the bottom over my head. Then I grab the edges of the comforter and begin to tunnel toward the back. The temperature inside my office is approximately seventy-four degrees, but inside this duvet, it's more like twenty-eight hundred degrees Fahrenheit, which would be superconvenient if I were trying to melt structural steel.

I shove and bunch and sweat, and when I believe I have everything situated, I exit the duvet's birth canal. Grasping the comforter at two corners, I shake it out, hoping everything will fall into place.

Everything does not fall into place. In fact, everything is skewed. The dimensions of the comforter versus that of the duvet are diametrically opposed. Why? Why is this? Why aren't the damn duvets shaped like the comforters? Why is there no standard? Beds are standard sizes so sheets can fit, so why hasn't anyone come up with a benchmark in regard to duvets and fillers? How much easier would that make everyone's lives? Although I'm prone to favor smaller government, I would GLADLY support a National Bureau of Ensuring Shit Fits Properly.

I rip out the comforter and turn the whole thing ninety degrees to the left before starting the process again. I keep a death grip on the end of the comforter, guiding it through the Amazonian rain forest that is the inside of the duvet. Once I'm in the belly of this thing, I'm aggravated because there are all these long strings hanging down on the seams. Way to make the inside of your product raggedy, *Pottery Barn*. Sheesh.

Before I can do anything else, I have to immediately remove my shirt or else I will pass out, and I'm not kidding. Rivulets of perspiration roll down my back, and my ponytail is practically saturated. All the stupid strings are tickling my neck and I keep thinking they're ticks, leading me to have a series of mini heart attacks.

I have to hold open the bottom part to get a breath of air, and that's when I notice that there's a binder clip on my floor.

Wait a minute. Could that work? What if I were to clip the comforter to the duvet with the binder before I shake it all out? Yes! Genius!

But before I can do that, I have to line up the rest of the comforter. By now, I've generated so much heat inside the duvet that my whole office is roasting. I figure the most expedient thing is to remove my pants, too, because I'm simply not built for heat.

So I'm pretty much scuba diving inside the covers when all the exertion causes me to—how do I say this delicately?—honk, poot, step on a duck. I've just managed to Dutch-oven myself. I suddenly, deeply regret having consumed antique seafood salad at lunch. Granted, I noticed my lunch was long past its first blush of youth, but at eleven dollars a pound, I wasn't about to waste it.

Penny wise, pound foolish.

Breathing through my mouth, I manage to position everything in place, and I'm able to extricate myself once and for all. Still undressed, I grab my box of binder clips and secure the entire north end of the operation. Then I stand back and give the bedding a vigorous shake and . . . success! Everything falls into place! Cheese cutting be damned, this duvet is filled perfectly and aligned exactly as it should be!

I'm cheering and jumping around when Fletch enters my office. I'm not sure what specifically is the most off-putting—the prolific sweat, the unexpected underpants, or the fetid fug of indigestible Neptune salad. Openmouthed, he gawps at me until I say, "Got that duvet thing worked out."

He nods and backs out of the room, without ever having said a word. The dogs come dashing in the open door and immediately hop on all my hard work.

From her spot on the edge of the bed, Maisy's nose wriggles before she eyes me warily, clearly communicating, "This is what shame smells like."

Yet this is a victory. Plus, for the first time I feel like I out-Martha'd Martha. That's not only cause for celebration, but also another revelation in the lately dormant Tao: The universe can be built only once a proper foundation is laid.

Had I not been so intent on learning Martha's processes, I'd have never freestyled my duvet solution. I feel like I should write in to *Living* and tell them that I've discovered the right way to stuff a duvet.

Maybe this is the X factor for which I've been searching?

Maybe this is my opportunity to share my own bit of Martha-inspired breakthrough with the world!

Yes!!

But first I'll get dressed.

I'm mentally composing my Duvet Treatise when it occurs to me that all those stupid strings may have served a purpose. I pull up Potterybarn.com and I read the description of my new bedding:

"Duvet cover has interior ties and a hidden button closure."

Wait, are interior ties the same thing as fabric tape?

According to MarthaStewart.com, yes. Yes, they are.

Turns out all I needed to do was use the flappy strings to truss the comforter into place, *exactly as the* Homekeeping *manual instructed.*

Maisy watches me as I huff and sigh. "Sweetie, your mummy is a dummy." I sit down next to her and plant a kiss on her wide, flat head. "But at least the bed looks pretty now."

In response, she thumps her tail and practically nods and says, "So there's that."

I'm at lunch with the girls when the call comes in.

I knew what would happen next was coming, but I didn't think it would be today.

On the other end of the line, Fletch is understandably upset.

"One minute everything was fine, and the next . . . I can't . . . It's just . . ."

"It'll be okay, honey. I'll deal with it when I get home."

Tracey's, Gina's, and Stacey's eyes are trained on me when I hang up. Stacey puts a comforting hand on my shoulder. "Do you have to go?"

"What's wrong?" Tracey asks, voice full of concern. "Did something happen with Maisy?"

Oh, my God, they think . . . "What? No! I'm so sorry; she's good. A little tired, but not so much that she's not still bossy. That's not why he called. Remember when I told you guys about One Kings Lane? And how my card expired and I was waiting for a couple of shipments? Apparently everything arrived today."

One of the reasons I'm such a fan is because OKL is ultracareful with breakables. The first thing I bought was this little ceramic bird, maybe the size of my fist, and they shipped it in a box that was easily twenty-four inches wide and twelve inches high.

"So there's a lot?" Gina asked.

I laugh, imagining Fletch's distress. "He says there's a tower of boxes outside the front door that's about five feet high by six feet wide. He can't get out the door. He said he looked outside and saw a sea of brown—he thought we were having a zombie apocalypse."

"Is he disappointed?" Stacey queries.

"Probably."

We're all still chuckling when our regular waiter comes up to take our order.

"Ladies ready?" he asks, folding his hands behind his back. I'm perpetually stressed out when the waiter doesn't write anything down, despite the fact that, A) we get the same lunch every single week, and B) they've yet to not deliver everything we order. But the not noting the order—why is this a thing everywhere now? I hate this. Yes, yes, we're all impressed that you remember that Stacey likes her eggs scrambled well-done, her bacon burned, and fruit instead of potatoes, and that I prefer my bacon floppy as opposed to crispy. If you're my server, please just humor me and take a note, okay? You don't even have to give it to the kitchen. Otherwise, I'm going to spend the next twenty minutes obsessing over your memorization skills.

"I'm going to have the breakfast burrito, but please hold the avocado," Gina says.

"Oh, are you allergic?" the waiter asks. "Because I'm allergic. Can't have avocados at all, even avocado oil." See? This is why I get anxious when he doesn't jot down what we want. Every damn week he forgets that he's told us all about the avocado thing.

As our waiter launches into his tale of avocado woe, he doesn't even notice that we're all laughing into our napkins.

Sometimes happiness is a warm puppy, sometimes it's Fletch's beard, and sometimes?

Sometimes happiness takes the form of a flatulent waiter.

P.S. I love my room makeover.

F·O·U·R·T·E·E·N

THE AMBIEN DIARIES

The top five best things that ever happened to me in my life list out something like this:

Meeting Fletch—Self-explanatory.

Adopting Maisy—Again, self-explanatory.

Deciding to Pursue a Writing Career in Lieu of Being a Corporate Drone—Which pretty much changed everything. (Please refer to *Bitter Is the New Black* with any specific questions about the process.)

Moving to the Suburbs—Peace! Quiet! Privacy! Free parking! One hundred percent fewer crack-induced knife fights in my driveway!

Discovering Ambien—This may require more explanation.

By the way, my top ten includes the Nespresso coffeemaker, no-chip manicures, Spanx, in-dash GPS, and the end of the Cold War, even though I'm bummed that no one pens song lyrics about nuclear winter anymore.

But back to the Ambien—I can't fall asleep. Ever. I can stay asleep with no problem, but getting there unmedicated? Nope. All of my little neuroses come out to play the second I slip into my jammy pants. Despite how busy I've been during the day, no matter how much physical labor I may have exerted, or how much mental energy I've had to expend, the minute I hit the sheets, my brain switches into hyperdrive and I'm suddenly overwhelmed by racing thoughts.

I'm not necessarily even contemplating the world's problems (or my own); it's more like every idea, notion, or question I've ever had pushes all Japanese commuter–style into the Tokyo Metro that is my brain. The floodgates open and suddenly I'm staring at the ceiling, wondering what ever happened to that kid named George in the fourth grade who used to wear all those silk shirts. How come the hair grows on my legs every time I sneeze? How many people touch the handrail on the revolving door into the Sears Tower every day? Do workers in that building have a higher instance of cold and flu than in smaller buildings? And will any true Chicagoan ever call that place the Willis Tower? (FYI? No.)

Complicating matters is that now the Internet exists and I can actually find out the answers to my burning oh so stupid questions, and then that leads me down the rabbit hole that is Google, because George is alive, well, and living in Ridgefield, New Jersey, with his wife and teenage children, one of whom loses her shit over One Direction, which is a band that got their start on Simon Cowell's *X Factor* in Great Britain. What's interesting is that 1D didn't even win the competition; nor did they start off together as a group. Niall, Zayn, Louis, Liam, and my favorite, Harry, originally auditioned as solo acts, but after they didn't make it, they . . .

Do you see what I mean? The thoughts are relentless.

To sleep, I require an off switch, and that's how Ambien works eighty-five percent of the time. I take my pill, read a bit, and then, like magic, I'm lulled into slumber by the absolute solitude inside my head. I sleep deeply and wake up refreshed; it's borderline miraculous.

Or would be, if it weren't for the ten percent of the time that it all goes horribly awry and I end up parading around the house in a shower cap.

I'm no science-tician, but from what I understand, Am-bien quiets the executive function, which is how it puts me to sleep in the first place. But once in a while, with my executive functions dulled, I go to my computer instead of going to sleep. This phenomenon led to the first Great Barbie Head Kerfuffle of 2007 and the 2008 Entire New Set of Bedroom Furniture Incident.

However, since we moved to the suburbs, Ambien shopping hasn't been much of an issue, because I specifically put my desktop on a different floor from where I sleep. Once in a while there's an iPad run-in, like the night I ordered both skinny jeans AND an airplane seat-belt extender. (What was my thought process here? "I'm so fat! No, wait, I'm so *fabulous!*")

For the most part, though, the shopping thing is under control because our master bedroom is on the first floor, as far away from my office on the second floor as physically possible. That's why I now end up in the kitchen instead of on the Internet, making sandwiches instead of purchases. Granted, I don't need the calories, but I *really* don't need a new master suite.

At our holiday party, our friends Kim and Wes brought us the greatest hostess gift of all time—a Williams-Sonoma caramel apple. I've been obsessed with these ever since Stacey told me it's her go-to Christmas present for business contacts. Because I can't do math, for years I assumed the apple's twenty-two-inch diameter meant radius, leading me to believe the apple was as large around as an old-growth oak tree or Lil Wayne's spinners. But still, twenty-two inches is just shy of a bowling ball, so trust me when I say it's more crunchy chocolate and ooey-gooey caramel than one person could ever inhale on her own.

When we received our magical treasure orb, I immediately shoved it in the back of the fridge, lest any of our guests believe it was for sharing. Over the next week after the party, I'd crack the fridge door all Gollum-style, peering at it while murmuring, "My precious . . . my precious."

And . . . then I got busy, filled the refrigerator with other items, and kind of forgot about the whole thing, until one Ambien-fueled night when I decided it was time to have a crack at the apple.

I blame Fletch for what happened next.

Or, rather, what happened first.

I'd recently purchased a pair of Ray-Ban Wayfarer eyeglasses, assuming they'd be as flattering as my sunglasses. What I didn't account for was how thick the lenses would look in such a large frame. (Imagine Mr. Magoo, only more myopic.) I'd been in my bathroom getting ready for bed and I realized I was out of my makeup removal cloths, so I had to wash my face the regular way. My sink is supersmall, so I always end up splashing myself, which is why I opt for the Olay Regenerist wipes.

So, my face was clean, but my nightgown was covered in wet splotches. Then I dotted a couple of blemishes with Mario Badescu drying serum, yanked my hair into a knot on top of my head, and threw on my massive glasses. I got a kick out of how unattractive the whole combination was, so I had to point it out to Fletch. I went marching out of the bathroom, announcing, "Hey, hey, here comes the sex machine!"

Then he laughed at me.

Which would have been fine, because I knew I was the opposite of adorable at the moment; that was the whole point of my announcement.

What I didn't expect was for him to literally double over, clutching his sides, with tears pouring down his face, for *two straight minutes.*

"Okay, that's enough," I said. "Stop it, please."

He couldn't stop.

"I'm serious; it's not that funny," I said.

He was gasping for breath, and when he tried to straighten up to look at me, he doubled over again.

"Quit laughing at me; this is insulting!" I insisted.

Through ragged breaths, he said, "But the trundling . . . oh, God, the way you were trundling along like a penguin, and the wet spots . . . and . . ."

Then he guffawed to the point that I briefly contemplated giving him a slipper-based colonoscopy.

"I'm going to go read with the dogs in the other bedroom until you can pull yourself together," I huffed.

Which is what I did. Then, every thirty seconds, I'd hear a burst of intermittent laughter through the connecting doorway.

"I'm sleeping in here because I hate you!" I shouted.

He could barely get out an "okay" before he burst into another fit of giggles.

That's when I took my Ambien.

After it kicked in, I had a brainstorm. He'd hurt my feelings—okay, my pride—and I was mad. I figured the best way to exact revenge on the Braying Jackass I married would be to eat the caramel apple myself right that minute.

Yes. This was genius.

I scurried down the hall, dogs in tow, to claim my great prize.

Quietly as I could, I retrieved the apple from the back of the fridge. With much stealth, I grabbed a cutting board and a sharp knife. Bracing the wealth of riches with my left hand, I sliced into paradise.

Here's a bit of Discovery Channel for you—apples don't last forever. They can stay fresh for a long time, especially when refrigerated, but definitely not forever, and certainly not from December into the month of March. My beautiful precious had turned brown and awful. What made the whole situation worse is that the caramel and chocolate surrounding the rotten apple were totally okay, like a diamond-enrobed turd.

I'm not sure exactly what brought Fletch scurrying into the kitchen, but it may have been all my anguished screaming.

At this point, a non-Ambien-addled person would have swept the whole mess into the trash, whereas I . . . found the perfect opportunity to channel Martha Stewart.

"Hello," I said to Fletch. "Welcome to *The Martha Stewart Show*. Today I'm going to show you how to salvage your delicious Williams-Sonoma caramel apple. Now, first, we're going to—"

"Hey, Martha, hold up a second—I'm going to need to get my camera for this." Were my executive function functioning, I'd have known never to do stupid shit around a man perpetually five feet away from a camera. Yet such is the price of sleep. Fletch raced over to the charging station to grab his iPhone and quickly adjusted his settings. "And we're live in five, four, three, two . . . rolling!"

Then, in full sex-machine regalia and without benefit of a bra, I proceed to demonstrate the process of extricating the stinking brown apple flesh from the heart of the caramel center, before artfully spreading the good parts over a few stout slices of multigrain bread.

"The magic happens in the microwave," I told my imaginary studio audience, comprised entirely of drooling dogs. "And don't be afraid to use a little butter." By a little, I meant half a stick.

After I assembled all the ingredients, I took an enormous bite of the chocolaty, buttery, slathered shamewich, and without even a hint of irony, I told the camera, "The Williams-Sonoma salvaged caramel apple sandwich; it's a good thing."

And then I winked.

Fletch showed me the video the next morning, laughing possibly even louder than he had the night before.

Although I'm impressed with my Ambien-fueled knife skills, there's not one second of the recording that doesn't induce paralyzing mortification, from the topknot, to the free-range, braless swingability, to the wink.

I guess the good news is that shame often induces realization, and this incident allowed me to uncover another fundamental in Martha's Tao: Revenge is a dish best not served at all, unless you're camera-ready.

Using the threat of death, dismemberment, and divorce, I've since convinced Fletch to delete the incriminating footage. He promises he has.

I'd like to believe him.

Of course, if I were him, I'd save the footage to use to ensure getting my way at some point in the future. Sometimes marriage isn't about love and companionship as much as it is a fine balancing act involving mutually assured destruction.

For insurance purposes, I've since convinced him to get his own prescription. As yet, I've not filmed him swimming around the shallow end of the bedroom, but rest assured, I will.

Anyway, in calculating my own personal Ambien odds, eighty-five percent of the time, everything's fine when I take it, and ten percent, it's not. But what really keeps me on the zolpidem pony is the five percent I haven't mentioned.

The five percent is pure genius, and I mean *actual* genius and not the caramel-apple-sandwich kind.

I'm fresh off an Ambien episode induced from watching the Bradley Cooper movie *Limitless*. In it, he begins to take a drug that increases his mental acuity by, like, a million percent. "So it's Adderall," Fletch remarked while we watched it.

Later that night, I decided that Ambien made me limitless as well, and I demonstrated my superpower, which involved my running sideways faster than anyone else on earth. Sometimes I sleep in the newly decorated adjoining bedroom, like whenever Fletch snores or laughs at me. With the way that bathroom lies, the whole thing forms a big circle that is really the perfect avenue for crab-running while shouting, "I am limitleeessssssss!"

Or so I'm told.

Anyway, I'm in the second bedroom, reading with Maisy curled up next to me. She doesn't climb into bed with me much anymore, ever since I toured earlier this year. Fletch replaced her old crappy bed with something called the Snuggler, and she's madly in love with it. (The tall walls make it feel like a massive pillow fort. Hell, I'd nap in it myself if it were a little larger.) But here she is now, all pressed up next to me, and between the combination of warm dog and sleeping pill, I'm inspired with my best idea yet.

"Fletch, Fletch, come here!" I shout.

He does not come running.

The last time I shouted, he came running, only for me to demonstrate how my new foot brace had turned my whole leg into a robot. I'd finally seen the podiatrist for treatment after Fletch caught me trying to use a Swiffer mop as a cane. So a portion of my ongoing treatment involves the use of a night brace.

Anyway, my robot leg kept kicking him, which I explained was not my fault. I was all, "Dude, I have no control over robots; what do you want?"

He eventually ambles in and then I share my brainstorm.

"We're going to be married ten years in three weeks and that's a big deal. We should celebrate somehow."

Before Martha, our old holiday traditions entailed doing nothing to commemorate an event; ergo last year we spent our anniversary drinking canned beer in the pool. By the end of the day, I kept telling Fletch I'd become "more fish than man."

"I agree," he says. "What do you propose? Have you got some big Martha party idea you want to try?"

Maisy leans into me and I run my hand over her sweet head. "Yes and no. We're going to have a party . . . but *you're* going to throw it. I want you to be in charge. You figure out the food and the drinks and guest list. You make the invitations. This will be your baby and your gift to me."

He narrows his eyes at me. "Has your Ambien kicked in?"

"Absolutely! But I must have gotten a good one tonight, because this really is a fantastic idea. Hear me out—in order to be a better hostess, I want to come to one of my own parties. I'd like to be my own guest."

"Meaning?"

"You know how you always see the hotel owners on *Undercover Boss* checking into their own properties? That's what I want to do. But not in disguise. You'll know I'm here, because it's my anniversary, too."

He nods grudgingly. "This is not the worst idea you've ever had."

"I know, right?"

We discuss details for a while, until I can't keep my eyes open anymore and I happily nod off to sleep.

Ambien, you're the gift that keeps on giving.

A week later, we're having coffee after walking Maisy and giving her a subcutaneous treatment. We're getting to be such pros at this. We got all her fluids in less than ten minutes! She even took her pills without trickery, so I can tell already today's going to be a good day. Granted, Dr. Thornhill said she's regressed a bit, so we're back to fluids twice a day. Hopefully this is just a phase.

Fletch has a couple of folders in front of him and hands the first to me. "Okay, here are the catering choices—with our budget, we can select three items from each tier. Please go through and circle what you'd like. I've highlighted the items I think would be the most guest-friendly, according to their allergies and preferences. Now, our order isn't large enough to have anyone here helping serve, but they will come and set up, which is half the battle."

I scan the list of hot and cold appetizers, trying to do the math in my head. "Are you sure you have the pricing right? I can't cater a party myself for the cost of the ingredients."

He nods in a way that seems almost officious. "Positive. I triple-checked prices and cross-referenced the number of guests with the optimal number of servings per person."

If he is, in fact, correct and he can throw a party together for less while employing professionals, then . . . then . . . then this whole year of living Martha-style has been a lie.

"You've got to be wrong. That's the only explanation."

He purses his lips at me and I amend my statement.

"Fine," I concede, "I do end up either throwing out two-thirds of all the party food I make, or we eat it ourselves until it goes bad."

"I recall having Independence Day hot dogs for lunch until July tenth this year," he says. "I was ready to go Boston Tea Party on them and dump them all in the pool, but I figured they'd float and you'd just fish them back out."

"What you're saying is that a caterer can't do a party *better* than me; she can just do it differently."

Technically this is not a win for me, but I won't pursue the point.

Fletch flips through the folders. "Anyway, here's what we're looking at in terms of liquor. I'm making a Costco run later this week and with the beer we have left over from the Fourth, we'll have plenty."

"Cool, thank you."

Why isn't he sweating?

Where's the swearing and crying?

Throwing a party isn't this easy; trust me—I've tried.

I point out, "The house is filthy. I've been so busy with Maisy that I've not kept up like I want." Aha, here comes the sweating and crying!

"Not a problem. I have a cleaning service coming in that Thursday."

"You'll want to spot-clean the rugs, though." In the diminishing battles between the New Girls and the Thundercats, the upstairs carpet has borne the brunt of the tail end of the cross fire. I'm not exactly sure how taking a whiz on the carpet establishes one side's dominance over the other, but that's what's happening.

Also? I was having trouble getting meatball stains out of my workout shirts, and Fletch determined that the problem was our twenty-four-year-old washer, so we invested in a new set. We left the door open on the new front-loading washer, and last week one of the cats pooped in there. I really have to teach these assholes to journal their feelings so they can stop with the biowarfare.

He glances down at his list. "Stanley Steemer's coming on that Friday."

I'm not sure how the man who forgets to put the milk back in the fridge every day is so on top of this, but I'm not going to argue. Am I going to be all, "No! Stop! You're going too good of a job here!"

And yet he's making me look bad.

"What about the broken faucet in the powder room?" Okay, now I've got him.

"The plumber will be here tomorrow."

ARGH.

I mean, thank you. This is going to be an incredible anniversary, but ARGH. Why is he already better at this than me? He hasn't been poring over Martha's entertaining books for the better part of the year; nor has he filled his days watching a massive TiVo cache of old show episodes.

Is it possible that some people are more predisposed to party planning?

Wait, at least I'm on the ball about something.

"Oh, forgot to tell you—I picked up a couple of cans of Off! at the grocery store yesterday. The mosquitoes have really being going crazy at dusk, so I bought enough for everyone." Weather permitting, we hope to hold the party outdoors.

"No need. I've scheduled the exterminator to spray for them."

I grit my teeth. "Great, then I can concentrate on the decor." I'm sure that this will be my oeuvre. I'm going to construct pretty paper lanterns and poufs and hang them in the apple trees.

He consults his stack. "The landscapers will string up twinkle lights in the backyard over the weekend."

DAMN IT.

"And this falls within our party budget?" I mean, he went all Imelda Marcos and the shoe closet here, surely. That's why the anniversary gathering is going to be fab, right? We're going to be eating cornflakes all winter because he tapped into our reserves. Or else I'll have to squirrel away more party hot dogs or something.

Fletch slides a spreadsheet across to me.

He's not only on time but under budget, so much so that I can now have a cake made.

If smug were a drug, he could sell it by the gram. (Ten points for catching the Vanilla Ice reference.)

He neatens his stack and says, "Of course, I sent the save-the-date e-mail a few days ago, and the hard copies are going out today."

I guess I can't be surprised at how on top of things he is. When Fletch planned his high school reunion earlier this summer, he used Martha's site for guides on everything from suggested vendors that would print and mail invitations to an online RSVP system.

Oh, *that's* it.

He didn't do this on his own, not really. He had Martha's help! That doesn't account for why he's better than me at party planning, but it does give me some comfort that he's not, like, a soiree savant or something.

He shuffles his folders again. "There's one area where I might need your help."

"Pfft, finally. I thought you had this on lock."

"For the most part, I do. But I'm having trouble with the love tree."

?

"I'm sorry. The *what*?"

"Your love tree. When we discussed the party the night you had the good Ambien, you demanded I plant you a love tree for our anniversary. So I talked to Rich and he'd never heard of a love tree, either, but he was going to check with Bob the Arborist. But maybe you can help us out—do you want something flowering or something that will be at its height at the beginning of September? Also, where in the yard do you want it?"

I'm still confused. I don't recall a single word of this conversation, as it must have happened deep in the Ambien fog.

"I asked you for a love tree?"

He nods. "You said you wanted it to"—he makes air quotes—"'sym-bolize our lives together' and we could plant it in the yard and 'watch our love grow every year,' preferably within eye line of the breakfast table so you didn't have to crane your head. You were real specific about that part, actually. Seems like a good idea, though. Rich suggested we plant it where the old ash tree was. I was thinking either dogwood or flowering maple."

He pulls out his iPad and begins to scroll through our options. Everything is gorgeous.

See?

This?

Right here?

Is why I live for that five percent.

Viva la Ambien!

The anniversary party is a rousing success. Almost everyone we love attended, including some of our out-of-town old friends who'd been to our actual wedding. Everything about the night was magical, from the company to the food to the music to the weather. Fletch was so proud of himself, and it was gratifying to step back and look at all we'd built in our lives over the past ten years of marriage.

And yet there's still a hole in my heart.

Maisy isn't going to make it.

As she slowly, steadily worked the crowd on Saturday night, I had the feeling she was saying her good-byes. By the end of the night, she was stationed on her dog bed, too worn-out to even lift her head.

When we took her to see Dr. Thornhill the last time, he was somber and didn't talk about her levels. We received no congratulatory handshakes. Every week when he draws blood, he runs a computer model on her functions, and for the past couple of weeks, they've been trending downward. When we asked about scheduling her next visit, he simply said to call him in a few days.

He knew, but he was waiting for her to tell us.

Maisy had a good Labor Day, though. She sat in her favorite lounge chair and quietly panted in the sun, a small doggie smile playing at the side of her mouth. Then yesterday, she and I were taking a stroll at dusk and we spotted three deer in the neighbor's yard. Instead of barking or losing her mind in the myriad ways she always used to do upon seeing another living creature, she simply looked at me and wanly wagged her tail, turning for home.

This is our last walk together.

This morning, Maisy doesn't bound out of bed. She doesn't nose after the cats or frolic with Libby. For the first time in ten years, she doesn't roll around and scratch her back.

When she looks at me, I know it's time.

And I love her enough to let her go.

Funny thing about grief—you can't run away from it. You can fill your days with activity and even leave town, but it follows you.

Grief is the ultimate debt collector.

After we say good-bye to Maisy, Fletch and I are at loose ends. We don't know what to do now that our days aren't filled with caretaking. I make some halfhearted stabs at Martha-based projects, but I can't seem to concentrate on anything. We don't even really eat, subsisting mainly on snacks from the "big box of happy" gift basket that Stacey made sure was delivered the day we lost her.

A week later, Fletch and I fly to Las Vegas in the hopes that getting away will help. It does and it doesn't. We're able to forget while in Vegas, but the minute we arrive home and she's not there, we experience the feelings of loss all over again.

Everywhere we look in the house, there are signs of Maisy, whether it's the ottoman she chewed long ago or the E-Collar I used to help steady her while we gave her fluids. Each time I walk past her love seat and she's not there, I break into tears.

The worst part of all this—outside of missing my girl every second of every day—is that I feel like I wasted three years of my life worrying about this moment. I mourned her long before she was gone. Despite all my anxiety, the worst happened anyway. I thought somehow I was bracing myself against the sadness by preemptively fretting, yet all I did was waste the time I could have had being happy.

That is, except for the past two months. I knew we were on borrowed time, so I made the most of every single moment, and when Maisy left this realm, there was no question in her mind as to how much we adored her.

The Tao of Maisy dictates that we need to be awesome, give awesome, and get awesome, but we're doing none of those things right now. We're just sad.

When Maisy was initially diagnosed three years ago, Fletch and I rescued the Thundercats, because I was determined that no other creature was going to die on my watch. But until we tear out all the floors and install bar grating so feline fluids can sluice through when they anger-whiz, we're steering clear of more cats.

The way I see it, we can spend our time mourning, or we can honor Maisy's memory by rescuing another pit bull.

Happiness really is a warm puppy.

"Everything about this dog is a lie," Fletch proclaims as the Red Menace bounds over the back of the couch in pursuit of Chuck Norris.

"No, it's not! She just got over her shyness. Like, really quickly."

Last week Elaine told us about a seven-month-old pit bull in need of a forever home. Although she'd not personally met the reddish-caramel-colored puppy called Whiskey, the foster parents assured her how sweet and mellow Whiskey was, so we wanted to meet her.

Elaine and the foster parents brought Whiskey over on Sunday and we spent a few hours introducing her to Libby and Loki to see if she might be a good fit. Libby loved her on sight—naturally—and Loki wasn't aggressive toward her. He didn't *like* her, but he didn't try to annihilate her, which was key. He would be far more difficult to win over, largely because he's an older dog. Think about it—most seventy-year-olds don't want to be friends with toddlers. But once they get to know each other, they can enjoy each other's company.

I counted on Fletch to be the voice of reason here, because three weeks after losing Maisy, you could lead Cerberus the three-headed hound from Hades into my house and I'd be all, "I LOVE DOGGIE SO MUCH!"

In terms of looks, Whiskey wasn't exactly the kind of pup you'd put on an adoption poster, either. She was awkward and gangly, too big to really be considered a puppy, but not yet grown into her frame. Also, her head was enormous and her weird yellow eyes were spaced really far apart, kind of like a horse or a hammerhead shark. Because her face was all one color, save for the eyes, she had absolutely no expression, save for a blank stare. Plus, she was shy and had such separation anxiety that the first family to adopt her sent her back to the fosters in three days.

So when Fletch looked at her and said, "I'd probably call her Hambone," I knew we'd found our new family member.

But Fletch is a little bit right: Hambone's not exactly as previously described.

Hambone, aka the Red Menace, is a *handful*.

We had our first inkling of this on Sunday night, when we tried to put her in her crate when we went to bed. Elaine said that whatever we did, we had to make sure she bunked in her crate, and that she wasn't allowed to sleep with us until she found her place in the pack. She said that even if Hambone cried, we were to Ferberize her.

Which would have worked fine, had Hambone not disassembled her cage around her. We'd heard she'd done the same thing at the first owners' house, but we figured they were stupid and didn't have their crate properly assembled.

Sorry I misjudged you, strangers.

As Hambone clambered into bed with me, curling up in Maisy's old spot, all I said was, "Don't tell Elaine."

Then, the next morning, Fletch went upstairs to work in his office while I showered. Hambone didn't like us both being out of her line of vision, so she climbed up on the bathroom counter and barked until I rinsed all the shampoo out of my hair.

A week into her tenure here and she's proven herself to be stubborn, bossy, and mischievous. She's profoundly annoying to the cats, as every time they hiss at one another, she bounds over to break up the fight. She's making Loki crazy with her constant sucking up, and she's emulating all of the bad habits Libby learned from Maisy. We've started to train her, and as yet, she cycles through every command she knows, desperate to be rewarded with a treat.

I think she'll fit in here just fine.

BANANA GRABBER

My job now is to figure out what life looks like post-Maisy. I figure the quicker we get back to living our normal lives, the better off we'll be, so I dive back into my happiness project.

Immediately, I realize that in living like Martha for so many months, I've not made her macaroni and cheese once.

Did we lose a war or something?

Martharoni and cheese (not what she calls it, but she totally should) is absolutely one of my all-time favorite dishes, as it's a steamin' bowl of melted comfort. However, Martha's recipe is not so moist that it turns into a big soupy mess, oozing across the plate and sullying the green beans. The crunchy crust gives the macaroni much-needed gravitas, and the chili powder lends the perfect amount of zing. If I ever find myself on death row, this is *so* on my final menu. (I say this more to emphasize the tastiness of the dish and less as an ad hoc admission of a desire to commit a capital crime.)

I've intended to rectify my mac-free situation for a while now. Through proper planning, I've had my blocks of cheddar and Gruyère at the ready for whenever the weather finally cooled and the urge struck. But when I was cleaning out the fridge today I noticed that the cheeses are on the verge of breaking bad. I realize it's still warm out, but if I don't use these now they won't last, and I'll be so mad at myself if I end up wasting these ingredients.

Now I'm determined not to let my sadness (and possibly a bit of the fall TV season) get in the way of meal preparation. I hate when I wind up throwing away all kinds of formerly beautiful produce and previously delicious dairy when I *meant* to make dinner but I wasn't in the mood. I particularly feel guilty when I don't cook the hamburger or pork chops I've defrosted in time. Knowing that some noble beast gave his life for my dinner and then I couldn't even do him the honor of eating him before he spoiled because I was busy having All the Feels and ordering Thai and watching Teresa Giudice plot against her younger, firmer sister-in-law gives me existential angst.

(Also? Melissa was not a stripper, *capisce?*)

At one point over the summer, we realized we'd been wasting so much that Fletch insisted I make a list of all the foodstuffs I had to toss and promise that I'd stop buying them. (RIP, farmers' market beets, barrels of marinated olives, and an ocean of premade tuna salad.) Granted, I was able to salvage a few items by freezing them, and now the fridge is stockpiled with no fewer than eight thousand overripe bananas.

What is it with me and banana hoarding, by the way? I like bananas well enough, yet I'm not exactly ape over them. (My apologies for that truly despicable pun, but I'm in a weakened emotional state and I couldn't help myself. Do you want me to cry? Do you? No? Then the pun stands.)

I mean, seed-specked dragon fruit, impossible-to-navigate pomegranate, and boring old apricots would have to become extinct before bananas even cracked my Top Twenty Favorite Fruits list. But the second they begin to grow spotty and lose their solid constitution, they morph into something more precious than rubies, and I squirrel them  away in the chilly confines of the freezer as fast as I can.

I keep telling Fletch that I'm going to use this vaguely phallic stockpile to craft the world's most delicious and nutritious smoothies, but when I finally attempted to do so recently, I discovered that in order to access the stupid banana, I needed to have peeled them before giving them the full-on Han Solo carbonite treatment. Peeling a frozen banana is like breaking into Fort Knox, or being Taylor Swift's long-term boyfriend: patently impossible! I've also learned that defrosting them first renders said bananas both useless and liquid-disgusting, so I no longer try that route, either.

Once science figures out a way to de-peel a frozen banana, I'll be in the catbird seat. Until then, there's still plenty of room in the second fridge in the laundry room. Also, we've been pricing deep freezers for the basement. See? It's all fine.

Anyway, I'm determined to make macaroni and cheese tonight for Fletch's birthday dinner. It's time I got back in the kitchen. I plan to start the process shortly, as soon as his present gets here. I'll do a quick wrap job and then I'll start the second phase of the meal. The short ribs have been braising nicely for the past three hours, and all the dogs are hanging out by the oven, closing their eyes and inhaling really deeply. Dogs are supposed to be able to sense every element of a dish, so I hope they appreciate how I slowly built the layers of flavors by caramelizing the mirepoix (diced onions, carrots, and celery) in pancetta fat and then deglazing the pan with stock and merlot. If the short ribs taste half as good as they smell, we're in for a very happy birthday indeed.

In terms of prep, I've already cubed the zucchini (yeah, still bitter over the garden) and squash, which I plan to toss in olive oil and a rosemary-sage salt, for pan-roasting. I need only to chop a little bacon for the frisée salad. I consider adding a poached egg to the salad, but the rest of the meal is so heavy that we don't need it. Now the kitchen is immaculate, the birthday white chocolate cheesecake is chilling, and the wine is waiting to be decanted.

Seriously, Google "organized" and you will see a photo of me.

Well, technically if you Google "organized" you'll see a bunch of stuff about the Mafia, but the point is, I've got this shit on lock and Martha would be proud.

So, the rest of the day should go: present wrapping, then macaroni making, dinner eating, present opening, and television watching. (*Mindy Project*, I luff you!) Yes, this should all work out nicely.

I ordered Fletch a coat for his birthday, which, frankly, seems like a crappy gift, right up there with savings bonds and roadside assistance memberships. But he seemed really excited about the prospect of a new coat and it's his day, not mine. Coat it is. I found a place online that could deliver what he wants today and that was that.

Please note that I didn't argue with him over his bullshit gift, like he did when I mentioned what was on *my* birthday wish list.

"I would like an aquarium," I said.

"Pfft, out of the question," he replied with a wave of his hand, like he was dismissing the notion of anything fish-based entirely.

"Whoa, what do you mean 'out of the question'? Who made you Birthday King? It's fish, not a damn pony. Plus, I didn't say no to your stupid coat. I mean, *I* don't want a coat, but it's not *my* day. See, that's how birthdays work."

Patiently Fletch explained, "Yes, but an aquarium is ridiculous; A) we have no room for one, and B) you wouldn't take care of the fish anyway."

I replied, "Alphabet back at you! A) I'm not looking to build a wall of shark tanks like the lobby of the Mirage hotel or some *Miami Vice* drug lord, and B) shut up. C) I don't want a saltwater monstrosity that requires a PhD in marine biology to maintain, and D) I just thought it would be neat to have something small to put in my office on the black credenza, like twenty gallons or so. E) I figured it would be relaxing to hear water bubbling while I'm working, and the cats might get a kick out of it, too. Maybe watching fish would calm them down, and F) they wouldn't pee everywhere."

Unmoved by my A-to-Z argument and enumerated salient points, he shook his head. "A fish tank is a terrible idea. You'd never clean it. I remember the algae farm you used to have when we started dating. Bio-hazardous. You had to scrape through the green to even see the fish." To punctuate his point, he shuddered.

"Yet you forget that Oprah Winfish lived for five years after that."

My other goldfish, Sally Jessy, Geraldo, and Ricki Lake, didn't last nearly as long. Typical.

He suddenly became very interested in scrolling through the TV listings. "I . . . don't remember that."

I was resolute. "You don't remember having to lug a half-empty tank to three new apartments because I refused to give her a premature burial at sea?"

He simply frowned in return. "No tank. Rather, no, *tank you*. Heh."

"Yeah, hardy-har-har."

Yet I didn't press the point, because sometimes I like him to have the illusion that he's running the show.

Trust me, though, on my birthday, there *will* be fish.

Presents in mind, I head to the front porch to see if my box arrived yet. The dogs would normally bark their fool heads off when UPS arrives, but they're so enamored with the smell of braising meat that a battalion of squirrels could set up camp on the lawn right now and they'd not notice.

I peek out the window and see no conspicuous cardboard box; then I open the door to make sure it's not propped up against it. Nope. Nada. Which is weird. I was very specific about ordering using UPS, since they're far more reliable than our postal carrier. Only about a third of the items we're supposed to receive via the post office actually arrive.

(Although I have no proof, I'm pretty sure my mailman drinks.)

(Otherwise, why don't we receive our mail until five p.m.?)

(Addiction is more forgivable than incompetence, FYI.)

I zip up to my office to reread the coat shipper's confirmation e-mail; then, just to be sure, I recheck the UPS tracking number. Wait, what does this mean?

SHIPPER FAILED TO PLACE PARCEL OUT FOR
DELIVERY PRIOR TO CUTOFF TIME

As it turns out, even though I ordered in plenty of time, somehow they didn't get Fletch's coat on the truck and now it won't be here until tomorrow. ARGH.

I make some calls and I may or may not get a little snippy at the third-world customer service rep after she explains that somehow this is *my* fault for purchasing the kind of outerwear that people forget to put in an outgoing shipment prior to cutoff time.

Going forward, can someone please, please empower customer service reps to say the following magical words: "I'm so sorry. I understand you're frustrated. How can I make this right?" It would really save some strain on everyone's vocal cords.

I tell Fletch what happened and he's totally fine with not getting his present until tomorrow. But what if it suddenly drops forty-five degrees and snows between now and then? And what if my theory of not unwrapping something on your actual birthday leads to a year of bad luck? What then?

Unwilling to chance it, I jump into the car and drive to the cute little Williams-Sonoma in town. For the past couple of years, I've been giving Fletch their matching glassware for the bar, slowly replacing our piece-meal collection of (thus far unbreakable) one-dollar wineglasses. That was pretty much the plan for this year until we had the big coat conversation a couple of days ago.

While I wait for the clerk to wrap the martini glasses, I notice a jar of macaroni and cheese starter. Now, *that's* interesting. However, this stuff can't possibly be a good as what Martha prescribes. And yet . . . most of the ingredients are exactly what's in the original recipe: milk, butter, flour, nutmeg, and salt—there's nothing in here I can't pronounce, and there are no additives or preservatives.

What this looks like is a jar of someone else having made the appropriate effort. So I could skip the hard parts of making the béchamel and just use this jar?

Could it be that easy?

At this point, it's already coming up on six p.m., and the idea of a shortcut is not without merit. Martha would resoundingly disapprove (unless it were her brand), but she probably would have thought to ask Fletch what he wanted for his damn birthday more than two days before the event, and thus would have plenty of opportunity to implement a plan B if the present didn't arrive in time. Then again, Martha's not pre-occupied by bursting into tears every time she finds a bit of Maisy's fur on her fall clothes; nor is she attempting to re-potty-train the Red Menace and hand-scrubbing all of her soiled rugs, so I'm cutting myself some slack.

Anyway, the jar's fourteen dollars, but with the amount of time and the ingredients I'll save, the price seems worth it. I ask the clerk to add the jar to my total, and once everything is wrapped, she helps me carry my bags to the car. My car's normally black, but I hate paying for the fancy hand car washes Fletch demands, so right now it's kind of gray. (I love the four-dollar washes at the gas station with the big revolving brushes, but Fletch says we may as well rub the car with steel wool.) (I still sneak into them sometimes.) The clerk likely regrets assisting me, as my fender stripes her apron with road grit. Then she comments on how dirty my car is and I feel less guilty.

When I'm back in the kitchen, I arrange my blocks of cheese and begin the hunt for my grater. The stupid grater is another reason why I don't make the mac as often as I'd like. No matter how careful I am, no matter how hard I try, it's impossible for me to grate cheese without also shaving off the tops of my knuckles. What's for dinner? My DNA!

As I poke around the disorganized cabinets, I run across the food processor. Fletch loves this thing and uses it all the time, but I've never quite gotten the hang of it. I have an odd prejudice against food processors, largely because it bothers me that Fletch is more adept at something in the kitchen than I am. But as I inspect the various blades, I notice there's one that looks like it might be appropriate for shredding.

Again, could it really be that easy? Is it possible to finally make this dish without making myself bleed?

It is and I can! My victory tastes like Gruyère as I gloat over my perfectly proportionate mounds of shredded cheese. My pasta's ready (Martha, forgive me, but I prefer cavatappi noodles over elbows), so now all I have to do is heat the jar of sauce, stir in the cheese, and shove the whole thing in the oven. Dinner at seven p.m., just like the good Lord intended!

I pop the lid and try to pour the macaroni starter into my enamel-covered cast-iron pot. I was anticipating the sauce being all creamy, but actually it's more of a big, gelatinous cube. I urge the mixture out with the help of a spatula and it lands in the pan with a gratuitous plop. I slowly begin to warm and stir, careful not to scald the mixture. Martha says to be really cautious with anything containing milk, because it's so easy to ruin when the heat's up too high. Like, have you ever had a horrible latte and couldn't grasp why it was so bad? Burning is why.

After about five minutes, the béchamel is creamy and just a little bit bubbly. Again, I don't bring it to a full boil, because I'm about to add the cheddar and I don't want the sauce to break. Excessive heat makes cheese separate into oily and lumpy bits. Once the cheese breaks down, it never gets smooth again.

The thing is, I've watched just enough *Top Chef* (fine, *Hell's Kitchen*) to know that you HAVE to taste your food before serving, or, in this case, before adding almost twenty dollars' worth of high-end cheese.

And I'm so glad that I did, because this sauce is rank. Somehow this mixture manages to turn my tongue dry while making the rest of my mouth water. The whole thing manages to be bland, yet also bitter and awful, but I rationalize that that's because I haven't added any of my seasonings. I love Williams-Sonoma and I want to give them the benefit of the doubt. I reason that this isn't a complete sauce, so as soon as I add salt, pepper, and garlic, it should be delicious.

Should be.

But is not.

Not even close.

According to the ingredient list, there's nothing in the mix that should make the sauce taste this way. So what's the deal? Then I quickly scan the Williams-Sonoma Web site to see a dozen similar complaints and that the product is no longer available online.

The good news is, this is not my doing, but the bad news is that it *is* my problem.

From the corner of my eye, I see Martha's confident visage grinning away on the cover of her *American Food* cookbook, and I steel myself for what comes next.

I scrape the whole fourteen dollars' worth into the sink and begin to make the sauce properly.

In the scheme of things, fourteen dollars is nothing, yet in the Big, Bitter Book of Accounting that lives in my head, I'll file this transgression next to the seven dollars I never received for babysitting for the creepy family who didn't have a television, the meathead who used to steal my *Chicago Tribune* when we lived in the bad neighborhood, and my college frenemy who never chipped in her twenty-six dollars for the hotel when we saw U2 in Indianapolis in 1988.

Bitter forgives, but Bitter doesn't forget.

Or I could just return the bottle to the store and get my money back. You know what? That's a better idea.

Anyway, in less than ten minutes, I have a batch of silky béchamel that is so creamy and perfect that Williams-Sonoma should be bottling what's on *my* stove. I toss in the cheese, adding a little bit of fontina and smoked mozzarella, because there's no law against adding a few personal tweaks to your favorite recipe. Case in point? I often don't have white bread for the crust topping, so I improvise with buttery bread crumbs. I

promise you it's equally tasty.

Dinner's delayed by fifteen extra minutes and there's suddenly a sink full of dishes, but the end result is well worth the wait.

The short ribs steal the show, but the macaroni proves itself to be worthy of the pairing. Fletch declares this to be the best birthday dinner he's ever eaten.

And just when I least expect it, Martha illuminates another tenet of her Tao: Save your shortcuts for road trips; do it right or don't do it at all.

Now, if she could just show me what to do with those damn bananas, I'd be all set.

S·I·X·T·E·E·N

MY KINGDOM FOR A CROCK-POT

I've hit a wall and now I need a project.

I need to stay in motion.

The minute I stand still is the minute I begin to fall apart.

Maisy's been gone a month, and I have to find a way to stop obsessing. Missing her has become a physical ache. Every time I think, "I'm better now!" I have a setback. I'm somehow regressing in my grief and I don't understand why.

Maybe it's finally sinking in that she's not coming back, especially since we received the urn with her ashes. We placed her on a shelf in the great room, surrounded by the ashes of all our cats. I arranged her in such a way that she'd be able to see all the doors as well as the main hallways of the house. Had she been able to haul her ponderous bulk up there, this is exactly where she'd have wanted to sit.

Still, and even with the addition of Hambone, I'm struggling.

Rationally, I not only understand that it was her time, but also that

allowing her to go was the most compassionate action we could have taken. I appreciate what a gift her life was, and if I hadn't lost her, I'd have never come to realize the Tao of Maisy.

The best way to honor her life is to get on with my own.

She'd want that.

Mind you, I'm aware that she was a dog and couldn't grasp the complexities of human emotions like grief. But I can say that whenever I've been sad or down in the past ten years, she'd do something to try to pull me out of my funk, like the Naughty Run. If I was in my office, she'd nose through my trash until she found a Starbucks cup and she'd pry off the lid to lick the contents. Then she'd sit there grasping the cup, which would look comically large between her paws, and she'd always remind me of an Olsen twin.

Her need for physical proximity was her trademark, and I can attest that it's very hard to stay upset when a sixty-five-pound pit bull tries to climb into your shirt or attempts to hump a cat. Maisy could even time a fart in such a way that it broke the tension; her comedic sensibilities were second to none.

In many ways, having Hambone is a godsend, but at some point in the past few weeks, she careened into adolescence. Any vestiges left of the advertised "cute, timid puppy" have been replaced with "awkward teenager with a sassy mouth and a penchant for biting her brother in the face."

Every day it's something with this dog. Her power move last week was exploding out of the screen when she thought it was an open door.

Her Facebook "likes" include Running Through the Muck on the Edge of the Yard and Then Jumping on the Beds, and the Coalition of Dogs Who Prefer to Whiz Indoors.

Yesterday she tore open a six-pack of toilet paper while we were out, and for a second I thought it had snowed in three rooms upon our return. I've been calling her Osama Bone Laden, because she's terrorizing all of us.

Someday Hambone will be my best friend and the love of my life, and I'll have spent a decade telling her my secrets. Someday I'll nurse her and hand-feed her every bite and fret over each breath she takes because I love her so much it hurts, and I'll live to make sure she's comfortable and content.

Today is not that day.

Today, I picked up four mountains of her poop in the living room. And then I took it all out to the trash, and while I was gone she not only crapped in the laundry room, but then stepped in it and Dirty Sanchezed me in her zeal upon my return.

Maisy would have found Hambone hilarious, which actually gives me comfort.

But the fact remains that if I'm not occupied with a project, then I ruminate on what I had and not what I have.

While I was busy cooking Fletch's birthday dinner, I felt like the old me, the one who isn't consumed with loss and sings (badly) into her spatula while she's making sauce. Truly, there is a joy of cooking. (Quick, someone use this as a title for an iconic cookbook!)

Although I once despised all things meal-preparation-related, I've been cooking enthusiastically ever since I wrote *My Fair Lazy* and upped my previously nonexistent culinary skills by taking classes. But I've made very little since July that wasn't specifically to feed Maisy. Between giving her fluids and trying to coax her into eating and taking her on nightly walks, by the time dinner rolled around, delivery seemed the easiest option.

I need comfort; ergo I need comfort food. So I believe the best way to live My Year of Martha currently will be to head back to the kitchen. I'm going to cook every single day for the rest of October. I mean, meal making feels the most Stewartesque action, considering she built her empire on a catering business.

I'll begin the process by asking Fletch what he might want to eat.

He doesn't even hesitate with his answer. "Anything in the slow cooker." And then he smirks.

Crock-Pot cookery does not normally lend itself to smirking, except in this circumstance. Back when we lived in the city, I started hosting an annual eighties party. Everyone would don Lycra and leg warmers and Members Only jackets and we'd throw down to new wave music with John Hughes movies on in the background.

Nothing's more retro than neon food, so Stacey told me how to make Day-Glo orange Rotel dip, which is comprised of exactly two ingredients, the second being Velveeta. Open the Rotel, cube the cheese, turn on the slow cooker, and voilà! Four hours later, I have the kind of liquid gold that guests will mainline, given the chance.

Except I had a shitty old slow cooker and ended up burning my Rotel dip. Two ingredients! One step! Ruined! (I ate it anyway, but grudgingly.) So, before our next party, Fletch bought us a new slow

cooker. He was in charge, as slow cookers are somehow under my mental auspices with other things-that-I-need-but-won't-pay-for, along with oil changes and car washes.

He brought home a beautiful cranberry-colored KitchenAid slow cooker in which the entire ceramic part lifted out. We used it a few times in our old house with great success. But then we moved and we lost the cord in the shuffle. I found this out the first time I tried to make Rotel in the new house. (Fortunately the microwave can do the same thing, three hours and fifty-five minutes quicker. Score!)

Fletch offered to pick up a new one, but if I'm too stingy to buy a new slow cooker in the first place, the last damn thing I want is to fork out the cash to replace one that's perfectly good.

I tore this house apart for *two years* looking for the cord. I knew it was here somewhere, and the minute I gave up and bought another one, then I'd find the original cord. Not happening.

When Angie was visiting last week, we got onto the subject of slow cookers.

". . . so I'll send you the recipe—it's so good!" she told me, recounting a dish she'd made for a faculty party.

"Can't, no slow cooker," I replied.

"I thought you had a nice one," she said. "Didn't we make Rotel dip in it?"

"Yes, but the cord's missing. I've pawed through every box in this house multiple times, but I can't find it anywhere, including the garage. And we had great movers. They didn't even break a single wineglass. Everything we owned arrived here in perfect shape, so I refuse to accept that they'd lose this one tiny, stupid thing."

At that point in the conversation, Fletch came into the kitchen for a Diet Coke. He went first to the butler's pantry, where we store the soda, and then to the glasses across the kitchen, and then to the ice maker. Exhausting! Why not just keep the sodas in the fridge and drink them cold from the can? What Fletch calls "being a nudge" I consider "being a paragon of efficiency." Although when I pointed this out, he asked, "Are you really burning gray matter in trying to figure out how I can streamline my beverage consumption?" I kind of didn't have a response to that.

Angie smiled in greeting to Fletch and then said to me, "Can't you just order another one online?"

Exasperated, I replied, "You'd think, but no. After officially having a missing cord for two years, I decided to compromise by buying a replacement cord. I figured it could be expensive, but not as much as replacing the entire unit. But KitchenAid doesn't make them!" I'm not kidding; I spent days trawling all the online sites for a solution.

"Replacement cord for what?" he asked, standing at the head of our extra-long dinner table. The old home owners had a tiny table in here, plus a whole seating area with a couch. Mind you, I love a good couch and I'm a huge fan of comfortable seating, but if everyone's gathered in the kitchen, it's to eat and drink, not lounge, so we found a table that seats eight normally and ten with the leaves installed. I plan to have this table for the rest of my life, and that gives me a great sense of stability. I feel like that quote from *Fight Club*, all "no matter what goes wrong, I've got that [sofa] table thing figured out." (Of course, I'm less on board with the movie's line, "Fuck Martha Stewart. Martha's polishing brass on the *Titanic*; it's all going down, man." But kudos to our gal for being woven so deeply into the tapestry of pop culture!)

"The slow cooker. But no one makes one."

Fletch pulled out a chair and sat across from us. He sipped his soda and said, "I don't believe that."

"What's not to believe? I went everywhere online, and I mean everywhere. I can find you a new drive assembly part for your KitchenAid ice-cream maker, or a rubber foot for your Pro Line coffee grinder, but a cord? No. Replacement cords do not exist for that unit."

Fletch folded up a napkin and placed it under his drink. "That can't be. You must have looked for the wrong thing."

Argh.

"I didn't look for the wrong thing—I even Googled every iteration of 'cord,' 'plug,' and 'power,' but there's nothing. Not to go all H.W.'s reelection, but read my lips—no new cords."

Fletch pointed to Angie's Kindle. "Can I see that for a minute?" and then he conducted his own Internet search.

"Maybe you should look under 'magical electricity-bringer rope,'" Angie suggested.

"Ereplacementcords.com is the most comprehensive place to search," I offered.

He tooled around on the Internet while Angie told me about her summer teaching in China. Angie had such an adventure there, yet she returned home with a profound appreciation for advancements in American plumbing. She says every time she flushes, she's all, "USA! USA! USA!"

He closed her Kindle with a frustrated snap.

"Honey," I said gently, "this doesn't need to be an I-was-right kind of thing. Rather, these cords simply don't exist."

I *was* right, though.

I just didn't need to *say* it.

"Where is the slow cooker now?" he asked, rising from his spot.

"Butler's pantry, right side, bottom shelf."

Before Angie could describe what Walmart's like in China, Fletch marched back in the room carrying the Crock-Pot.

The Smug arrived two seconds before him.

"What's with the smirk? Was the cord inside the removable ceramic part?" Angie asked.

I had to roll my eyes. "Oh, like I didn't check there ten million times?"

In one deft move, Fletch flipped the Crock-Pot on its side to display the bottom . . . where the cord was neatly wrapped around the prongs.

Damn it.

Angie barked with laughter while Fletch explained, "The more you

talked about the cord, the more the day I bought it came back to me. I remembered my thought process as I weighed my options. There were nicer units, but I said to myself, 'Jen will likely lose a cord in the chaos that is our drawers. I should get the model with the attached cord to prevent this from being a problem. I'll buy this one.'"

"Then why didn't you tell me it was attached during the two years I looked for it?" I was delighted to have my slow cooker back, but aggravated at all the time I wasted. Am I not a paragon of efficiency, after all?

"She never asked?" Angie offered.

"She never asked," he confirmed.

Point?

I've found a project to occupy my time and my mind: slow cooking for the win.

And I shall call this month CROCKTOBER.

"What's for Crocktober dinner tonight?" Fletch asks.

"Pulled pork with a side of red cabbage."

He nods appreciatively and rubs his beard. "Mmm. How long till it's ready?"

"We'll eat at six thirty."

"Great!" As he retreats from the kitchen, he turns back to say, "The house smells like McDonald's right now, and I mean that in the best possible sense."

I nod in agreement. He's dead-on with that assessment. The air is fragrant and heavy with the scent of warmed meat, even though I'm braising pork and not frying beef. I bet the similar aroma stems from the ketchup in the recipe. There's something inexorably linked about McDonald's and the smell of ketchup.

I'm excited about serving this particular dinner. Pulled pork is one of those dishes I never had any idea how to make. I routinely buy it premade by the pound at various grocery stores, and I'm always disappointed because it tastes so much better when homemade. Had I any clue how simple pulled pork was to fix at home, I'd have started years ago! The only difficult bit was making sure I started dinner eight hours before we wanted to eat.

With the advent of Crock-Pot meals, my organizational skills have been put to the test. As I was a competent home cook before, it could be six p.m. and I'd have no idea what to serve, yet I could always whip something together before Bill O'Reilly came on at seven p.m. (Don't judge; I find his bloviating highly entertaining.)

But now I plan not only the morning of the dinner, but often days before, so I can shop and stock all the needed ingredients. I feel so . . . domestic. In terms of the Martha Stewart Experience, Crocktober has been among my favorite parts. Our roles in this house are fairly nontraditional in that I'm the primary breadwinner, and Fletch is more likely to take care of the day-to-day business of our household. He runs the laundry and washes the dishes and scoops litter boxes. He's the one who schedules vet appointments and picks up prescriptions and drops off dry cleaning while I'm at work. (Generally working involves my sitting at my desk in yoga pants without benefit of a shower, but still.)

But in living my life like Martha, I've taken back the mantle of domestic responsibility. Through diligent time management and a growing sense of organization, I've been able to better balance both household and professional tasks. I'm always at my best when I'm busy, so instead of feeling overwhelmed, I feel accomplished.

With my stepping back into the picture, Fletch has had time to start a small telecom consulting business. He's still in the early stages of establishing a client base, but he's deriving a great deal of pleasure from building something on his own. Plus, his being in an excellent state of mind is absolutely improving my own.

Since we're not quite so enmeshed in each other's day, we actually have stuff to discuss at the dinner table now, other than Bill O'Reilly. Which is lovely.

As Crocktober has progressed, I've come to accept exactly what a state my kitchen has been in for the past two years. Again, everything appears neat and clean, but there's neither rhyme nor reason to any of the cabinets. What it looks like is that we moved in and I immediately had a book due, so I threw the contents of every box into any open cabinet. (That's because it's exactly what happened.)

Before I started any projects in the kitchen, I sat down and brainstormed on kitchen priorities, which were basic, yet painfully lacking. I wanted:

- like items, such as flatware, china, and glasses, grouped in a way that makes sense. I want day-to-day items in one spot, and entertaining items in another. Sounds so simple, and yet . . .

- a spice rack where I can easily grab what I need without pawing through every herb I ever bought

- a dedicated baking cupboard

- an orderly freezer where chuck roasts don't come flying out to hobble me

So, every day, once I set up my Crock-Pot meal, I've been working on organization. I started off in the spice cabinet, as Fletch had previously claimed that looking for garlic salt was "like an Easter-egg hunt, without the fun."

By using Martha's advice from her "How to Stock: Home Essentials" checklist on the Web, I quickly culled half of my spices. I gave them the sniff test, and the ones that were no longer fragrant were tossed. (FYI, you do not want to snort cinnamon. Trust.)

I also evaluated my own purchasing habits and cursed myself for having three kinds of allspice. WTF, allspice? I can't think of one dish that requires allspice, let alone enough to require three bottles! I did cut myself a break on the four bottles of chili pepper, because that had Fletch's fingerprints all over it.

I cross-referenced the spices Martha recommends to keep on hand from *Martha Stewart's Cooking School* and restocked accordingly. The only one I didn't buy was Szechuan peppercorns, figuring I could muddle through with my black, white, red, and pink peppercorns, as well as my favorite Williams-Sonoma smoked pepper. (Which totally makes up for the macaroni sauce debacle.)

Then I put everything back in alphabetical order.

Oh, my God.

Rather, ERHMERGARD!

Do you have any concept of how much easier life is with alphabetized spices? Everything I need is right there, in the exact same spot, every time I go to grab it. Assembling ingredients for a meal now takes seconds, not minutes.

Who knew?

Okay, maybe everyone else in the world already knew this, but I feel like Helen Keller the first time she figured out the word for water. Fletch says this makes him my Annie Sullivan. Oh, really, Annie Sullivan with your spices arranged by *country of origin*? No.

After I tackled the spice rack, I felt confident and emboldened and I rearranged all the dinnerware. I finally donated the plain diner-style dishes we received for our wedding, because the stupid lip on them made it impossible to balance a knife on the side. Instead, we're now officially using the brightly patterned stuff I bought for a dinner party a while back, and Fletch no longer has to sneak off to enjoy their wide-lipped bounty.

My ultimate plan in here had been to convert the gun cabinet to a baking cabinet, but as Fletch works on it (he insisted), I realize that it's too pretty to use to store flour. Also, Loki's bed is right in front of it, and I don't want to upset him every time I make a pie. (Which has been often—Crocktober has also turned into Sweettober, as I've been trying various pie recipes like crazy in order to have my Thanksgiving offerings down pat.)

So the gun cabinet will be a china cabinet, which means the butler's pantry will be rededicated for baking.

But first I have to tackle the Cabinet of Shame.

The Cabinet of Shame is far worse than the Drawer of Shame, due to both size and necessity. With the drawer, everything's stashed away to protect stupid cats and dogs from ingesting items that could hurt them. The cabinet? Well, that's just laziness. This is prime kitchen real estate, located directly across from the stove. But is it filled with cookware or pantry supplies?

Not even a little bit.

Among numerous other items, I remove the following:

- my entire collection of *Mad Men* Barbie dolls, as well as my bonus Iggy Pop action figure

- six bottles of tanning lotion for electric tanning beds, none less than four years old

- a single mitten

- three kinds of pastel Easter grass, not bagged or contained, just pretty much sitting on a shelf with other bits of effluvia like quarters and screws nesting in it

- a garage door opener to an apartment we vacated in 2008

- three empty bottles of bug spray

- a copy of *Life* magazine with Richard Nixon on the cover (to be fair, we'd been antiquing recently)

- eight thousand loose AA batteries

- two chewed-up dog hairbrushes

- nine broken Christmas ornaments

- three packages of plastic caps to go on the cats' claws to keep them from destroying the furniture/one another

- phone books, phone books, and more phone books. Because apparently the Internet no longer exists

- one set of 1970s mustard-yellow salt and pepper shakers shaped like mushrooms (In and of themselves, this is a reasonable item to house in a kitchen cabinet. Yet Joanna and I purchased them because they closely resembled the photo our friend received of one guy's junk and we thought it would be funny to send them to her . . . except I fail at execution.) (Also? Naked Dude who thought he was being sexy by sending unsolicited shots of his gentleman business? For future reference? This photograph was passed around the table at Moto on the night of my birthday in 2010 at least a dozen times. Other tables even got in on the action. For Christ's sake, we showed the same waiter who later appeared on *Top Chef*. Many, *many* laughs were had at your expense. Sending someone a picture of what's in your pants is not a good way to flirt. However, it *is* an excellent way to have the story of your poor decision memorialized in the Library of Congress, so let this be a lesson to you.)

As I work, I have to wrestle almost every one of these items away from Hambone, as Libby has taught her the finer points of counter-surfing.

Oh, Hambone. Once the cabinet's emptied I'm able to wipe it down and restock with the overflow of pastas and rice from the other cabinets. That's when I realize that all the times we've been to the grocery store and I've said, "Do we need more bucatini?" we did not.

After I finish my purge, I chop the red cabbage and toss it with a little cider vinegar

and coarse salt. The acid in the vinegar will cut down on the crunch factor, and its fresh tang will complement the rich pork. Hambone begs for a bite of cabbage, and I hand her a chunk. Her jaws snap as she relishes this delicious treat.

A word about the Bone?

I appreciate her enthusiasm when it comes to food. Loki's always been fairly laid-back about dinner. He likes what he's served, but he's never been one of those dance-around-the-kitchen types. He has too much dignity. Until our old, toothless cat Tucker started eating his leftovers, Loki would often leave half his dinner until later. Loki likes to lie down while he eats and chews slowly, savoring his meal. Libby's easy to please, and she'll take what she's given and will consume in a manner best described as "polite." She's the kind of girl who'd place her napkin in her lap, given the chance.

For the last couple of years, Maisy was decidedly fussy about her dinner. Of course, she was always hungry, yet still quite picky. Being sick really brought out her finicky side. I was constantly striving to find the proper mix of wet and dry food in order to make sure she ate. She started on prescription food last winter and she despised it. So it was my job to flavor it enough to make her kidney kibble more palatable. She was always changing her mind, too. One day, she'd love Evanger's canned beef, and the next she wouldn't want anything to do with it; then it would be her favorite again later. (After August, she was on palliative care, so I didn't worry about her prescription diet—it was too important to load her up on any sort of calories.)

My point is, I've never had a dog that was as enthusiastic as Hambone is about eating, and I appreciate that. Every single thing she tastes is her favorite dish ever. There's no begging when I feed her, no doctoring. I just set down her plate of dry kibble and in ten seconds, it's spotless. Recently she discovered that the apple tree is more than a source of superfun red balls to chase. I almost died laughing the day she ran to the door looking like a luau pig, pink eyes bulging, with an apple crammed in her maw. Now she's got the other two turned on to apples, and every time I glance outdoors, they're all happily munching away like a bunch of horses in a field. Stacey says to be careful, because if the apples are on the ground too long they'll ferment and the dogs will get drunk.

Yeah, a drunken Hambone is just what I need.

Anyway, I still have time for another project before dinner, so I decide to tackle the freezer. I have a general idea of what's where in here, and I've tried to keep the same kind of meat on the same shelf. Unsuccessfully, apparently.

I find a number of containers of mystery items, some creamy and white, some bumpy and red, and I let them defrost. We're not going to eat them, but I'm curious as to what I thought was important enough to save. (The contents turned out to be ancient Bolognese sauce, bacon grease, and maple cream-cheese frosting for cinnamon rolls.)

Fletch bought a number of plastic bins to better organize his already impeccable workspace in the basement, but I make the executive decision to commandeer them. They're the perfect size for packages of meat, and they make the process of categorizing everything far simpler. Then I label everything in the fridge, so going forward I can stick with this system.

I still have time to spare, so I start to clean off the big kitchen table. The bananas are on the verge of breaking bad, so I go to toss them in the freezer, because that's what I do. Then I notice that one of the bananas has busted open and there's what I believe might be a couple of tiny maggots at the bottom of the fruit bowl. Whatever they are, they're . . . writhing.

My stomach heaves as I dump every last piece of fruit in the trash and fill the sink with boiling water to scald the bejesus out of the bowl before running it through the dishwasher.

And just like that, I step into the laundry room and toss my entire collection of frozen bananas. Although I can't promise that I'm done being a Professional Banana Grabber forever, I'm definitely through for now.

I give Fletch a tour of the new and improved kitchen before we sit down to pulled-pork sandwiches. He fakes crying with joy, but I can tell he's pleased.

The truth is, I'm ridiculously proud of myself right now, and I haven't had time to feel depressed while I work through my project list. There's something about having physical evidence of my hard work that's deep-down soul satisfying. But do I wish Maisy were here right next to Loki on the bed, eyes trained on me, watching while I get it all figured out? More than anything. There will always be a pit bull–shaped portion of my heart reserved for her. But the more I accomplish, the more I'm able get out of my own head and move forward. Progress, definitely. And despite all evidence to the contrary, Hambone is helping.

Fletch settles in with a Diet Coke as I finish up the pork. What had been a tough pork shoulder eight hours ago is now so tender that it's falling apart before I can even break it up with a couple of forks.

"On a scale from one to ten, how impressed are you right now?" I ask, dishing up his dinner on one of the plates he loves.

"Ten, absolutely. But you realize that this entire project has been you coming around to my way of thinking," he replies.

I glance up from the Crock-Pot. "How so?"

"Well, you're finally using the right equipment and becoming organized. I've been begging you to do this for years, but you've perpetually thwarted my efforts. Really, you can thank me." He considers this statement for a moment and runs his hand over his chin. "And you can thank my beard."

But I don't offer a snappy retort; nor do I stab him in the neck with my fork, because I'm aware of one of Martha's most relevant portions of the Tao: Prison sucks and you'd miss your pets. Avoid at all costs.

Besides, I'll need my fork for pie.

S·E·V·E·N·T·E·E·N

EVERY DAY IS HALLOWEEN

I hate Halloween.

Despise it.

Loathe it.

Detest it.

I actively screen Halloween's calls. I block Halloween on my privacy settings. I slash Halloween's tires and secretly subscribe it to NAMBLA newsletters. Given the opportunity, I'd go all Travis in *Old Yeller* on Halloween's ass.

Mind you, I'm not trying to justify my disdain of Halloween; rather, I'm simply sharing a somewhat nonsensical feeling. For the record, Halloween is not my only vaguely irrational, deep-seated prejudice. I also harbor an intense dislike of all things Kardashian and . . . Abraham Lincoln.

Yes, you read that right.

Listen, I *understand* Lincoln was a great man. I *appreciate* how he pulled himself up from humble beginnings to be the sixteenth president.

I *know* he issued the Emancipation Proclamation. I'm *well aware* that he was all about honesty and integrity and stalwart leadership during our country's darkest time. (Also? Vampire hunting.)

There's no rational basis for my dislike, yet every time I spot his big ol' mole on the penny or see a stovepipe hat, I feel twitchy. And that four-score-and-seven-years-ago business? Would it have killed him to say eighty-seven? Was he being paid by the word for that address?

Point? I realize it's way better to be thought a fool than to speak and remove all doubt, yet here we are. I don't claim that my own personal narrow-mindedness is anything less than ridiculous, especially since Halloween used to be the best day of my year.

As a child, I much preferred Halloween to the more obviously kid-centric Christmas. I mean, sure, I could appreciate that Christmas meant the celebration of the birth of the savior and his promise of life everlasting (and also receiving gifts). But for me, *nothing* could be more miraculous than a pillowcase stuffed to the brim with free candy. Anyone who grew up in a household where carob passed for chocolate and apple pies were actually filled with zucchini will feel me here.

(Seriously, what was up with the zucchini? Clearly I'm a fan, but what was so unhealthy about a freaking *apple* that it required a vegetable surrogate?)

Every year as Halloween would approach, I'd make meticulous plans for my costume, agonizing over each nuance. No detail was too minute for my scrutiny. "I shan't just don my brother's Little League uniform to portray some generic baseball player—I'll paint on a handle-bar mustache, grab an Oakland A's hat, and go as Rollie Fingers!" Or, "Look at you garden-variety witches in your gym shoes; everyone knows the real Wicked Witch of the West requires fancy Mary Janes and properly striped socks!" Or what about, "All you weak-sauce, drugstore-costume-wearing fake Wonder Women can suck my Golden Lasso." I was nothing if not boldly authentic.

My best effort ever in terms of costume was when I hit the mean streets of Teaneck, New Jersey—the wealthy burb on the other side of the street from my middle-class home in Bergenfield—in full Ace Frehley regalia. To this day, I fixate on how much better my moon boots would have looked had I simply been allowed to spray-paint them silver, rather than being forced to wrap them in aluminum foil.

I was one goddamned can of Krylon away from officer candidacy in the KISS Army, *Mom.*

Sigh.

As I grew up, Halloween transitioned from a sugar-fueled, door-to-door beg-a-thon to youth-group basement costume parties, then to bobbing for apples in friends' garages, eventually followed by haunted-house outings. The pinnacle of high school Halloween festivities was the year my nerdy Masque and Gavel drama club compatriots and I piled into Carol's car for a pizza party at our coach's house, with an eye toward later telling ghost stories in a graveyard.

We were totally sober, by the way.

(Did I mention the nerdy part, or was that truth already self-evident when I said "drama club"?)

Carol had just inherited her grandparents' Cadillac, a vehicle slightly smaller than your average aircraft carrier, and almost as easy to maneuver. But because of the car's color—a startlingly vivid turquoise, despite being twenty years old, with bonus white hardtop—I felt my costume should reflect my ride.

So . . . I dressed up as a prostitute.

Much as I used to sweat the details on my costumes, I didn't have an inkling of what a *real* working girl might wear in 1984. And how would I know? Cable television wouldn't arrive in my neighborhood/sheltered little universe for ten more years, and the Internet was but a twinkle in Al Gore's eye.

My only frame of reference for Ho Couture was Jamie Lee Curtis's character in *Trading Places*, and she spent the bulk of that movie running around in a Fair Isle sweater. (And, BTW, never *actually* having sex with men for money.) So I truly believed that my white, ruffled, high-necked, puffy-sleeved poet blouse, knee-skimming miniskirt, and opaque tights were *exactly* how a hooker would dress.

Regardless, I felt superhot in my outfit, and I was pretty sure that before the night was over, one of the cute drama club guys would want to make out with me against a mausoleum.

As the singular nod to any sort of authenticity, I'd warned the other dorks not to mess with me, because my pimp would be arriving shortly. About an hour into the evening, our buddy Trey showed up in full Huggy Bear regalia, thanks to a visit to our community theater's costume cache. He sported a fedora with a two-foot-long feather protruding from the brim, and a silky shirt unbuttoned to his waist, over which he layered a dozen gold chains. His platform shoes added four inches to his height and were completely ensconced by the depth and breadth of his phenomenally funky bell-bottoms. Trey's commitment to working his look was so awesome it *almost* made up for my not being allowed to paint my boots years before.

Almost.

When we reached the ghost-story portion of the evening, we sat in the damp night air, trying hard not to disturb the frigid tombstones. Certainly *some* of us were grateful for having the foresight to wear thick tights. My rationale was that women working street corners would be loath for their legs to get chilly. (At no point did it occur to me that if pros were all about rational thought, they likely wouldn't be doing blowies for a sawbuck. Seriously, set up a phone sex line and charge five bucks a minute like the girls in the movie *For a Good Time, Call. . . .* That's a much better business plan.)

Anyway, our geek squad clung to one another as we spun our terrifying yarns, our breath forming misty puffs in the darkness. And we reveled in our abilities as thespians when lines like, "The calls are coming from inside the house!" and, "He found a hook latched to his door handle!" caused the boys in our group to shriek even louder than the girls.

I didn't realize that all the drama club guys were gay until I had Facebook years later, but that's neither here nor there. Although this discovery does neatly explain why no one wanted to make out with me against a mausoleum.

Once the elements of liquor and straight men were added to the mix, Halloween exponentially improved. Playing the "Monster Mash" at a junior high bash was always fun back in the day. But hearing the same song while swilling grape trash-can punch with my sorority sisters, all done up in matching cat costumes?

Incomparable.

Even the silliest bits of Halloween, like carving pumpkins, were fun when executed with my best college buds.

So I can honestly say I *loved* Halloween.

Until I didn't.

Maybe it was because the party invitations stopped rolling in after graduation, when no one wanted to throw down in a Princess Leia outfit on a Tuesday night. Possibly I lost my passion for the day because I was so broke as a young professional that I couldn't afford to fill anyone's pillowcases with something fun-size.

Most likely what soured me was seeing grown-ass adults wearing costumes to their day jobs. I had a lot of cognitive dissonance when I'd receive my day's assignments from someone dressed like Dorothy from *The Wizard of Oz*. Does your little dog want me to complete a spreadsheet, too? I didn't enjoy sitting around the conference room while Count Dracula and Mr. Clean droned on about go-to-market strategy; nor was I a fan of having to elect health care benefits with Tony the Tiger in HR. And the day I went to deposit my paycheck with the teller dressed in a gorilla suit? Suffice it to say I did not go ape for the bank's new mon(k)ey market accounts.

To date, I've successfully avoided Halloween for more than a decade. Back when Fletch and I were too destitute to go out for dinner during peak trick-or-treat hours, we'd cover the windows with garbage bags, which made our place look vacant and unintentionally spooky. We'd turn out all the lights and sit in the dark watching TV while wearing headphones. When we moved to the place with a big security fence, we padlocked the gate and headed out for Thai. And I have to be honest—when it came time to buy our first home, we picked the one at the end of a long, wooded drive on a sparsely populated street, partially in hopes that roving bands of Gypsies and Elmos would pass us by.

And for the past two years, they have . . . largely because with all the lights off, you can't even tell there's a house here. The first year we went to a movie, but last year we stayed home and watched television (no headphones!) upstairs. I didn't have candy, but I figured if anyone braved the long, dark walk, then they'd be rewarded with a chocolate–peanut butter PowerBar.

Hey, those things are two bucks apiece—so, *you're welcome*, Yoda.

But this year, everything changes.

Martha goes all out for Halloween; ergo, so will I.

Or I'll go all John Wilkes Booth on myself while trying.

Which is an option I've not yet ruled out.

To get into the Halloween spirit, I first need to make this place look festive. I have to set the stage for trick-or-treaters so there's no confusion that we're open for business on the big day. Yet one of the (myriad) things I despise about Halloween is tacky yard decor. I don't want to fill my lawn with fake tombstones, and I'm not about to make the landscapers weed around them. Frankly, after dulling their mower blades with hidden plastic Easter eggs and fallen piñata candies all summer, they're not my number one fans.

Anyway, I have a strong aversion to decor that is gross, so I eschew decorating with fake blood. Ditto for guts or eyeballs. Don't even start me on how much I abhor the super-realistic scary stuff; there's a house in town with a mannequin hanging from a noose, and every time I pass it on my way to the post office, I lose a year of my life. And anything with a skeleton on it makes me feel fat.

But I don't hate pumpkins.

That's where I'll start.

When I was a kid in New Jersey, my family once trooped out to the boonies to visit a pumpkin farm. I loved everything about this day—the pastoral setting, the corn maze, the pick-your-own pumpkin-patch part, the bags of misshapen gourds—but what really won me over were the cinnamon doughnuts and hot apple cider served in the snack booth. This last bit made an indelible impression. Fletch and I have been together for eighteen years now, and like clockwork, the minute October hits, I stock up on cider and doughnuts. But somehow, it's never quite the same. I keep saying that one day I'll find a pumpkin farm with proper cider and doughnuts, but I've never quite gotten there.

For decorating inspiration, I find a video clip where Martha features the Shelton family pumpkin farm in Connecticut. That's when I decide that instead of hitting Home Depot, I'm going to pick my own pumpkins this year! Yes! This can happen! A quick Google later I find an authentic pumpkin patch less than ten miles away. Woo-hoo!

(While I have Google open, I also do an image search on "prostitutes.")

(Yeah . . . about the tights and poet blouse? Big mistake. Big. Huge.)

The patch is really close to where we bought our trees this summer, so I won't even need to use GPS to get there. This is so exciting! I'm all anticipatory over grabbing a little red wagon and then selecting pumpkins at my leisure. I want a couple of really big ones for the door, and then a bunch for carving.

I've been consulting *Halloween: The Best of Martha Stewart Living* for design ideas, and I've already downloaded a couple of carving templates from her Web site. I love the wood-grain faux-bois pattern, and I'm torn between whether I want my theme to be witches or black cats. Maybe I'll just go elegant and do the one with the ginkgo leaves.

The closer I get to the patch, the more wound up I am. I haven't had proper outdoor hot cider and fresh doughnuts in thirty-five years, and I just know the experience will have been worth the wait. My only regret is that Fletch isn't with me, but he's busy finishing a painting project.

As I approach the entrance, I find myself stuck in a line of traffic. Huh. I wonder what happened here? Maybe there's an accident up ahead? I hope this delay doesn't have to do with difficulties with the deep fryer.

Five minutes later, I discover the source of the stoppage—it's not an accident. Rather, the holdup stems from the dozens of SUVs waiting to enter Pumpkinfest.

Shit.

What I see before me isn't a twee, rustic farm in the middle of the New Jersey wilds . . . Instead, it's a gourd-themed festival, with petting zoos and performance stages and honest-to-God carnies manning the ring-toss booths. There are no hayrides, because why would you want to tool along on the back of a horse-drawn wagon when you can zoom around on a mini roller coaster? Or defy gravity in a moon bounce? Or have your photo taken with a baby kangaroo?

I pull in and begin to maneuver across the massive expanse of the field currently being used as a parking lot. The nearest spot I can find is literally three-tenths of a mile away from the entrance. I quickly calculate exactly how far I'm willing to carry a pumpkin from point A to my car, and realize that if I don't get within spitting distance, Pumpkinfest is not going to happen, particularly since my foot isn't completely healed from this summer's plantar fasciitis. I mean, I walk slowly, but I never walk backward.

Twenty-five minutes of fruitless searching for a closer spot later, I'm so frustrated that I want to weep, yet I can hear Martha's voice in my head saying, "There's no crying in Halloween."

(Unless no cute nerds want to do the Monster Mash with you in a graveyard.)

I ask myself what Martha would do in this situation, and then I remember that she has an endorsement deal with Home Depot. So I'd be perfectly justified in leaving the patch to buy my pumpkins there.

That's when I realize I've inadvertently uncovered another piece of Martha's Tao: Practice the homemaker's version of Occam's razor, which is the law of parsimony. The most succinct path is almost always the correct path.

Consider this—Martha's a huge proponent of simplicity. Her undertakings are successful because she never overcomplicates them. She concentrates on doing the right activity at the right time. That doesn't mean her projects can't be complex and multistepped; rather, it's that she doesn't fight the natural flow of the universe. She's not one to plow blithely on when environmental factors are against her. For example, if she wants to do a show segment on canning, she's not about to undertake this in March, when the only tomatoes available are from South America or her own personal greenhouse. She'll wait until they're ripe everywhere for everyone. So although the canning process may be complex, she'll undertake it only once nature properly sets the scene. That makes so much sense.

I take a big step back and assess my current situation. My goal for the day is to have some pumpkins to carve tonight. They don't need to be local, organic, or self-picked; they just need to be orange and round. The point of today was to *buy* pumpkins, and not necessarily to *pick* them. And the most succinct way to *buy* them is to visit Home Depot. I can park out front, wheel all my purchases to my car in a sturdy cart, and I'll be in and out in ten minutes. Thus I'll have preserved my energy, which I can then channel into carving.

My sense of relief in not having to deal with the crowd and the walk is palpable as I steer out of the parking lot. Still, as I make my way to the Depot's impressive and affordable selection, I pledge to find a more remote pumpkin patch, because I'll be damned if I miss out on doughnuts one more year.

"Let's do this!" I exclaim.

Fletch and I are sitting at the newspaper-covered kitchen table, each of us with a stack of stencils and a variety of carving tools at our sides. We figure we'll practice on a couple of smaller pumpkins so that we'll be ready to tackle the big guys. I explain my vision of a sea of glowing pumpkins cascading across the front porch and down the step, flowing all the way to the end of the bluestone walkway. The pumpkins are beautifully carved, and their warm golden glow lights up the whole front of the house. In my head, the scene is downright majestic, and I feel like Martha would be proud!

"I can't tell you the last time I carved a pumpkin," Fletch says.

"Me neither. But how fun is this going to be?"

He exhales rather loudly through his nose. "That remains to be seen."

I look over to where he's currently frowning at the big orange orb in front of him. "Hey, you don't trust me here, do you?"

He eyes me warily. "Do you blame me?"

As I've approached various projects on this endeavor, he claims I keep Tom Sawyering him. He'll see me doing something badly (his opinion, not mine), and when he tries to offer suggestions, I'm defensive. More than once I've retorted, "Oh, yeah? Well, I'd like to see *you* do it better!"

Which he then does.

Actually, Fletch couldn't join me on my expedition today because he was busy finishing one of my botched (again, his word, not mine) home-improvement projects. He said he couldn't stand watching me slop paint all over the gun cabinet I'd decided to convert to a china hutch, so he sanded everything back down to bare wood and started from scratch. Then he proceeded to work his paintbrush like he was Michelangelo and my ex–gun cabinet the Sistine Chapel, and the project went from the course of one afternoon to two full weeks.

He was less than pleased.

I give him a big hug. "Luff you! And I love my fab new china cabinet!"

He grunts in response, then mutters something about how those were two weeks of his life he'll never get back.

I return my attention to the task at hand. I plunge my knife into the top of a pumpkin. I kind of have to shove it in, because the blade I'm using is a bit spindly, even though it's specifically made for this task. In my distant memories, I recall my knife slipping through the pumpkin's flesh as though it were warm butter, but that's definitely not the case here. I stab again—repeatedly—and I finally gain purchase.

I saw back and forth and feel like I'm trying to hack through a log with a nail file. Why is this so hard? Are these unripe or something?

"Do you remember it being so hard to slice up the pumpkin?" I ask.

He shakes his head vehemently. "No. No, no. You are not doing this to me. I am not going to be your pumpkin bitch. As it is, I can barely move my shoulder from all the damn painting. I'm not carving your pumpkins for you."

I'm taken aback. "Didn't ask you to; I'm just commenting on this being a little tougher than I remember."

"Uh-huh."

I keep plugging along on the top of my pumpkin. "But the skin is thicker than I recall. That's all I'm saying."

"Mmm."

The force I'm exerting on the blade causes it to bow and the whole damn thing almost snaps, at which point it would have slashed the tender skin between my thumb and forefinger. "Shit! I almost stabbed myself!"

Fletch's lips tighten as he works. His deft but delicate swipes cut a smooth swath through his own pumpkin and he's quickly able to remove the top. He is the Pumpkin Whisperer.

"Hey, Fletch, that was so easy for you! Will you demonstrate how you did it?"

With a fake Southern accent, Fletch drawls, "'Say, Tom, let *me* whitewash a little.'"

"I was just—"

"Going to offer to trade me your apple core for the opportunity to carve your pumpkin? No."

I grumble something about liking to see him do it better, but he doesn't rise to my bait.

Oh, crap. He's right. I actually *do* Tom Sawyer him. My bad.

Eventually I'm able to remove my own lid, and I begin the process of scooping out the pumpkin guts. In retrospect, I should have allowed the pumpkins to come up to room temperature first, because not only is this process slimy and disgusting—it's also freezing. Every time I grab a handful of innards, half of the stringy goo gushes out and squirts all over the newspapers, and the other half ends up on my shirt. When I use a spoon to scrape down the sides, my wrist quickly grows sore, and picking up stray seeds is tantamount to trying to catch a greased pig.

I scrape and squirt, slosh and spill. This is gross.

There's not one satisfying aspect to this whole process.

And now I stink of gourd bowels.

"This is nauseating," I comment.

"It sure is," he replies placidly. That's when I notice that he had the presence of mind to put on rubber gloves before disemboweling his pumpkin.

"I'm not enjoying this." I sulk. This is not his fault, of course. (But I don't tell him that.)

"Listen." He waxes philosophical while smoothing out the sides of his perfectly rounded pumpkin-lid hole. "There's a reason we stopped carving pumpkins years ago. Bet this is a lot like dyeing Easter eggs. In your head you spend all year fantasizing about how fun pumpkin carving is going to be, but in reality, it's just foul-smelling and labor-intensive, and ultimately all your hard work will be eaten by rodents."

I reply, "You may be onto something."

He wipes a stray bit of pumpkin gut from his cheek with the back of his hand. "Martha's created an industry out of home-based initiatives, but her success came because people enjoy doing the activities she's taught them. It doesn't matter if you can perfectly sculpt your pumpkin if you actively despise every minute of it. So I say, if you don't enjoy the process, then stop. That idea applies to anything in life, not just gourds."

I glower at my stupid, cold, slimy pumpkin while he talks. I'm so aggravated with this project that I'm not going to order my usual pumpkin latte next time I'm at Starbucks. No, wait, I will order a VENTI latte, because that means more pumpkin had to die in order for me to drink it. Ha! Yes. That's exactly what I'll do.

My workspace is glopped with pumpkin innards, and small shards have embedded themselves in the rug underneath. The newspaper covering is moist and sticky and starting to fuse with the tabletop. Pumpkin ooze is winnowing its way into the wood grain. I glance at my hands and they're stained orange and with layers of pumpkin flesh layered under my nails.

This?

Right here?

Is why I hate Halloween.

While he speaks, Fletch removes his gloves and wipes his hands on a paper towel. "Jen, I'm sure there are plenty of other festive ways to decorate with pumpkins that don't require us to perform surgery on them. There's more than one way to skin a cat, and by cat I mean pumpkin. Can't you just dip them in glitter and call it a day?"

I need a minute to process the genius of what he said.

Without even realizing it, Fletch has just elucidated another facet in the Tao of Martha, which dovetails so neatly into what I discovered about opting for simplicity earlier today: There's more than one path on the road to beautiful.

Glitter pumpkins it is.

I completely reimagine my Halloween display using whole pumpkins as the focal point, instead of jack-o'-lanterns. Apparently Martha regularly glitters the shit out of pumpkins and gourds. This is a brilliant alternative to the hassle and filth of carving, and I'm delighted by this turn of events. And Fletch was so pleased at not being stuck dissecting great gourds last night that he agrees to get his doughnut on with me at a pumpkin patch about an hour away.

Today's the most perfect specimen of fall day imaginable. The skies are impossibly blue and cloudless. The sun's strong enough that we're able to shed our jackets, but it's not so hot that we complain of an Indian summer. We're both in excellent moods and we laugh all the way to South Barrington . . . where we discover that the entire population of greater Chicagoland has had the exact same idea today.

WTF?

If the Pumpkinfest by our house was like a carnival, then what's happening here is more on the scale of Disney World. Apparently this veritable Pumpkinpalooza is in the middle of nowhere because it's so damn monolithic. Traffic to get onto the road leading to the festival is backed up for half an hour, and the parking lot is larger than that of Kings Island. If I thought having to lug a pumpkin three-tenths of a mile was bad, that pales in comparison to the literal mile we'd have to hoof to the entrance.

Suddenly, contending with a few dozen SUVs doesn't seem so bad.

Fletch is exactly as fond of crowds as I am. We both grimace at the flannel-wearing, stroller-pushing, pumpkin-carrying mass of humanity standing between us and the hot cider.

"I've never seen anything like this," Fletch says.

Even though I've completed physical therapy on my foot, it's still painful and I'm very cautious about walking long distances. "I'm not sure I can make it all the way to the entrance. Would you want to drop me off and meet me after you park?"

"I am not your pumpkin valet."

"Damn."

He surveys the line of traffic again. "So . . . how important are these doughnuts to you?" he asks.

Not enough to force the natural flow of things.

I tell him, "Not enough to risk walking with a limp for the next month."

"Would you have a fit if we skipped it?"

"Honestly?" I study the ocean of cars and tentatively flex my foot. Ouch. "No."

It takes us another twenty minutes until we're able to turn the car around and head back up north. Our ride home is less festive, since we know that there's no prospect of cider or doughnuts waiting for us at the end.

However . . . all is not lost!

As it turns out, the universe really is Team Doughnut. Or possibly Team Simplicity.

Fletch takes a different route home, and on our way we pass the first Pumpkinfest. Suddenly, the crowd and the parking situation seem very manageable, and I'm able to get to the entry without once hobbling.

Fletch insists we ingest some protein before we complete our mission, so we feast on brats and burgers and roasted corn. Neither one of us can resist the siren song of a lemon shake-up, so we wash our meal down with a couple of small bucketsful.

After wandering around the event—and briefly debating if I want to have my photo taken with a baby kangaroo—we order two hot ciders and half a dozen doughnuts directly out of the fryer. We're content to work on our drinks before the doughnuts are cool enough to touch.

As we perch on a bench across from the Tilt-A-Whirl, Fletch takes the first taste.

"What do you think?" I ask.

He cocks his head to inspect his doughnut before taking another cautious bite. He chews thoughtfully, and answers me only once he swallows, and that's when a huge grin spreads across his face. "I . . . finally understand why you've been obsessing about these for thirty-five years."

I take my own bite, and the sugary spice is all that I remember and more. The warm cake is delicate and ever so slightly redolent of apples. The crunch of the coating is the perfect contrast to the soft, doughy middle, and the whole experience is enhanced times a million with a sip of the cider.

We stay on that damn bench until we inhale every single one of those doughnuts and the last dregs of our cider. That's when Fletch turns to me and says, "Do you want to throw up now?"

"Little bit," I concur.

Of course, the plan was to purchase more pumpkins for glittering

and a few gourds, but we quickly come to realize that the event isn't crowded because everyone is inside in line waiting to pay for their purchases.

Martha's Tao dictates it's time to leave.

Also, Fletch says our indulgence has triggered his heretofore nonexistent diabetes, so we head home. Fletch collapses on the couch in sugar shock, but I still have supplies to buy for my outdoor display. I kiss him good-bye and make my way back to Home Depot.

When I was here yesterday, I bought a bunch of mums along with the pumpkins. In previous years, I'd set a pot or two out on the porch and call it done. But yesterday it occurred to me that by arranging mums around the dried grasses in all my planters, I've discovered *an entirely new planting season.*

This is huge for me.

I live for the spring, when I can finally chase away the dull grays of winter by filling my planters with pansies and hardy ivy. Sometimes the only thing keeping me from going all *The Shining* during the long, dark Chicago winter is imagining finally working in the garden again. Then summer's even better when I'm not limited to designing with the most frost-resistant varietals.

But having the opportunity to redo my planters again *in the fall?*

I feel like I'm through the looking glass here.

After I planted my containers yesterday, I had a couple of extra mums. So I plan to take the stupid hollowed-out pumpkins from last night and, following Martha's lead, use them as cachepots. I'll toss in a couple of ornamental cabbages, prop them up on hay bales, and then scatter the whole display with a variety of gourds, and boom! #WINNING!

I'd hoped to circle the porch columns with big stalks of corn, but once I grab a couple of bundles, I realize the folly of this idea. I thought cornstalks would be light and airy, but they are not only ridiculously heavy, but also terribly cumbersome. After hamstringing a couple of unsuspecting Home Depot shoppers with my bunch (not entirely my fault; they were busy texting), I put the bundles back. Even though I parked close, there's still too much potential for this project to go all Three Stooges.

I pay for my pumpkins and gourds and I'm loading everything into the car when I feel the first twinge in my abdomen. In retrospect, I probably should have stopped after the first ear of corn. Or doughnut. Also? The whiskey sours I made to appease Fletch last night aren't exactly helping either. Guess I forgot to read the memo on moderation.

Michaels is just around the corner from Home Depot, so I'm sure I can get in and out and home before any unpleasantness.

Of course, that's what I think every time I go to Michaels.

To preface what comes next, I readily admit that I'm on the wrong side of forty and I've never met a carb I didn't like. I desperately need a cut and a color, and there are only so many ravages of time I can hold back with injectable cosmeceuticals. Also? I dress like a page from an L.L.Bean catalog, circa 1983. The sexiest shoe I own is a tasseled loafer. I'm aware that I do not inspire anyone to say, "I'd like a piece of *that*," when I pass, unless they're referring to the cake I'm carrying. Yet every time I step into a craft store with its subgenre of cat-sweatshirted, bowl-cut, non-hipster-yet-still-gigantic-plastic-glasses-framed patrons, I feel like Gisele-freaking-Bündchen.

I park and enter the store. My stomach, or possibly an intestine or two, registers its displeasure. I feel something cramp low in my belly. Okay, I've got to make this quick.

I'm committed to using Martha's specific brand of glitter (girlfriend don't put her name behind no dogs), but her stuff isn't located with the rest of the tubes of shimmer. Why? Why wouldn't all the glitter be in one place? That's nonsensical. (Not as nonsensical as disliking Abe Lincoln's face, but still.) As a matter of fact, very little about this store makes logical sense. Similar items are spread across as many as three different aisles.

While I prowl the store in search of sparkles, a thin sheen of sweat begins to bead on my upper lip. That's when I notice that the channel's been changed on the in-store radio station. I'd been listening to the dulcet tones of Taylor Swift a moment ago (love her; shut up), but now they're playing an absolutely horrific doo-wop station.

Ugh.

Mind you, I'm neutral on most types of music. My issues arise not because of genre, but because of personal-space invasion. For example, I actually kind of love old-school rap like Eazy-E, unless you're idling in front of my house with "Gimme That Nut" thumping so hard my walls vibrate. Then? Not so much. So I don't mind most music, save for Norwegian death metal . . . and anything doo-wop. There's something about greasers and four-part harmony that makes me want to slap babies.

Doo-wop is audible waterboarding for me.

Play me one verse of "Duke of Earl" and I'll happily provide the Taliban with the code for the nuclear football.

I pick up the pace on my Hunt for Red (Glitter) October while the singer on the sound system muses on who may have put the ram in the rama-lama-ding-dong. What could this possibly even mean? Was some A and R guy all, "Yes, I love this track, as long as you also sing about putting the bom in the bom-bo-bomp-bom-bomp, too." How was this song ever a hit? I thought no one in America started doing drugs until the late 1960s.

The torturous music has definitely lit a fire under me to finish my errand posthaste. While I unsuccessfully navigate around be-sweatshirted cat ladies, my digestive tract begins to protest in earnest. You! Beatles-bangs! Move!

I'm desperate to shout at the slow-moving crafters about finding a damn sense of urgency already, but truly, there's nothing inherently urgent about the home candle-making process. Plus, these women aren't doing anything wrong by taking time to browse, unless not getting out of my way is considered a crime. (Someday, though, amirite?)

I finally find the glitter display and I double over with another cramp. While I'm bent down, I begin to toss in every vaguely harvest-related color I can find, along with glue and brushes, because basic principles of gastroenterology dictate that I need to get out of here sooner rather than later.

I clutch my stomach with one hand and my shopping basket with the other and I race to the checkout counter.

Bad things are happening down there.

Very bad things.

(Is this my karmic payback for disliking Abe while living in the Land of Lincoln?)

As I approach the cash register, a cache of cat ladies swoops in right in front of me. Normally I'd not let this kind of aggression stand, but I feel like my body is a live grenade right now and someone's already pulled the pin. One false move (or one bit of officious voice raising) and I'm going to have to dispose of these pants.

My whole lower half twists and I feel like I'm having a contraction, about to deliver the Worst. Baby. Ever.

To distract myself, I flip open my iPad. Tracey's sent a group e-mail to all the girls to see how their weekend is going. She tells us she's snuggled up with Maxie watching football, while Stacey and Bill are having a wonderful time at their family retreat. Gina's still recovering from a fancy event the night before. I reply, "In line at Michaels buying sparkles. Kill me now."

I'm almost to the front when a woman with glasses the size of salad plates begins to quibble about a coupon for yarn. No! Nooooo! Stop! Please! I'm not sure how much longer I can clench. It's only fifty cents! I beg of you, let me cover the difference!

About. To. Blow. Five, four, three, two . . .

That's when I think to myself, "This is how pride comes to an end. This is how dignity dies. My hubris is about to shart itself at the craft store to the tune of 'Yakety Yak' while I am buying glitter paint."

Fortunately, that's when the Silhouettes' "Get a Job" begins to play and my entire body seizes up from all the hate. The only force more powerful than what's about to befoul the checkout line is my passionate abhorrence for the lyric "Yip yip yip yip yip yip yip yip / Mum mum mum mum mum mum / Get a job," so I manage to hold everything together. I throw a wad of bills at the cashier and then sprint like Jackie Joyner-Kersee to the car. I drive the four miles home like I'm piloting the Batmobile, while praying hard to the Patron Saint of Green Lights.

Exiting the car without incident is touch and go for a second, but by Kegeling everything from the bra down, I'm able to narrowly avoid ignominy. Thus, I'm able to keep my favorite pants.

I can offer no Tao of Martha principle related to practicing moderation when it comes to fresh doughnuts and hot cider.

Because that's plain common sense.

By the time I sit down with all my crafting materials, my attitude has devolved. Glittering is the path of least resistance, yet I'm grumpy and my stomach still hurts.

My plan is to cover the six smallish pie pumpkins with three colors of glitter as quickly as possible. In the *Martha Stewart Handmade Holiday Crafts* book, she uses gold, bronze, and champagne-colored sparkles. Her display is perfect on the page, but come on, when isn't it? I imagine my reality will pale in comparison, but I'm committed to at least trying.

Now I'm supposed to brush glue on one side of the orb, and then let it dry for an hour before attempting the other side. So I diligently get out my glue and start working. I'm not thrilled with wasting my night on this, but it's far less labor-intensive than carving, so here I go.

On the pumpkin-sparkling segment of Martha's show, she holds her pumpkin by the stem at the exact moment she reads the cue card and tells the audience that's the wrong way to hold it when applying glue. She laughs and shrugs and it's all adorably self-aware. But my takeaway is, if she can grasp the stem without incident, then so will I.

Works like a charm.

Then I grab the champagne-colored offering and begin to sprinkle. A little bit goes a long way and coats the glue completely. I sit back to cast a critical eye on the results.

Um, is it just me . . . or is this thing *freaking gorgeous*?

Wondering if this result may be a fluke, I continue to paint the first half of all the pumpkins, arranging them on the drying surface shimmery side out.

I stand back and appraise again.

This is not a fluke; these are incredible!

What were a bunch of boring old pie pumpkins ten minutes ago have been transformed Cinderella-style into something dazzling and elegant. How can a few shiny bits of powder so change the look of something? I've never in my life been interested in glitter before, but suddenly all the sparkly things in the universe make sense, like drag queens and participating in *Toddlers and Tiaras*.

I planned to address these six items and be done, but the plan has changed. As I transform each gourd, I feel borderline euphoric. I must have Sparkle Stockholm Syndrome, because now I have the overwhelming desire to glitter-spackle *everything in my kitchen*.

I collect the apple-size pumpkins I've scattered on shelves throughout the first floor and I coat them all in glue before dousing them in white glitter. The effect is that of sugared fruit, and I love it so much I want to hug something.

I grab Hambone, who's sitting next to me begging for gourds. (FYI? Three weeks after the fact, she'll still be shimmery.)

I'm awed by how such a tiny amount of effort and a few cents' worth of materials have so altered the gourds' appearance for the better. So now I'm on a mission.

Last week, I'd topped my mantels with decorative gourds, but now I round them all up for their shine coat. In addition to the sparkle powder, I also bought a clear glitter paint that leaves everything with a glossy sheen of iridescence. I line up my dozens of minigourds and get busy.

Three hours later, my work is done.

Yet I'm finished only because I ran out of items to which to add sparkle. (Fletch gave me implicit instructions not to glitter any of his

stuff. I know; I asked.) The aftermath of the project has left the whole kitchen shimmering like fresh snow on a bright winter morning. Libby and Hambone are twinkling like a Cullen in the sunlight. The floor between the table and counter gleams like the Yellow Brick Road. Personally, I'm shinier than Ke$ha right now, and I have so much glitter in my lungs that my breath is phosphorescent.

But I don't care, because I positively adore the end product.

Okay, Halloween.

Game on.

TRICK OR TREAT!

At the last minute, I decide that the mantels full of gourds and hay bale–and–cachepot-strewn steps aren't quite festive enough.

If I'm channeling Martha—and I believe that the glitter opened that gateway—then I'm committed to doing things up right for the trick-or-treaters. So I decide to decorate the front hallway, too.

I find creepy old black draping online and I spread this spooky, holey fabric across the tops of the hall bookcases. Then I adorn them with realistic crow and rat figurines and I

cover the wall on the way into the dining room with big black paper spiders. Even though they're only two-dimensional, they stop my heart every time I come down the stairs. The paper arachnids made Fletch yelp the first time he saw them, so I can verify they're totally bank.

(Yes, I'm still trying to make "bank" happen.)

I also spread some of that awful spiderweb stuff you always see on people's bushes, but it's so sticky that I quickly abandon its use. Later, when I catch Hambone not only taking a dump in the laundry room, but also tangled in a cloud of webs from the banister, I'm glad of this decision.

As for me, the time has come to face my most personal of demons . . . the purchasing and wearing of a costume. I thought that a banana suit would be a hilarious choice, à la *Arrested Development*'s Gob Bluth, but the shipper couldn't guarantee delivery until mid-November. Um, no.

Ironically, I pick an outfit inspired by my great dislike of doo-wop music. I find a complete fifties-girl ensemble that comes with everything from a chiffon scarf to a crinoline to puff out the poodle skirt. I make this choice because it's about the only thing I can find that doesn't have "sexy" in its description. Also, being plus-size severely limits my options, so it was this, sexy opera singer, or sexy pirate wench.

With the costume business under my belt, I can concentrate on the main event: the treats. Because candy was so important to me when I was young, I want to do something extraspecial for the kids who trick-or-treat at my house. Martha had wonderful plans for spooky sugar cookies and popcorn balls, but I'm not sure how homemade treats would be received, so I'm going the more traditional route of packaged candy.

The first few groups of customers will receive the most adorable custom treat bags, in their choice of witch or witch's broom. I spend two hours putting them together, and they're each filled with more than ten fun-size bars apiece.

Seriously, come on!

TEN fun-size pieces?

I'd have to go to ten houses for ten fun-size pieces as a kid! That's an entire city block! And I still remember when I'd go to the cheap people's houses and they'd give me a freaking peppermint or a single Life Saver. I put on Ace Frehley makeup for *this*? Or what about the guys who'd give out pennies, and not even a handful, just a single coppery (hateful) Lincoln? Are you kidding me? Why bother answering the door? Why not cover your windows in garbage bags, Mr. and Mrs. Whatever-the-Halloween-Equivalent-of-the-Grinch-Is? You and your crappy apple can kiss my moon boots.

Point? I kick *ass*. I'm going to own Halloween. And this makes me very happy.

My friend Joanna's a dietitian, and she tells me when she first started getting trick-or-treaters years ago, she'd pass out Halloween-themed pencils and stickers, because she figured the kids were already getting enough sugar. As soon as she married Michael, he insisted on doling out proper chocolate, rationalizing that he didn't want to spend the day after Halloween scraping jack-o'-lanterns and black cats off his car. He wasn't wrong.

Because I feel a real karmic debt for shuttering my home for the past decade, I'm going all out and giving away full-size candy bars after the badass treat bags are gone. Heck, I still remember who gave me big bars almost forty years ago, so I love the idea of being the house that kids recollect fondly when they're adults.

And . . . if full-size candy bars keep local kids from playing mailbox baseball at my house when they become teenagers?

Then all the better.

Such is my Halloween spirit that even Fletch participates. He dons his army-surplus gear and straps on his ridiculously realistic Airsoft BB guns with bonus ammo vest. He settles in at the dining room table with me to

wait for the hordes of local youths hankering for ten ccs of Twix bar, stat!

I'm ready. Let's rock this.

At four-oh-one, one minute into the official Lake Forest trick-or-treating hours, our bell rings. Showtime! Fletch answers the door while I dash to retrieve the tray full of booty. With my back turned, I hear the mailman gasp when Fletch's body armor/arsenal pretty much scares the pants off him. Judging from the mailman's reaction, I guess he doesn't usually deliver certified letters to the fully armed.

Clearly he's never carried mail in the city of Chicago.

Fletch then compliments the postman on his realistic costume and the guy doesn't even laugh a little bit.

Pfft. No candy for you, pal.

While we wait for business, I anxiously rearrange my enormous silver candy platter. Why the hell do I feel nervous? I used to get tense when I was trying to dodge the trick-or-treaters, so afraid they'd catch me unprepared.

But today?

I couldn't be more ready for them today.

The house is superfestive, the favors are bangin', and we're both in costume, with bonus positive attitudes! Fletch is particularly compliant because he's secretly proud that his ensemble scared our feckless mailman.

He had me take a bunch of pictures of him in his costume and then posted them on Facebook, adding a caption on how he was dressed as an Army Special Forces guy, and not a Navy SEAL. He wrote that you could tell he was a Green Beret because his hands were in his pockets. I said that would make no sense to ninety-nine percent of the world, particularly since he wasn't wearing a beret, but he promised me that his

enlightened followers on Facebook would find that absolutely hysterical.

Um, yeah.

I'll have to take his word on that.

(A week later, we see Stacey for my birthday and she compliments Fletch on his authenticity with the whole esoteric hands-pockets thing. He positively beams, completely unaware that she's messing with him.)

Anyway, I feel an odd little twist in my stomach, and today it's not because of doughnut overload. I don't understand why I'm edgy, because I've executed an outstanding version of a *Living* Halloween. This day has Martha's stamp of approval all over it. I really put in the effort to make everything special and elegant. Given that my last go-round at a Martha-type event on the Fourth of July turned into a redneck, white-trash, hee-haw hoedown, I raised the bar here exponentially. As I take in my surroundings, I'm confident in my creation and I wouldn't change a thing.

Yet I'm jittery all the same.

My commitment to Halloween planning has given me a real sense of satisfaction and the kind of peace of mind I've been hoping to gain ever since I started this project in January. Once I came to terms with my initial misgivings and threw myself into the process, I've had the best time. In fact, when I was glittering my gourds last Saturday, I couldn't stop saying, "This is so fun! I can't believe how much I love this!"

When I was decorating yesterday, I realized I was singing to myself. Badly, of course, but that's not important. Breaking into song is my good-mood barometer, and I haven't done it since we lost Maisy. This is so significant. A month ago, I honestly worried I'd never feel joy again. I couldn't get through a day without crying. But here I am, moving on, letting happiness in without feeling guilty for it.

Turns out I've not only embraced the Tao of Martha finally, but also the Tao of Maisy. This realization causes my anxiety to magically melt away, and I address my tray with renewed vigor.

I merchandise the big bars in attractive rows and I group the treat bags together. I decide I'm going to let the kids decide if they want a full-sizer or, if they'd like to pick what's behind curtain number two. (Personally, I'd go for the unknown. Could be a bag of candy; could be gold bullion!)

As I survey the bounty, I hope I made the right choices. From what I understand, children need to be hermetically sealed in a bubble until the age of eighteen, so I'm concerned certain chocolate bars may be an issue. Joanna's sister-in-law recently told me that in her kid's pre-K class, there were four peanut allergies, one strawberry allergy, two gluten-frees due to issues with wheat, one corn allergy, and one lactose-intolerant child. This is out of fourteen total students! What do parents bring in for birthday treats? Pencils and stickers?

"Is it okay that some of these candy bars have nuts?" I ask Fletch.

"What do you mean? All the best chocolate bars contain nuts. Everyone knows that. See, you've got your Baby Ruths, your Snickers, your Paydays, plus Reese's cups and Mars. Also, Butterfingers count because they use ground roasted peanuts. Candy bars with nuts are at the top of the sweet-based food chain. Fact." He pauses thoughtfully and then makes a face. "Except for Almond Joy. Those are just wrong."

"Yeah," I agree, though I'm not convinced. "But what if parents give us shit for passing out bars with nuts in them?"

He shrugs. "Then I'll suggest that they stop encouraging their children to take candy from strangers."

"Is that the Tao of Fletch?"

He nods and goes back to his Facebook page on his iPad, waiting for everyone to comment on his hilarious pockets joke. Suspect he'll be waiting awhile.

Speaking of waiting . . . er, hello? It's four fifteen p.m. and we've seen no one. Nary a ghost nor Power Ranger has even walked past the house, let alone come down the drive.

Four twenty p.m.

Nothing.

Four thirty p.m.

No one.

Four thirty-five p.m.

I open the front door and yell, "Kids? I have lots of candy! Please come ring my bell!"

Fletch comments, "That didn't sound menacing or creepy *at all*."

Four forty-five p.m.

I'll just have a little glass of wine while I wait.

Four fifty p.m.

Did I turn the porch lights on? I double-check. Yep, they're on.

Five p.m.

Yo, yo, yo, where my trick-or-treaters at?

Five-oh-five p.m.

Maybe I'll have a splash more wine. Possibly two splashes.

Five fifteen p.m.

"Yeah, you can top off my glass, Fletch. It's not like I'm *busy* giving anyone *candy*."

Five thirty p.m.

More wine. New bottle. More wine.

Five thirty-five p.m.

Spill my glass, prompting Fletch to exclaim, "Please don't lick wine off the furniture."

Five forty p.m.

I tweet: "COME AND GET YOUR DAMN CANFY BEFORE I AM TOO DRUNK."

Five forty-five p.m.

It's wine o'clock somewhere. But mostly here.

Five fifty p.m.

I tweet: "I am Linus in the GD pumpkin patch right now. Come get your stupid candy, you stupid kids. AUGH, I HATE YOU."

Six p.m.

"Maybe all the neighbors have been busy with soccer practice and dinner and they're just now getting to trick-or-treating," Fletch suggests.

Six-oh-five p.m.

Then I'd better fill up before the onslaught.

Six ten p.m.

Onslaught? Onslaught? Anyone? Onslaught?

Six fifteen p.m.

How long does it take them to remove their cleats and eat some chicken fingers?

Six twenty p.m.

Yes, I will have more wine, thank you.

Six thirty p.m.

Am starting to see two Fletchers. One of them has his hands out of his pockets. Must be a Navy SEAL.

Six forty-five p.m.

"What are we doing for dinner?" Fletch asks. I respond by chucking a Milky Way at his head. He says nothing, opting instead to bring me more wine.

Seven p.m.

I open the door and shout, "I HAVE FULL-SIZE CANDY BARS, YOU LITTLE ASSHOLES! COME AND GET THEM RIGHT NOW SO YOU CAN HAVE YOUR MAGICAL MARTHA FUCK-ING MEMORIES AS AN ADULT."

Behind me, Fletch mumbles something about needing some pizza to sop up all my excess Halloween cheer.

Seven ten p.m.

I kind of forget what happens after this.

Eleven forty-three p.m.

I wake up in full poodle-skirt regalia, my cat-eye glasses tangled up in my high ponytail. I'm surrounded by snoozing dogs, an empty pizza box, and one very smug spouse.

Fletch tells me that he had to keep me from accosting the pizza guy when he rang the bell a minute before the official trick-or-treat end time of eight p.m. Fletch sent him on his way with an extra-large tip and a couple of Snickers bars. I have no recollection of this, but I suspect he's telling the truth. (Green Berets are notoriously honest.)

I'm still a little groggy as I change out of my costume and don my pajamas while I reflect on the whole Halloween experience.

I did it.

I faced my enormous fear of Halloween and, with Martha's guidance, I got through it.

In fact, I got *over* it. I don't despise Halloween anymore.

I'm not sure I love it, but I'm no longer going to go all Jehovah's Witness in the face of it.

I began traditions this year that I'll continue. Maybe I won't ever wear my costume to the bank, but I sure as hell will glitter up some gourds. I'll decorate my house. Maybe I'll even host a party for my friends' kids, because, damn it, someone needs to receive some full-size candy bars, even if they're not my neighbors.

In terms of personal contentment, I feel exponentially better about life at the end of October than I did at the beginning. Working on this project allowed me to focus on something other than missing Maisy, and proved to me that I can absolutely be happy again. I was able to strengthen bonds with Fletch. I started having fun so much so that I was able to share it with readers on social media.

By embracing the Tao of Maisy, I was able to be awesome, give awesome, and get awesome back in return. I really believe that this project is working! And all it took was a little sparkle powder and a couple of doughnuts.

Perhaps Lincoln was a wee bit right when he said, "People are just as happy as they make up their minds to be." So the Martha Tao tenet I've taken away from this experience is: Seize the opportunity to create new memories and traditions.

Hey, Halloween?

You and I are officially cool again. I'm putting you back on the buddy list. Maybe now I'll even reconsider my feelings on Abraham Lincoln. (I don't like that man. I must get to know him better.) We'll see.

But the one thing I can say for sure is that I am glittering the shit out of Christmas.

N·I·N·E·T·E·E·N

LIVING, ZOMBIE STYLE

As I've lived my year of Martha, I've been searching for an X factor, a project I could take on and make my own, pairing what I've gleaned from Martha's Tao with my own sensibilities.

A challenge without training wheels, if you will.

Achievement is a cornerstone of what makes me happy, so I've been anxious to carve out my own niche. Of course, finding a domestic venture that Martha hasn't already mastered—*and* secured the merchandising rights for—hasn't been easy. Cooking? Pfft, covered. Cleaning? If it's not included in the 744-page *Homekeeping Handbook*, then it doesn't need to be done. Crafting? She's glittered the whole DIY universe. Pets? Her dog's been to Westminster; mine tosses his salad for sport. Entertaining? Oh, honey . . . bless my own heart.

Martha's ubiquity has been a boon, up until now. I want to plant my own flag in a tiny plot of uncharted territory.

So what's left?

What could I do that she'd approve of, but hasn't already covered extensively?

As always, the answer lies in Fletch.

A lifetime obsession with zombies and George Romero's (*Fill-in-the-Blank*) *of the Dead* films have left Fletch one black helicopter shy of turning into a complete nut job.

Bless *his* heart.

It's not that he believes we're actually going to be overrun with flesh-devouring undead (or so he says). Rather, he's always talking about our society becoming zombies in an allegorical sense. For example, Fletch hypothesizes that personal electronics are turning their users brain-dead. Like, every time we'd leave the house when we lived in the city, he'd point to hipsters wandering into the street because they were too busy texting about a new PBR-serving dive to look for oncoming vehicles. At Whole Foods he'd gesture toward moms so fixated on their iPhones that they didn't see the homeless drifter chatting up their toddlers over by the almond butter.

Fletch also harbors major concerns about CDC-type outbreaks that could occur if we were hit with biological warfare or some horribly virulent strain of flu, as seen in the movie *Contagion*. (Two enthusiastic thumbs up, BTW. Any film that offs insufferable Gwyneth Paltrow in the first ten minutes is aces with me.)

Anyway, all of the above led him to start perusing army-surplus Web sites, snapping up items like military-issue sleeping bags. I argued that if the zombies were indeed coming, then I would rather they eat my brains while I slumber on my actual mattress inside my climate-conditioned home instead of a tent in the woods, but sometimes it's easier not to argue.

Fletch's stockpile grew to include disaster-ready items like a short-wave radio and batteries and lanterns, which really didn't seem like a terrible idea, given how often we used to lose power when we were un-employed and couldn't pay our bills. (Sometimes the only thing standing between me and stark raving madness was the ability to read a book by the wan glow of a 4D LED light. God bless you, Coleman corporation. God bless.) I stayed out of his way while he happily prepared for the end of days, humming along in his tinfoil cap.

So, like someone who lives with a chronic whistler or travels with the kind of person who feels compelled to read every billboard out loud, I eventually learned to tune out his Chicken Little–ing and all was well. Then we moved to the suburbs. Although everyone is decidedly much slower-moving up here (seriously, Lake Foresters, you're deciding between soy or skim, not life and death . . . Pick up the pace already!), they compensate by paying attention, which I greatly appreciate.

And Fletch's zombie war obsession went dormant.

Until he started watching *The Walking Dead*.

Yeah, AMC.

Thanks for that.

He keeps telling me that I'd enjoy the show, but judging from all the screaming, shooting, and breaking glass I hear from my office every Sunday night, I'm pretty sure that's the opposite of true.

He's also crazy in love with National Geographic's *Doomsday Preppers* series, which has grudgingly become one of my favorites, too. I generally hate the people who've been featured, and if they're who survives after an apocalypse, I'm going to dip my head in ranch dressing so the zombies will sup upon me first.

As this is practically the one show on which we agree, we've seen every episode, often more than once. Each time we view, we find more reasons to mock the participants. Not all of them, mind you. Some of them are the kind of ex–Special Forces, hard-core, badass warriors whom I'd wish to have my back in a fight. Or how about the industrious old hippie who turned his postage stamp–size backyard into a massive vertical garden capable of sustaining not only his own family, but also a portion of the community with his magnificent eight-foot butternut squashes? LOVE HIM, particularly after having my own stupid garden go sideways this summer. Granted, I harbor a few concerns that his family seems inbred, but the man can grow a fine beefsteak tomato from seed, and that's what's important. I care far more about his ability to produce the means to make a proper BLT than I do about his relatives' proclivities.

There's a particularly contemptible Texan prepper on the episode we're presently watching, and we have to keep pausing to talk shit about her.

"Her contingency plan is to *hike thirty miles* outside of the city to where her car is parked?" he says during a commercial break. "Wow, what could possibly go wrong in that scenario?"

"Yeah," I agree, "why wouldn't she leave her car, say, *twenty-seven* miles closer? Houston's not that big; there's no reason to park so far away! And when you're in the middle of roving bands of marauders and the onset of an apocalypse, wouldn't you want something more between you and them than, say, a JanSport backpack? What are you going to fight them off with, your Trapper Keeper?"

Fletch nods as he forwards past a commercial for a prepacked survival food that piques my interest. "Parading through the streets carrying all your worldly supplies seems like an invitation to be beaten and robbed. Or worse."

"Right? Also, maybe before you park thirty miles away, you should verify you can actually, you know, *walk* thirty miles."

Listen, I'm never, ever going to ridicule anyone's weight or fitness level. Your body, your business. And as someone who's jealous of everyone cruising through Costco on a Rascal, I'm well aware that I have zero right to pass judgment. (Personally, if my path to salvation hinges on thirty miles of road marching, then I'm going to be sitting right here with a whiskey sour and a TiVo full of fine, fine Mark Burnett programming. Come and get me, zombies/terrorists/aliens/etc.)

All I'm saying about this woman is that if physical strength and endurance are the key components to your bug-out plan, you should do "some" training, as opposed to "none."

I decide to actively despise her only when I hear of the next step in her genius plan.

"She's going to show up at the Mexican border once she finishes the marathon to her car," Fletch says.

I nod. "Sounds like it, yes."

"And she's confident the border guards will simply stand there with open arms, all, 'Oh, apocalypse in the USA? So sorry. Come on in, friendly Northern Neighbor! You're totally welcome to all our resources! Here, have a chimichanga, señorita! You must be tired after your long trek.'"

"Pfft, I can't get past the cat."

The linchpin of her increasingly ludicrous plan is to *shoot her cat in the head* before she leaves town once hell rains down. Because that's way more humane than allowing her cat to roam free and feast on the plentiful rat community spawned as a direct result of the apocalypse.

Asshole.

As the season progresses, we see one episode with a gal who calls herself the Martha Stewart of prepping, and she demonstrates how to make gourmet meals out of her hoarded cans of goods.

Also? She has bouncy hair.

Hmm.

I was passively interested; now I'm actively so.

Plus, having an emergency store of food that I could turn into tasty dinners doesn't seem like the worst idea I ever heard.

Seriously, *cat execution*, anyone?

I do a little research, and I'll be damned if the Domestic Diva herself hadn't addressed basic emergency preparedness on a show in May of 2007.

Again, hmm.

At any point in time, I have false eyelashes and lash glue in my purse in case I suddenly have to appear on TV, so it's not like I don't appreciate the notion of planning for various contingencies. (No one has ever spontaneously asked me to be on TV, but when they do, I'll be there with big, be-fringed Zooey Deschanel eyes.) What I'm saying is, I've put forth so much effort in lugging around day-to-day preparedness—dental floss! extra socks! spare string of pearls!—that I never really considered emergencies outside of not being properly accessorized.

Mind you, I'm not worried about an actual zombie war, *Fletch*. Rather, my concerns are more pedestrian—tornadoes and blizzards, mainly. Maybe some high winds in the mix. I live in a particularly wooded community on a tree-heavy street. I can't walk anywhere except to places with more trees, so it would make sense to be ready for what might happen in case the roads are blocked by felled limbs.

I also want to be on top of it if a tsunami occurs on the other side of the globe and suddenly production is halted on important everyday items, like moisturizing color-care shampoo and the toilet paper with lotion in it. In fact, I'm still congratulating myself for having the foresight to stock up on o.b. ultra tampons before Johnson & Johnson's inexplicable two-year supply interruption. (P.S. They're back and for sale at Drugstore.com! Don't be suckered into buying a box for seventy-nine bucks on eBay.)

Mainly, though, I'm leery of economic problems, at the macro and micro levels. I worry about the country's finances as well as my household's. Go broke once and I promise you will never forget it. That memory is always right there, looming on the edge of my consciousness.

Ergo, there are a dozen excellent reasons to lay in a few supplies, particularly as this project seems so Martha-esque. Martha's previously detailed the specifics both in print and on video on packing an emergency evacuation bag, as well as tips on readying a first-aid kit.

Even Martha's adorable French bulldogs, Francesca and Sharkey, have gotten in on the act, using their blog to advise pet owners on how to keep animals safe in inclement weather. Prior to Hurricane Irene, Martha posted photos on her blog about tying up wisteria vines. My assumption is that if she has time to worry about wisteria, then she's got the basics like food and water down cold. I have to assume that variations on prepping are at the top of her mind, even if I can't find a specific *Living* piece on exactly what supplies I need to shelter-in-place.

Wait a minute. This is it!

This is my X factor!

I'm going to pursue emergency preparedness as my super-extra-credit Martha project. And I'll have Fletch help . . . even if having him do so confirms that he was right about the zombies the whole time.

Argh.

I guarantee that the basement in Bedford is stocked to the rafters with beautiful beets and gorgeous green beans and zaftig zucchini, all harvested and stored at the peak of freshness, because Martha's perpetually featuring canning recipes and techniques.

Maybe she's been so diligent about canning because she fears nuclear winter, or maybe it's just because this was a great year for apples and tomatoes and she's a huge proponent of seasonal produce. (FYI, she even offers free canning label templates on her Web site, and they are *supercute*.) In her book *Whateverland*, daughter Alexis dishes on how Martha hates to get rid of anything, so I guarantee that if she's in her kitchen filming a segment about canning, then those items will be stored, rather than pitched.

Regardless, the specific reason she might keep extra canned goods on hand is not important; that I believe with my whole heart that they exist is what's key here.

However, the idea of putting up my own fruit and veg scares me. So many things can go wrong, from an exploding pressure cooker to botulism stemming from improperly sterilized tools. The act of canning seems a clear and present danger far more than anything zombie-related. Also? See: *Failure, My Garden, 2011–2012.* I don't have any fresh produce to can; even the frozen bananas are gone now.

This is going to require some research.

Four highly productive weeks of prepping later, I'm at lunch with the girls.

"You guys hear about the storm that's supposed to hit New York? I wonder if it'll impact our trip to Philly?" I ask.

Every year when Stacey's new book comes out, she sponsors a preorder contest that culminates in the two of us heading to a different city to take a reader and his or her best friend to lunch. Last year, we visited Dallas, where I learned an important lesson on why to never request that the stylist make your hair "big" while in Texas. This year's winner lives in Philadelphia, and we're going there week after next. (Shout-out to Jon!)

"I'm sure we'll have no trouble. This hurricane will be like Irene," Stacey says. "Everyone will panic and sandbag the hell out of the entrances to all the Starbucks and then it'll be nothing."

"I don't know," Tracey counters. Tracey is totally Team Fletch when it comes to disasters potentially leading to zombie wars. "What if it's not? They're calling it a superstorm."

"No, they're calling it a Frankenstorm, and now I can't stop saying that word. Frankenstorm, Frankenstorm, Frankenstorm. I even said Frankenstorm in a dream last night," I add. "Frankenstorm is supposed to turn the whole East Coast ass-over-teakettle. Read all about it on WeatherChannel.com."

Stacey's unmoved by my prowess in meteorology. (She's previously been unmoved by my prowess in practicing medicine, stating that a broadband connection to WebMD doesn't mean I'm a doctor.) (No free diagnosis for you, then!)

"Philly will be fine and New York will be fine," Stacey assures me. She practically pats me on the head as she says it.

"You know, Karyn told me when she lived in Brooklyn, she had a hard time getting renter's insurance because of hurricanes," I say. "She was all, 'But this is New York—we don't have hurricanes.' Then I said to her, 'Doesn't Brooklyn sit right on the ocean? Wouldn't it stand to reason that could be a strike zone?' She said the beach was a mile away, but it was a shitty beach, so it never really occurred to her that she could be impacted."

"God, I love Karyn," Gina says. "You talked to her lately?"

"Actually, Karyn and I e-mailed all day yesterday because I showed her this." I gesture to the photo on my phone.

Tracey squints at the small screen. "Is this your basement?"

I can't suppress my enormous grin or overwhelming sense of pride. "Indeed this is my basement, which is no longer just a repository for old Rollerblades and a place for dogs to poop. Check out my emergency readiness, bitches."

The photo does no justice to what's currently happening on the eight-foot-long span of shelves at the bottom of the stairs. I've been systematically snapping up and storing emergency food supplies.

What I'm doing *looks* like hoarding, but would a hoarder have an impeccably organized stash of two months' worth of emergency rations?

Would a hoarder make sure she not only had shelf-stable regular milk (white and chocolate), but also soy milk, evaporated milk, sweetened condensed milk, and powdered milk?

Would a hoarder find and buy not only canned tuna, but also canned salmon, canned beef, canned turkey, canned chicken, canned ham, and canned bacon? (That's right. Canned bacon. It's a real thing.)

Would a hoarder keep a dozen cans of brown bread so her twelve jars of peanut butter, six jars of marshmallow fluff, three quarts of jelly, and industrial-size jar of Nutella wouldn't have to be eaten by the spoonful? (Note: I have no issue with eating Nutella by the spoonful.)

Okay, a hoarder might well have all these items, but she likely wouldn't shelve them all lined up, labels out, by classifications such as "pasta" and "canned fruit" and "soups/chilis." She damn sure wouldn't keep them all organized on a spreadsheet by expiration date for proper stock rotation, either.

I started by purchasing a case of Beefaroni because it could—at least according to my experience coming home drunk from the bars in college—be eaten directly out of the can. I also bought a couple of cases of vegetables and tuna, and I figured that was an excellent start. After all, I wasn't going to become one of those lunatics I watch on TV, right? It's not like I'm stocking up on bullets for the cats.

Then I started researching how to create an emergency pantry, and I fell down the prepper rabbit hole when I realized exactly how woefully unprepared I was. Not only did I not have an nth of what I needed in emergency food stocks. I'd completely overlooked nonedible supplies, like those related to health and hygiene and cleaning. I found extensive lists about what items are most likely to disappear after a disaster. I assumed that there'd be a run on batteries and candles, but did you know that in post-Katrina New Orleans it was almost impossible to find stuff like writing paper and garden seeds and aluminum foil (for hats?) and dog food? I sure didn't.

The more I read, the more I exercised the "buy now with 1-Click" option on Amazon, and my UPS guy is starting to get suspicious about all the clanking boxes full of heavy metal stuff every day.

And now?

Well, let's just say that I'm ready for Frankenstorm, even if I do live a thousand miles away from the ocean. Also? I have a new respect for the participants I see on the show.

Except for the cat killer.

She's still a jerk.

"Funny, I can't recall an instance of Martha going all doomsday," Stacey says. "Is she crocheting gas masks? Perhaps providing tips on elegantly appointing your bomb shelter? This can't possibly dovetail into your project."

"*Au contraire,*" I reply. "Martha has actually done numerous shows about prepping. Look it up."

This is a lie, but it *feels* true.

Stacey's not convinced by my explanation, yet she does stop directly pursuing the Martha argument. She peers at the photo. "What are all these tiny boxes on the right side of the shelf?"

I tell her, "Sardines."

"You *hate* sardines," she says.

I shake my head and cross my arms. "Not true."

"Pfft, *absolutely* true. When you used sardines to lure the Thundercats back home last summer, I clearly remember you almost horking when you got sardine juice on your hand."

Ooh, she's got me with her legal mumbo jumbo.

"Well, sort of true," I admit. "But I don't hate sardines if there's no other source of food. See, my plan was to buy stuff that's cheap and protein-packed, but not so tempting that I'll want to wander down to the basement while on an Ambien bender. Also, this is a source of food for the cats, too. According to the Internet, sardines are a must-have in any competent prepper's pantry."

"According to the Internet, Elvis is alive and well and working at a Krispy Kreme in Michigan," Stacey argues.

"The King did love his doughnuts," Tracey reasons. "*I'm* really impressed with your stash, Jen."

"Thank you. Then my sardines are your sardines and you're welcome in my bunker," I assure her.

Stacey simply rolls her eyes.

"Is there wine in your bunker?" Gina asks.

I nod. "Plenty. We have something like thirty bottles left over from our anniversary party."

"Then I'm in, too," Gina says.

"I've also stocked up on various inexpensive vodkas and tequila for bartering and fuel," I admit. "Between my booze cache and sardine surplus, I plan on making my fortune on the black market when the balloon goes up."

"You let me know how that works out for you." Stacey snorts.

The smug is strong in this one.

"Oh, really? Okay, then—if Frankenstorm knocks us on our asses or if the Huns invade Chicago or something and you're like, 'Jen, Jen, we're starving. Can we come to your house?' I'm going to be all, 'Sardines aren't so funny now, are they?'"

"I promise to apologize to your sardines if the Huns invade," Stacey assures me.

"Fine. Then you can share my sardines when the time comes," I concede.

But she's not having any of my Pop-Tarts stash.

That's for damn sure.

Frankenstorm, now known as Hurricane Sandy, doesn't impact our trip to Philly, but the nor'easter that follows it does, and now we won't make it to Philly until next year. In the storm, Karyn's old hurricane-proof neighborhood is slammed, as is so much of the rest of New York and New Jersey.

I don't have anything funny to say about the hurricane or its aftermath. There's no feeling of impotence greater than sitting on a basement full of bounty with no way to directly share it with those in need. Fortunately, some industrious Brooklyn residents found a way to set up Amazon registries so donors could send items directly to those in need. (The item I donated the most? Ironically, new underwear.)

The scope and breadth of the storm, coupled with the government's inability to quickly aid the affected, has caused me to redouble my efforts in terms of prepping. The concept of "having enough" is so important to me, and the act of stockpiling has been a huge mood elevator. Every time UPS drops off a box, I feel like I'm taking a positive step to ensure our futures. Back in the *Bitter* days, we had an inkling of what it was like to want for basic needs, and I vowed that was the last time this would happen.

I will never be caught without my pants on again.

(Underpants, either.)

T·W·E·N·T·Y

GOBBLE, GOBBLE

"Lemme see. . . ." I glance down at the packing checklist. "Ah, in this box, we should have almond milk, coconut milk, powdered heavy cream, and powdered butter."

"Didn't know a lot of these products existed," Fletch says. We're standing at the table I've set up in front of my prepping shelves. I've had so many shipments come in lately that I need help getting everything unpacked and organized. I've had to annex another whole set of shelves to accommodate my supplies, and now all our holiday decorations are in freestanding tubs in the center of the basement. Fletch didn't want to cede the space, but I'm all, "You want a tidy place to store ornaments, or do you want enough pinto beans to survive a nuclear winter?"

Fletch picks up one of the cans on the table. "What are we going to do with powdered buttermilk?"

I look up from my list and push my sweaty bangs out of my eyes. "Isn't that the whole point of prepping? Right now, I'm not sure what we'd do with powdered buttermilk. But if there's an *event* and we need buttermilk? Boom. Ready."

He nods slowly. "I see."

Fletch, who was originally a hundred percent behind this endeavor, has started to sound more and more Team Stacey, especially now that the boxes of my supplies are too high to see over.

"Oof, this is heavy. Give me a hand, please?" I'm struggling under the weight of a giant rectangular box. "This goes over in pet supplies." He assists me and then I whip out my box cutter and busy myself unpacking all the canned dog food.

"I thought we were just feeding dry food now. Don't we have plenty of that already?" He squints meaningfully at the tower of airtight thirty-gallon tubs I have stacked beneath the stairs. Ever since Hambone saw me filling the tubs, she insists on sitting next to them when she's down here. She's currently standing guard. And drooling.

I hold up a can. "See, these serve double duty. That's why I bought Evanger's. Their dog food is made of human-grade whole foods without additives or preservatives. If things get bad and we burn through our cache of meats, experts advise eating dog food as a cheap, available source of protein. Check out this case of Hunk of Beef—it's like a mini pot roast! Maisy used to like this, and one time I was curious, so I tasted it. Needed salt, but otherwise, fairly tasty and absolutely something we could consume in a pinch. Throw the Evanger's, rice, and some dried veggies in boiling water? Instant stew!"

He crosses his arms and leans back against the furnace. "Good to know, especially since you're spending all our retirement money on dog food. We'll need the Evanger's."

"Wrong. My budget is what we'd been spending on Maisy's kidney medicine. So in a way, it's like she's looking out for us from the great beyond."

Fletch says nothing, only narrowing his lips in response, likely because he knows this is a lie, but he's never going to challenge me when I play the Maisy card. Although her meds were pricey, I've actually stopped buying anything nonessential, like clothes, antiques, or magazines, and instead have funneled all our extra funds into prepping.

He sits down on a large box and watches me arrange the dog food by expiration date. "What's in here?" he asks, pointing down.

I stand back and assess. "Mmmm, not sure. Could be all the big fake rocks we're going to use for rainwater collection under the drain spouts. Or maybe they're the WaterBOBs I ordered. Each bladder holds up to a hundred gallons of freshwater when placed in the bathtub. That reminds me—we should discuss our long-term water storage needs." I have to pause to blot the sweat rolling down the side of my face. Prepping is a great form of cardio!

I continue. "There's a retention pond about a tenth of a mile from here, according to satellite images, and, of course, there's that creek that runs through the Open Lands park down the street. Best-case scenario is getting water directly from the lake, but we'd need a motorized cart to get there, because it's too far to go on foot. I'm looking into those. I'm really intrigued by the ones that run on biodiesel."

"Who wouldn't be?"

"Back to water, though—we should figure out our purification strategy."

He scratches his beard. "Should we?"

I glance up from the box of medical supplies I'm unpacking. "Of course! You know the rule of three—you can go three minutes without air, three days without water, and three weeks without food. Water's too important to leave to chance. I thought we could do something with ultraviolet light, but if the water starts off cloudy, like you'd find in a retaining pond, or, really, Lake Michigan, then it doesn't work as well. Reverse osmosis is wasteful, and you need an electrical source for distillation to work. What if the grid's down?"

"What if, indeed?"

"A certified purifier is the best way to go, but boiling works in a pinch, even though I read it gives the water a funny taste."

"Wouldn't want a funny taste," he agrees.

"Are you humoring me?"

"Not in the least."

I set down my box and walk over to the second shelving unit. "Well, smarty, I've already accommodated for water that might taste bad. See? Look." I point to various cylinders all Vanna White style. "You'll notice that we have an almost unlimited variety of powders to stir into our water—Tang, fruit punch, lemonade, cranberry, and, if we're feeling festive, mojito!"

"I'd hate to think we were heading into the apocalypse without benefit of mojito-flavored water."

"Right? Anyway, help me find a space for these." I shove a handful of foil-wrapped capsules at him.

"And these are?"

"Potassium iodide—they protect your thyroid against radioactive iodine released during—"

"I know what they're for. I just didn't realize you'd ordered them."

I made a place for the pills between a bunch of vitamins and a year's supply of Tylenol PM, which, according to prepper handbooks, are a necessity because people have trouble sleeping during crises. "Good to have them, though, right? I wonder if they work on the dogs. Do dogs have thyroids? I'll have to check. Oh, and next time we're at Pet Supplies Plus, remind me to pick up Fish Mox Forte. Did you know they contain the same ingredient as human antibiotics? And you don't need a prescription."

"Yeah, I saw that episode with you."

"Oh, good, then I don't have to explain."

Fletch's stomach rumbles audibly. "Can you hand me some of those peanut butter–and-cheese crackers?" One of the prepping sites advised stocking lots of ready-to-eat snacks, because in emergencies, people need quick bits of comfort foods, as it makes them feel like things are normal. That's why I also have many packs of individually wrapped cookies, chips, trail mixes, and granola bars, as well as a shit-ton of left-over Halloween candy.

Stupid, nonexistent trick-or-treaters.

"Why do you want the peanut-butter crackers?"

"To eat. I'm starving!"

I shake my head vehemently. "Oh, no. No, no, no. Those are for emergencies."

"We have a hundred packages; I can't have one? Out of a hundred?"

"If we open up the peanut-butter crackers, then you'll have crackers and then I'll want crackers and then there won't be any crackers left when the big one hits."

"What *big one* in particular?"

"Whatever big one! You wanted me to be prepared? Well, this is what prepared looks like."

He sinks back onto his box throne. "This is unbelievable. I should just be hungry?"

"Better now than later. You'll thank me one day for being disciplined. Besides, I don't want to open any packaging. For long-term storage, we're going to need a bunch of those number ten buckets, as well as packets to prevent oxidization. And speaking of, I've been looking for a local LDS cannery—where the Mormons get their supplies. I found one in Naperville, but I'm not sure they sell to nonmembers."

Fletch idly thumbs through my "fire-starter shelf," which is full of waterproof matches, flints, and lighters, as well as mini camp stoves, lanterns, and Mylar blankets. "I have to hand it to you—you've really thrown yourself into this project."

"It made sense. Not only am I helping to safeguard our future, but I feel like I've embraced all the principles of Martha here. Although I can't say that my foray into prepping meets the letter of Martha's laws, I'm convinced that it satisfies the spirit of them. Everything Martha features in her books and magazines and on her shows—whether it's canning or building your own chicken coop, or just preparing a tasty apple pie—in some way improves people's quality of life. And I'm convinced being ready for the unexpected will absolutely improve *our* quality of life, you know?"

"I agree, even though I don't think one set of crackers is going to send our whole world crashing down."

"Probably not, but do you really want to take that risk?"

Truly, I believe that being ready in case of disaster is an important tenet in the whole Tao of Martha, that specifically being: Proper preparation ensures a better tomorrow.

"Well, I'm going back up to the surface to get a snack." He begins to climb the stairs, while Libby and Loki trail behind him. Hambone stays by the binned food. See? She appreciates my preps.

"Thank you for your help. I'm probably good from here." And I am good. I'm locked and loaded for whatever may come our way next.

He gets halfway up the stairs before poking his head around the corner. "Hey, I just realized—isn't Thanksgiving this Thursday?"

Shit.

How did I not realize that Thanksgiving is Thursday?
This Thursday?
As in four days from now?

How do I spend eleven months following in Martha's footsteps, only to screw up the one holiday that counts more than all the rest in the *Living* playbook?

WTF, self?

I feel like that marathon runner on *Seinfeld* who overslept and missed the Olympics.

Of course, Christmas is a big deal in the Martha universe, but that holiday entails events all month long, from baking to decking the halls to parties, yet everything comes down to one crucial day on Thanksgiving.

Thanksgiving is the big dance!

Thanksgiving is the Super Bowl of homemaking!

This day brings in every element I've been concentrating on all year, from organizing to cleaning to entertaining. And decorating and, duh, *cooking*. There's even a pet management element in regard to not letting dogs eat turkey bones (and keeping asshole cats off the buffet). And I didn't even realize it because I've been so busy rearranging cans of turkey SPAM.

What is *wrong* with me?

I knew Thanksgiving came particularly early this year, but I still wasn't expecting it for at least another week. Shoot, I haven't even reserved an organic turkey yet! ("I'll take 'The Most Overprivileged, First-World Complaint to Ever Be Uttered' for a hundred, Alec!")

I go directly to my office to look at my calendar to make sure he's not just messing with me. Please, please, please . . . Crap, he's not.

I gather up all my recipes folders and cookbooks and dash back to the kitchen to start making a list of everything I'll need to execute this day with so little notice.

Damn it.

Just doing the pies alone will take me an entire day, because I want to make crusts from scratch. I'll need to have the carpets cleaned, the linens have to be dry-cleaned, or at least laundered and pressed, I have to figure out a menu, followed by making an actual guest list, and then I have to grocery shop and buy liquor and I'm already overwhelmed.

I pound my fist on the table and scream in frustration and the dogs scramble.

Oh, great, now I'm stressing them out, too.

I just don't know how I let this slip past me, except that we have TiVo and I never see any commercials about Black Friday sales. Also, I don't work in an office, where all of us would have been counting down the days to this four-day weekend for a month.

If Joanna and her family were coming, she and I would have been discussing plans for weeks. Last year, I deferred everything to Joanna and her superior-registered-dietitian-industrial-kitchen management skills, and the day was outstanding. Our goal was to eat at five p.m., and we missed that goal . . . by a single minute, largely because we were half in the bag by then. However, her brother's coming into town this year, so she's hosting at her house. She's invited us there, but I feel obligated by the spirit of the project to do the day on my own.

I start tearing through my recipes and I'm getting more and more anxious. Haven't I been learning to improve my skill set since January so that I could take this holiday in stride? All I wanted last year at that fateful dinner party was to be able to make a nice evening for my friends and sit down and enjoy their company. And yet with my lack of planning and forethought on this event, I've pretty much guaranteed I'm still going to be a sweaty mess, thrusting recipes at guests when they walk in the door, and forcing them to help cook. This is not how I envisioned the day, at least not again.

I'm in a full-on lather by the time Fletch strolls into the kitchen. I've got stacks of magazines open next to half a dozen cookbooks, plus I'm concurrently Googling on my iPad and phone, while scrawling away on a piece of paper. He sees the state I'm in and settles into the chair across from me. "So . . ." he says, grabbing an apple from the bowl. "Excited for Thanksgiving?"

He snickers and then ducks as I whip a magazine at him.

"I'm sorry. I'm sorry, but you should see yourself right now. You look possessed. Maybe you should slow down."

I snap, "Maybe you should help me figure out a goddamned plan for this goddamned day."

"That's the spirit!"

I scowl and continue to frantically paw through all my material. He strokes his beard and watches me furiously tear out pages and make notes. Then he polishes the apple on his shirt and takes a juicy bite. What is it about people casually eating apples that's so infuriating? There's nothing inherently aggravating about someone eating grapes or an orange, but an apple? Puts me right into the red zone.

He takes another loud crunch. "You think Martha's busy swearing at her family right now?"

"No, I suspect Thanksgiving didn't sneak up on her like a criminal in a dark alley."

He munches some more and I feel my hands balling into fists. "She's likely pretty Zen about the whole day?"

"I'd imagine so, yes."

"Let me ask you something—do you even *want* to host Thanksgiving this year?"

I don't hesitate to answer. "Of course I do! It's our tradition! I want to make a huge meal from scratch and I want to have the house perfect and I want to have the Christmas decorations hung so as soon as we finish eating we can have a big Clark W. Griswold moment and light everything and we can all sing 'Joy to the World' just like in *Christmas Vacation*. I want to demonstrate everything I learned this year."

"As do I. But I have to wonder, if you were so into the idea of the massive, traditional Thanksgiving, wouldn't you have started earlier?"

"I didn't know, and it's not like you were reminding me!"

"Yeah, but did you even actively solicit that information? If you were so excited, wouldn't you have had your menu planned weeks in advance, like you did for the Fourth? You were finalizing shopping lists for that party at the beginning of June. Remember in 2011, when you were running through Target on July third looking for 'something flaggy,' you vowed that you would take your time and do the day up this year?"

"Which we did," I agree. "And we had a great time. Even as worried as I was about poor little Maisy that day, I was still able to enjoy the party."

He wipes a stray bit of juice from his beard and rolls the core into a paper napkin. "And what did you realize? What is the Tao in this situation?"

"Fletch, clearly you're driving at something. Just tell me, okay? I'd love your help and I. Do. Not. Have. Time. For whatever mystical shaman guessing game you're playing."

"Taoism's about going with the flow, about not swimming upstream, about not struggling against nature."

Exasperated, I reply, "Thank you, Professor Fletcher. Does that mean I should or should not make Martha's creamed onions with sage?"

"What does the Tao tell you?"

"The Tao tells me that your philosophizing is making me stabby. I need more doing and less thinking. Can you please call Stanley Steemer to see if they can come in the next two days and then check to see if the tablecloth is clean?"

He doesn't burst from his chair and fly into motion like I'd hoped. "Let me phrase it like this—do you want to live in the kitchen for the next four days, sweating your ass off while you make a meal it will take twenty minutes to eat? Do you want to attack a pile of dishes for three hours afterward? Do you want to spend a week eating old turkey and cranberry sauce because that's all we have room for in the fridge?"

I lay down my pen. Am I delusional from all the time I've been in the basement, or is he making sense?

"Of course not. At least, not when you put it like that. But we can't not have Thanksgiving, not after all of this." I gesture to the piles of recipes.

Yet the idea of *not* slaving away for four days isn't without appeal. I'm currently on deadline, too, and I hate to think of how far behind I'll be if I take the next four days off to cook and clean. Plus, I've been a little obsessed about what all the Hurricane Sandy victims are doing for the holidays. I've donated as much as I can, yet no matter how much I give, there's a part of me that feels really guilty about having a big celebration this year when so many others are having a terrible time of it. Seems . . . disrespectful.

"Can't we? What's stopping us from calling a TV time-out this year?"

"What about Gina, Lee, and Tracey? I'd feel awful bailing at the last minute."

The dogs have been monitoring my panic level, and it must be down an acceptable amount, because they've stationed themselves back around the table, each of them eyeing Fletch's napkin-wrapped apple core.

"Listen," he says, "we've monopolized them at half a dozen huge parties this year; is it possible that they have other friends and family who'd like to see them for a holiday? Be honest with them—they'll understand why we want to cancel."

Freaking out for the next four days really *does* seem counterintuitive to what I've been working for this year. The Tao principle that I keep encountering again and again is that all Martha's undertakings *seem* effortless because they *are* effortless, and right now throwing a proper holiday celebration seems like the ultimate haul upstream.

As I reflect, I realize that I've been so enthusiastic about disaster prepping because I want a system in place to shelter not just Fletch and me, but all the important players in my life. I don't need to stuff a turkey to show the girls how much I care; my sardines speak for me.

Of course, I've lost my head a little bit in the execution, but only because my heart's been so firmly in the right place.

I immediately get hold of the girls, and they're exactly as understanding as Fletch assured me they would be.

So it's a plan—Thanksgiving is canceled.

And the level of relief I feel at not having to coordinate the whole day tells me that this was the right call.

We have Thanksgiving with Joanna, Michael, and family, and it's lovely.

Martha spent her Thanksgiving sick in bed with salmonella poisoning.

She figured it came from all the raw turkeys she handled on the *Today* show.

This fact shouldn't make me feel better about my choice to bail on orchestrating the day, yet it does anyway. Martha didn't host Thanksgiving and the world didn't end.

Get well soon, Martha.

Christmas will be here faster than we think.

T·W·E·N·T·Y-O·N·E

NOT SEMIHOMEMADE

With the holiday season rapidly approaching, my thoughts turn to what kind of gifts I'll give this year. As Martha has devoted thousands of column inches and months of video to the notion of handmade presents, I can't exactly dole out Amazon.com gift cards this year.

(Again.)

I figure doing homemade gifts will trigger a number of my guaranteed happiness increasers—I'll have fun, I'll engage in the creative process while learning something new, I'll feel a sense of achievement once I'm finished, and I'll likely make my friends happy, which will lead to praise.

We're nothing but win here!

So, now I'm tasked with deciding what to make. Festive cookies are a no-brainer, of course. I've made holiday platters by the truckload every year since I had my first postcollege apartment in 1996. I could bake long before I could ever fix a non-sandwich-based supper. Baking is an excellent way to become familiar with the kitchen, because it doesn't require specialized knowledge, expensive equipment, or a vocabulary that includes the word *sous-vide*. If you can read and if you have a ten-dollar Pyrex pan, you can make seven-layer bars.

To be clear, if you're a shearling-coat-clad IKEA monkey—or Sandra Lee—you can make seven-layer bars, since all they require is dumping one ingredient on top of another. Cocktails optional.

(Yes, I still detest Sandra Lee and her semihomemade lifestyle. Throwing acorns on a store-bought Kwanzaa cake isn't cooking, and sticking a plastic plant in a pot isn't decorating, no matter how drunk you are.)

Baking's relatively easy if you use a recipe from a trusted source and are careful with measurements/oven temperature. Follow the directions and your end result will be edible. Granted, more complex, multistepped recipes exist—like the goddamned Momofuku crack pie I attempted for Thanksgiving that made me want to kill self-comma-others—but in general, even a novice can bang together a batch of oatmeal scotchies.

Yes, baking is science, but it's not *rocket* science.

Cooking well involves more experience and finesse . . . especially when freestyling a meal instead of following a recipe word for word. Time and practice are the most important ingredients in developing a palate, understanding how to pair flavors, and, most important, learning how to fix mistakes. Like if your stew seems overly salty? Did you know you can add potato chunks or milk or lemon juice? Is your tomato sauce New Black levels of bitter? Experienced cooks swirl in a little butter or baking soda. (As someone who spent years forcing Fletch to eat overly salty stews and bitter tomato sauces, trust me when I say I'm as proficient at employing fixes now as I was at ruining things previously.)

Anyway, food gifts are an absolute given, but cookies are a bonus gift-with-purchase in my mind. They're not a stand-alone present. I don't want to be all, "Thanks for the Jo Malone bath oil! Here, have a Snickerdoodle for your trouble."

(Hint: I would love Jo Malone bath oil, particularly Nectarine Blossom and Honey.) (No one's bought me any yet—likely because I don't deserve it—but hope springs eternal.)

I'm superpsyched for baking season to begin. I've been eyeing cookie photos on Pinterest for the past month. I'm still winnowing down recipe finalists, but the one treat I know I'm making is kind of a cheat. I always do white chocolate–dipped Oreos because they're fast, they're tasty, and they nicely contrast with my predominantly milk chocolate-based offerings. This year, though, I'm taking the little dippers to the next level.

I found a recipe on LulutheBaker.com where the author inserted sticks, turning the cookies into lollipops. Then she individually wrapped the top of the pop in clear cellophane and tied the bottom shut with  red and white craft string. So professional! These dipped pops look like something I'd happily buy at Fannie May for a buck apiece. I've already gathered all the materials, too, in case there's a run on clear cellophane in mid-December. (BTW, Martha makes the perfect striped craft string. Of course she does.)

What's going to make this recipe my own is using Trader Joe's Candy Cane Joe-Joes, which is like an Oreo, only it has a pepperminty center. The cream filling in the regular Oreos isn't thick enough, so the author suggested Double Stuf. The Candy Cane Joe-Joes are thin like regular Oreos, so my plan is to pry them apart and restick two cream sides together to make my own ad hoc Double Stuf. Then I'll take the spare cookie shells, smash them, and use them for piecrust. Brilliant! I'm like how the Indians would use every part of the buffalo, except with cookies.

But back to the business at hand—as for what else to make, I'm tasking myself with trying something new. Initially, I considered learning to sew, but sewing is completely unforgiving. Do it wrong and everyone can tell. I won't be happy if my presents make friends feel bad, all, "Shit, seeing Jen today. Better swap out my Kate Spade for the amorphous-blob sack she claims to be a purse."

Having had Fletch help me with a couple of seams over the summer, I finally accept that my inability to sew in a straight line is pathological. The sewing machine's gas pedal makes me supernervous, and I'm always afraid I'm going to stitch over my finger. As I want to have a little fun while I do the craft, sewing is out, because I don't see an upside and it makes me too anxious.

What else could I do?

My best option here is going directly to the source: the 1993 edition of *Handmade Christmas: The Best of Martha Stewart Living.*

A quick observation right off the bat—Martha uses Mario Badescu skin-care products, which I know because I bought them, too, based on her blurb. All the little jars are matchy-matchy and adorable, and I appreciate how cute they are in the basket next to my sink. Granted, sometimes I'm so tired when I get ready for bed that I just use a couple of pumps of hand soap, but that's not the point. The point is that Martha's on the cover of this thing, and she looks better now than she did twenty years ago—and she's served hard time since then! It's got to be the Badescu.

Right in the beginning of the book, Martha demonstrates how to make moss balls, which are strips of moss wrapped around Styrofoam forms. The end result is all organic and beautiful, and I envision these on white tablecloths and stacked in bowls.

To shape the balls, it's necessary to soak large strips of moss until pliable. There's a shot of a bowl of fetid moss water where Martha's squeezing out the extra liquid. Ugh. And mind you, this picture has been approved by whichever stylist worked on this book. So if the by-product is this level of gross while fancied up, I don't even want to know what it would be like in real life. Also, have you ever *smelled* wet moss? It's a lot like mold, only earthier. Frankly, if I want to get up close and personal with the stench of wet dirt, I'll hug the dogs. Think I'll pass on this project.

Next up is a handmade wreath crafted entirely with succulents, and it is stunning. However, with the amount of pricey succulents used to craft this magnificent wreath, I could buy something even more spectacular and have enough cash left over for a lunch (with wine!). (Then I could invite Sandra Lee!)

I freaking love the Christmas tree Martha's decorated with seashells and starfish bedecked in silver dragées, but that's more of a project I'd do for myself and not for a gift. Giving your friends handmade Christmas tree ornaments is like buying your friends a bra—like, the *thought* is there, but it's an oddly personal choice and almost certain not to fit. Moving on.

Okay, this? This I love. Martha's made an ornament tree, which reminds me of those big French profiterole desserts. Small round ornaments of various-size pearls and metals are all stacked together in the shape of a tree, and they're displayed in a vintage urn. I'm talking seriously elegant and gorgeous. According to the directions, the longer you have the tree, the more of an aged patina will develop on the ornaments. Perfect.

To make the tree, it looks like I'll need approximately 250 glass balls, a Styrofoam cone, and a hot-glue gun. Simple. Then I'll start gluing from the bottom. Once I hit the ornament with the hot glue, I'll hold it in place for a minute, which means . . . which means this project will take approximately 250 minutes, or a little over four hours.

Four hours?

Is this a joke?

Are you *high*, 1990s Martha?

I don't have four extra hours to do anything, and if I did, I'd certainly not use them to hold balls in place. Four hours! The only person who'd have four hours to glue balls is the one who's going all Benjamin Button on her book covers. So, no. Moving on.

When I page to the gift section of the book, I find that I can take acorns and turn them into tiny boxes, shaped . . . exactly like acorns. What? Acorn boxes would be the ideal size if I were gifting someone, say, a contact lens or a couple of rocks of crack, which *clearly I would have been smoking when I decided to turn an acorn into a present box in the first place.*

I don't mean to go all *Whatever, Martha,* here, but when I watch her show now and listen to her on the radio and read her magazine, every single thing she says is gold. Her projects are either useful or beautiful or mindful of the environment, and often all three. But this stuff from the 1990s? It's bat-shit, bug-fuck, banana-sandwich crazy.

I can't blame Martha, though. The 1990s were a weird time for many of us. No one was themselves. Dirty hair was in style, for crying out loud. When this book was published, I was running around in cargo shorts over long underwear, wearing ragg wool socks, Birkenstocks, and flannel shirts tied around my waist. I was the L.L.Bean version of grunge. What I'm saying is, people made bad decisions back then.

When I get to the point where Martha demonstrates how to dip my own particularly phallic-shaped candles, I'm done. I'm not going to be the gal who gives all her girls wax d-i-l-d-o-s for Christmas.

Maybe I'll just come up with handmade gifts on my own.

What might I be able
to make that doesn't en-
tail four hours, a hot-glue
gun, and six months of
merciless lunchtime teas-
ing due to an unfortunate
dick-candle incident?

I dig the idea of nee-
dlepoint and am desper-
ately in love with the

cross-stitch piece my friend Wendy made for me a few years ago. I adore
when the delivery of a sentiment is completely counterintuitive to the
medium in which it's expressed.

(This also neatly explains why any movie where kids swear is my
favorite. Love you, *Role Models*!)

While I was on my last book tour, I found myself watching *Ice Loves
Coco* (more charming than I imagined) (yes, I hate myself a little), and
there's an episode where Ice and Coco are looking at new houses. One
place had an amazing guest room, but that was a deal breaker for Ice.
Great guest rooms are so welcoming that they encourage people to stay
awhile, and Ice found that problematic. He said he wanted his guest
room to express the sentiment, "Don't get too comfortable here; motherfuckers need to *leave*," which I thought would be the best quote ever
to cross-stitch for a guest room pillow. However, needlepoint requires
reading glasses—over my dead, squinty body—and the ability to count.
So my filthy cross-stitch pipe dream remains just that.

I figure my best bet for inspiration is to wander around the craft
store. Maybe if I hit Michaels when I'm not five seconds away from a
moment of human urgency, I'll hate it less.

Off I go.

The jewelry-making section is at the front of the store, and I spend

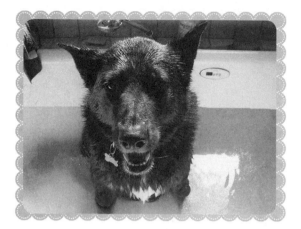

a decent amount of time contemplating this avenue. Martha doesn't do much with jewelry making on her Web site, but I do find instructions for making horsehair bracelets, which I really like.

Problem is, I don't have any horses in need of a haircut. All I have is a large black German shepherd with appropriately long bits of fur on his tail and flanks.

Would anyone want a Loki-hair bracelet? Considering we had him treated for both Swamp Ass and Jungle Balls again this summer, my guess is no. (It's a too-much-swimming-not-enough-drying thing. He's fine.)

As I wander the aisles, I muse on each offering. Turns out I am pro–nonpornographic candle making, but all the patterns I see would look best in Jack Tripper's apartment or perhaps as a hostess gift for Mrs. Roper's next party. Ditto on the macramé plant holders.

Nope, keep walking.

Glass etching intrigues me, but it seems pretty random. I'd probably go all meta and want to etch an image of a glass on a glass and no one would appreciate that but me.

I stroll and consider.

Love the idea of doing scrimshaw, but Michaels is fresh out of whalebone.

Years ago my brother used to practice whittling with a bar of soap and a butter knife. That always seemed fun, but if I give Stacey a bar of Irish Spring shaped like a duck's head, I'm never going to hear the end of it. As it is, she's still snickering about my Thanksgiving-killing dooms-day preps.

Back to the task at hand: I'm not painting/sketching anything, be-cause my entire artistic repertoire consists of primitively drawn pigs, bananas, and pineapples, and that brings us back to the whole awkward "Oh, no, she's coming over; hang the atrocity" business.

Besides, my friends with kids already have enough shitty artwork in their house.

I contemplate making everyone a birdhouse but suspect Fletch doesn't have time to Tom Sawyer them up for me when they go off the rails. Or, worse yet, when I have to use the power saw myself and I lose my middle finger. Then I'll never be able to drive in Chicago traffic!

In the back corner of the store, I finally hit pay dirt in the form of yarn. I've never successfully worked a knitting needle before, but as a kid, I had one of those little loom dealies and I used to make my Barbies all sorts of mod tube tops. I consider a long, straight loom that practically guarantees that any idiot could operate it. Hey, I'm an idiot! I bet I could work this! I suddenly envision many, many scarves in my friends' futures.

Looms are great, because they don't require knitting needles, so there's no need to be ultracoordinated. Simply wind the yarn around a series of pegs and then loop the yarn over with a little pick. Seems quick and easy, two of my favorite traits. Plus, unlike birdhouse making, I could knit in front of the television and keep all my fingers. Sold!

On my way toward the front of the store, I also grab a kit to make a latch-hook bald eagle tapestry for my friend Tracey. As she never once mocked me for my sardine cache, she deserves something extra special.

As soon as I get home, I bust open the yarn and begin to make my first scarf. It's slow going and, until I get used to the pick digging into my finger, the process will be a tiny bit uncomfortable, but in no way pro-

hibitive. The unexpected bonus while I make the scarf is that the knitting causes me to reflect on the recipient, which gives me an extra burst of happiness. I mean, ultimately isn't that what everyone wants? For their inner circle to spontaneously think nice thoughts of them?

The first scarf is for my friend Caprice as part of her housewarming present. She's really willowy and tends to get chilly, so I make this one extra thick and wide, remembering how the last time she was here, she cranked the temperature up to eighty degrees and shivered into her heated seat . . . on a fifty-degree day. I imagine her wearing the scarf I'm making and being grateful for its warmth. Plus, she's profoundly thoughtful, so I suspect she'll appreciate my attempts, dropped stitches and all.

I'm slowly learning that the old adage about the thought counting most isn't just something cheap people say to justify a chintzy present. The thought has become my call to action. When Caprice bought her new house in LA, my initial instinct was to send a Jonathan Adler gift certificate. She likes his stuff, and with a couple of clicks, I'd be done and I could put a big old check mark on the "Satisfied Housewarming Present Requirement" box. But my year of Martha has inspired me to do more than that, to make the effort. Ordering a gift would have taken moments, and it's one step removed from saying, "Here's a handful of five-dollar bills. Knock yourself out." So it's suddenly important that my housewarming gift be special, thoughtful, and personal.

Caprice moved to a famous old part of LA, so I felt my housewarming present should relate to her new neighborhood. I have another friend who collects really specific vintage postcards; thus I'm always on the lookout for her brand when I hit vintage shops. That's when I remembered that I'd run across all kinds of cool old LA postcards, so I headed to the antiques mall.

After searching through dozens of vendors' shoe boxes across the complex, I found five amazing black-and-white postcards featuring different shots of the Farmers Market back when it was hosted on a racetrack. Then I took them to one of the you-frame-it shops and put them all together in a collage that was not only incredibly cool and old-school, but also neutral enough to blend in with any decor. The picture is ready to ship, as soon as the scarf's complete.

My secondary purpose in knitting her a scarf is also utilitarian. What I'm making her is so thick and soft, it will neatly protect her framed postcards in shipping. In providing the one-two punch of considerate and practical, I feel like I just won at life!

When I do finally finish Caprice's scarf—and it takes forever—I'm struck by yet another Tao tenet: Semihomemade is as appropriate and welcome as, say, semiliterate, semisweet, or seminude. Which is to say, not at all. Give me actual homemade, or forget it.

Ooh, better yet:

Despite sometimes being affiliated with the pathological penny-pinchers, nothing says, "I love you" like a gift from the heart *and* the hands.

Although I have to wonder . . . where did I come up with the notion that handmade gifts were inexpensive? I've been working with a lot of baby alpaca and merino wool, and some of these pieces are running sixty bucks in material alone. Add in the cost of my time, and this scarf, this loopy, sloppy, love-filled scarf, would retail for more. Significantly more.

So I'm probably not going to quit my day job (as it were) to professionally loom scarves.

But I will have all kinds of fun making these thoughtful gifts for everyone I care about. And if in giving them I *happen* to receive some fine-quality Jo Malone products in return?

I won't complain.

I've developed a callus on my finger. Look at it, all hard and lumpy! Ha!

I'M A PROFESSIONAL KNITTER, BITCHES!!

I'm Aware Now, Damn It

Back in Crocktober, before I pledged my love everlasting to a skein of yarn, I was perusing Martha's tweets for inspiration. Turns out I found it . . . but not in the way I expected. While searching for ideas on the game night I hosted for my birthday, I ran across her tweet on how it's Breast Cancer Awareness Month. That made me think about mammograms. Mind you, mammograms are a shitty party theme, although I suspect our girl could pull it off. But seriously, they're a must, especially if you're over forty. So I quickly scheduled an appointment because I was overdue and then went back to sourcing the very best baked potato salad recipe.

Of course, I then *missed* my appointment because I'm an idiot who can't read a calendar when she's busy planning a game night. I was supposed to show up on a Thursday at one p.m., but in my head, I thought it was Friday. Damn it. Because apparently *everyone* calls to schedule their yearly scan in October (excellent job on raising awareness, all you purveyors of pink), this time I can't get in until the Friday after Thanksgiving, three weeks later.

I had my baseline mammogram taken last year, so I'm not particularly concerned about this time around. After just completing my well-woman exam, I'm reminded of what a big fan I am of any medical procedure that allows me to wear pants. I feel like I'd particularly excel at therapy. All that lying down fully dressed on big leather couches and complaining about the perceived wrongs in my life? That is *so* in my wheelhouse. I could knit while I was there, too. Plus, with the possible end result of having mood-altering pharmaceuticals prescribed? Yes! But I'm on an even mental keel, because I actively avoid situations that make me nuts, so mammogram it is.

The last time I came to the Women's Center for my exam, there were Quaker Chewy Granola Bars in lobby, but today there's only coffee. I'm not left waiting long enough to enjoy a cup or a (missing) bar, yet I'm disappointed all the same, because I brought my loom with me and I was hoping to get in a few rows before I'm called.

This knitting thing?

It's become an obsession.

I love the immediacy of knitting. In five minutes, I can create an entire inch of scarf. And if I make a mistake? Pfft, no big deal. Pull a few loops and it's like it never even happened. I've not yet graduated to fancy stitching or projects outside of scarves, but I'll get there. Plus, I'm naturally fidgety, so knitting gives me an outlet for nervous movement, and it really calms me down. And there's something about the wrist action of knitting on a loom that counteracts the wrist pain I feel when I type a lot.

When I sit down with a full TiVo cache and a skein of yarn, my whole being exhales. There's something incredibly calming about the repetitive motion. I'd say knitting produces the same kind of Zen as meditation for me, but when I'm finished, I have mental clarity *and* a new pair of socks.

The best part of this new, productive hobby is that both Laurie and Gina are knitters—who knew? Gina's even the founder of a local chapter of a drink-and-knit group called the Stitch 'n' Bitch. And Laurie? Laurie's up on all the hot knitting spots on the North Shore and introduced me to the most amazing yarn shop called Three Bags Full. (Never in my life did I predict I'd use the words "amazing" and "yarn shop" in the same sentence. Never.)

One of goals in living a year via Martha's dictates has been a desire to bond more with my friends. I love that by simply discovering a somewhat esoteric, mutually agreed upon, and highly productive hobby, I've advanced that mission. We're all about knitting get-togethers now and have an entirely new subject of conversation.

Anyway, I don't get to knit while I'm here in the Women's Center, but I also don't have to wait. I guess that's fine, too. I follow the nurse down the hall, and upon arrival in the digital imaging room I disrobe in front of the big machine. The technician twists and pulls my lady bits into place like so much bread dough, and it's more uncomfortable than I remember. She has trouble lining all my parts up properly and tells me, "Your breasts are misbehaving today, aren't they?"

I respond, "No, they're always like this," because what else could I say? What, like they need the naughty corner? Like they should go to bed without dessert?

The scans aren't as quick as last time and I'm not sure why. It's possible that the food baby I created at Thanksgiving may be to blame, because it's throwing off my whole midsection. Brussels sprouts lardons and raspberry cheesecake, I'm looking at you.

Regardless, I'm in and out in twenty-five minutes and right on time to meet Laurie for coffee.

"How'd it go?" she asks.

"Took a little longer than last time. The technician said 'the girls' were misbehaving."

Laurie is puzzled. "What does that mean?"

"I don't know. Considering they didn't just poop on the living room rug again or steal someone's identity, I'd say they were model citizens. I guess the issue was she couldn't get my . . . *stuff* to point straight." I give an inadvertent shudder, not only about the process, but also at almost saying n-i-p-p-l-e in the middle of Starbucks.

Laurie nods anxiously. "Mine never do either. Damn gravity. But otherwise everything was okay?"

I wave off her concerns. "Yeah, except they didn't have Quaker Chewy Granola Bars this time. Plus, breast cancer is the last thing in the world I'm worried about. I have so many other fears. Like rolling blackouts? Yes. Food shortages? Uh-huh. Getting my shoelace caught in an escalator and having it chew off my leg before help arrives? Sure, but less so once I bought a new pair of loafers. Zombie wars? Well, still no there, but I did finally watch *The Walking Dead* with Fletch last week while I was knitting and now I'm a little bit more concerned. But, honestly—the one thing I don't worry about is breast cancer—I never smoked and there's no family history."

"Not much on my side, either. One of my great-aunts had it in the fifties, but she lived another thirty years," Laurie tells me.

I stir my gingerbread latte before taking a sip. "The way I see it, between my terrible driving skills, my love affair with butter, and Hambone perpetually trying to trip me as I walk down the stairs, I'll meet my fate in an entirely different manner. S'all good." I blot a bit of whipped cream from my lip. "Ooh, speaking of good, guess what UPS brought today? Wait, you'll never guess, so I'll tell you. My Hostess cases!"

"Your what?"

Apparently Laurie isn't quite as keyed into the Wide World of Snack Cakes, so I explain how the minute I heard rumors of Hostess going belly-up, I stocked up on a case each of Twinkies, Fruit Pies, Ho Hos, Zingers, and cupcakes because that seemed like such a Martha thing to do. In fact, my foresight inspired a whole new tenet in the Tao: No one ever regrets positioning themselves ahead of a trend. (Within the auspices of securities and exchange law, of course.)

Laurie scrunches her brow. "Martha would *never* buy Twinkies. She'd create a far superior homemade version, with lighter-than-air angel food cake and decadent crème fraîche filling. They would be fabulous and she'd tend her herbs while they were in the oven." She says this without a trace of cynicism. When Laurie's sons were small, she'd tune in to Martha's show while they napped. She said Martha's world gave her a peek into the sanity and civility that would one day again be hers. Sometimes that was all she needed to recharge from chasing after two little boys all day.

I concede, "I'm sure you're right, but the larger point here is *business-related*, not cake-related. I swooped in right under the wire with my order, as the next day, Hostess announced they were shutting their doors. People are selling Twinkies now for a thousand dollars on eBay. I'm going to be rich, rich, rich!"

Laurie seems skeptical. "Are they *listed* for that price or are they *selling* for that price? Because there's a major difference."

Kind of like how my scarves are *worth* eight thousand dollars but no one would ever *pay* that?

"Um . . . I'll look into it." But I sure hope the Hostess products are fetching that price, because plan A is to hoard and eventually sell them for so much that I can buy a midsize island in the Caribbean. That is, if plan B—scarfing them all down myself after a bad day—doesn't interfere with my brilliant business model. "Also? I've had to hide the boxes from

Fletch. He doesn't understand that Twinkies are for *saving*, not for *snacking*. It's like he doesn't understand the first thing about personal finance."

We turn our conversation to more important things, like mohair vs. merino, books, Thanksgiving recaps, and how brilliant Claire Danes is on *Homeland* (I worship you, grown-up Angela Chase), and neither mammograms nor errant breasts crosses my mind again until the phone rings today.

"Hello?" I answer.

"Hello, I'm calling from Lake Forest Hospital—may I speak with Jennifer?"

"That's me," I say, already cursing Fletch in my head. I love that man with my whole heart, but if he can't eventually figure out our new electronic bill pay system, I will be forced to end him. Last month, he paid the gas bill three times and the cable bill not at all, which I learned only when I couldn't rent *Magic Mike* on pay-per-view. (Channing Tatum is a national treasure. There. I said it.) So I assume they're calling about an unpaid invoice and I will bring this up in calm but stern tones in our next State of the Why-Is-Quicken-So-Damn-Perplexing-to-You Union.

"Hi, Jennifer, I'm calling from the Women's Center about your mammogram. The radiologist found a point of interest and she'd like you to return for another scan."

Point of interest?

"Like . . . a scenic overlook or Yosemite National Park?" I ask.

"Er, no. Like a point of interest."

I flop down at the desk in the kitchen. "I'm sorry; I don't understand."

"The radiologist has asked to take another look."

I'm still not grasping why she's calling. "This isn't about a missing copay from my ER visit for food poisoning last year?" Oh, my God, that was awful. I was barfing so hard that I burst blood vessels in my eyes. "Word of advice? Avoid the pistachio mousse birthday cake from Rolf's."

"Um, I wouldn't know anything about that. I'm calling about your results."

I'm a little obtuse here. "Why?"

"Because there's a point of interest."

Um, no, there's not. I guarantee you there's nothing interesting about the ol' spice rack. Did I not mention I don't have a family history? Because *I don't have a family history.* I mean, you're welcome to call me about a bill Fletch spaced out about or a pending zombie war. That I'd believe. But the potential for breast cancer? No. Not happening. I say nothing in return.

"I'm sorry, Jennifer? Would you like to schedule an appointment while we're on the phone?"

When I went to my appointment on Friday, I wasn't supposed to wear any lotion, perfume, powder, or deodorant. Yet I knew they had wipes in the dressing room, so I figured I could be properly moisturized and stink-free while I ran my errands in the morning. I'd wipe away the evidence once I changed into the gown. So, does my point of interest have to do with using the antiperspirant that takes armpits to underarms in a week?

Well, now I'm mad.

What kind of cheap-ass wipes are they using that they don't remove all the deodorant, forcing the hospital to call people at home and get them all worried?

"The appointment? May we schedule it?"

I take a deep, calming breath before answering. "Yes, of course. Sorry. I'll take your next available, if possible."

"Okay, let me see. . . . I can get you in on December eleventh."

"That's three weeks from now! You don't have anything sooner? I mean, on the off chance that this isn't a deodorant issue, then I feel like I should come in sooner rather than later."

The caller sounds truly apologetic. "I'm so sorry, but that's the first open slot. However, if there's a cancellation, we'll call you. But the way that works is, we go down the list and we don't leave messages, so if we call and you're not there, we go to the next person." She repeats my home number to make sure that's the best way to reach me and then we say good-bye, whereupon I immediately begin to panic in earnest.

Normally the first thing I'd do is run to WebMD, but if I go there, I'll spend the next three weeks making myself crazy. Every time I cough, I'll assume that not only is it due to breast cancer, but it's now spread to my lungs and I won't have time to get my affairs in order or finish the taupe baby-alpaca scarf I'm knitting for Stacey. WebMD's all well and good when I'm diagnosing myself with nonexistent illnesses, but this has the potential to be *real*. There's not a thing I can do right now, so the less information I can twist in my head, the better.

The cruelest irony of all is that this is the exact kind of situation that calls for self-medication with fine, fine Hostess products, but they're my retirement plan and I can't touch them. Because my foot still aches enough that pacing's a burden, I instead channel my nervous energy into the loom. Before I even know it, I've knitted sixteen inches of stress.

That's when I'm struck with a particularly morbid thought—if I die, then maybe this scarf really could fetch eight thousand dollars.

Fletch spends the whole night trying to talk me down while I furiously loop my loom.

"You're worried, understandably so. But I looked it up—these things are almost always nothing," he reasons. "What the radiologist saw was probably just some spray tanner."

"Acknowledged," I say. "Yet what sucks is I have *three weeks* to worry about this until the nothingness is confirmed."

Fletch rubs my shoulder, which, because of my tension level, is up around my ear. "If the doctor thought this was a problem, you'd be moved to the head of the line, if for no reason other than their own liability. You're fine."

"Thanks, Dr. Fletcher."

"Now let's forget our troubles with some Fruit Pies."

"Not happening," I say for the millionth time.

Yet he has made me feel better. If this were a big deal, the hospital would bring me in sooner. That makes so much sense. This is nothing. Or this is something seriously stupid, like a smudge from where the doctor was eating an oily sub sandwich while reading my films.

You know, I did have this done on the Friday after Thanksgiving. Stands to reason that all the experienced doctors were off with their family and it was the B team in the radiology lab that day, with their bagged lunches of greasy Italian antipasto.

Yes.

That's totally what happened. The new gal on staff looked at my oil-and-vinegar-covered film and she couldn't differentiate between cancer and a tiny bite of capicola. Now, just to be sure, she's bringing me back in December because this is No. Big. Deal.

I'm fine.

Fine.

I'm so fine that I'm actually able to fall asleep at a normal time.

Fine.

I don't even toss and turn.

Fine.

Which is why I wake up so easily when the hospital calls me at seven thirty a.m. the next morning.

They want me to come in tomorrow.

Not fine.

Fletch comes to the Women's Center with me. Even though he has to sit in the main waiting area away from where I'll be, I feel better having him close.

I was much more careful this morning and pointedly ignored my usual lotioning/deodorizing/spray-tanning routine, hopping straight from the shower into my clothes. I'm a lot less cavalier today as I change into my hospital gown. The last time I was here, I removed my pearls because I wasn't sure if they could do the scan with them on. I wonder if that somehow skewed my luck. Today, I'm not taking any chances and I leave them on.

The last time I was here I locked my bag in my assigned cubbyhole. However, I may be waiting as long as two hours. I want to have all my personal electronics with me, as well as my knitting, so I carry my hand-bag into the waiting room with me. All the other women glance up at me, like, "Hey . . . *that's* a really good idea." Within minutes, each of them returns with her own purse. They don't don their pearls, but perhaps their talismans are different.

I must be with the point-of-interest crowd today, because no one is in and out like for a regular mammogram. Also? Everyone in here is completely quiet. The silence consumes us, wrapping us all in a layer of hushed, anxious reflection. Usually whenever there are two or more la-dies together, you can't help but start a conversation, e.g., "Hey, those are supercute boots," or, "Mammograms, amirite?" But not here, not now.

The women keep getting called to the back and then they come out and wait some more. That's when I notice that the slimmer women are wearing little hospital-issue button-up tunics, while the larger ladies are in the full-on gown tops.

Great.

So I have cancer *and* I'm fat. Today rocks.

I've whipped through about fifteen rows of my knitting when I'm finally called back for this round of mammograms.

"How are you?" the smiley technician asks as we make our way down the hall.

"Pretty nervous," I admit.

Worrying about what could be has cracked open a vault of fear and anxiety I haven't experienced since the dot-com crash, when we were on the precipice of losing everything. I wasn't even this afraid when Maisy was sick. At least with her, I knew I was ultimately responsible for making her feel safe and happy. So showered was she in love that she never had an inkling her health was deteriorating. Because of me, she had ten and a half years of utter happiness, and one bad morning. Having the ability to keep her comfortable was a massive comfort to me. But this? I feel like I have no control in this situation, and I hate that more than anything.

The worst part of our *Bitter* days wasn't the dramatic downgrade of our lifestyle. What made it so rough was the loss of choice. We were powerless as to what was happening to us, no matter how hard we tried to fight it. We were stuck living by other people's dictates. I think that's why I've been able to make peace with losing Maisy. There was never a treatment we couldn't pursue. We weren't encumbered by outside factors and we had control over the outcomes. We had the freedom to try alternative therapies again and again until Maisy herself decided we were done.

By recognizing and naming my fear, I'm hoping that will help me keep it at bay, or at least allow me to feel like I have a modicum of control.

And yet I have a keen appreciation for the work I've done stockpiling happiness. If I weren't in the positive state of mind that I've been in, this would be a million times worse.

"Seriously," I say, "I'm borderline petrified right now."

As we walk, the tech nods understandingly. "Most of the time, this is really nothing. What's likely to happen is that we take this set of films, the radiologist has another look, and all is well, so we send you home."

I exhale hard. "So . . . it's probably just spray tanner?"

"Uh, I'm not familiar with that being a problem, but let's find out for sure."

Buoyed by her positive attitude, I attempt to stop terror-sweating—ironic, because in a situation like this, I really could use some antiperspirant. I adjust my pearls, because that's pretty much the only thing under my control right now.

I notice the poses I'm put in are different from last time. The tech seems to be concentrating on the exact area where my underwire digs in on my right side when I slouch. I can't stop trying to rationalize causation other than the Big C. "Is it possible the weird results came from my bra? Like maybe it's scar tissue or a callus or something?"

I mean, I did develop one on my primary pick-wielding finger, so it stands to reason that my body would respond in kind to a pokey bra.

"Did your bra cause any sort of trauma?" she queries.

"You mean, outside of my being the only girl wearing one in sixth-grade gym class?" I ask.

Why?

Why do I do this?

Why am I compelled to turn every stressful situation into *The Jen Lancaster Amateur Comedy Hour*? I attempt to shake off my ham-handed attempts at humor and answer seriously. "No. No trauma."

"Well, have your breasts been causing you any problems?"

Okay, stop. Get ahold of yourself. Do not deliver your stupid panic-induced punch line. Do not say, "Problems? Like kiting checks?" or "Like grand theft auto?" or "Like they're all of a sudden cracking corny jokes à la Henny Youngman in the middle of a serious medical procedure?"

I take a deep breath.

Do not try for the funny. You will fail and it will not make you feel better.

"Problems like truancy?"

Oh, my God, self, *shut up*, *shut up*, *shut up.*

The tech seems puzzled, so I give her another nervous laugh and say, "No, no problems."

Today's scans are extra squashy-making, and I literally have to bite my tongue to not blurt out anything pancake-joke related.

As we walk back to the waiting area, the tech explains next steps. "The radiologist will look at your film now. If she's satisfied, we'll send you home. If she has any more questions, we'll have to do an ultrasound."

"Well, then I hope I'm knocked out before I make it to regionals," I say, settling back into my seat. ARGH.

Someone please find me some surgical tape that I can slap over my stupid mouth. Perhaps I need to knit myself a gag. Unsure of what else to do, I pull out my loom.

My thoughts turn to Martha, and I imagine her stress-knitting in the early days at Alderson Federal Prison. She seems so real to me right now. Oddly enough, this is the first time I've really thought of her as an actual person with thoughts and feelings and anxieties, rather than the face representing the entity of Martha Stewart Living Omnimedia. Yet it wasn't MSLO who handled prison with dignity and grace; it was Martha herself.

Before I can ponder more, the tech returns, but she's not as smiley as before. "We want you to come back again—the radiologist needs to see a few more views."

My tension level ratchets up another notch and I touch my pearls for luck. This is where she's *supposed* to tell me that I'm fine and I can go home.

There's more posing, more squashing, and more sweating, but no definitive answers yet. As we return to the waiting area, the tech says, "Now, don't worry if this takes a while. There are a couple of films ahead of yours, so the delay doesn't mean anything except that the doctor is busy, okay?"

I thank her and return to my knitting. That's when a nurse asks the woman with the bobbed hair to come in and speak with the doctor. The woman pales in her shorty gown and gulps audibly. There are eight of us in this waiting room. Statistics say that one out of eight women gets breast cancer, and I wonder if I'm the only one in our group doing the math right now. I don't wish any bad on anyone, but given the choice between me and someone else? I choose not me.

When the tech returns, she needs more film, and that's when I start to hyperventilate. She's all business this time and tells me, "We're going to have to do an ultrasound. After I take these, I'm bringing you right to the ultrasound room."

So I make it to regionals after all.

I walk on wobbly knees to the darkened room across the hallway. My hands are shaking too hard to grab my knitting this time as my mind begins to race. No one's said there's any kind of problem yet, and I'm ninety-nine percent sure that everything I'm having done is simply about being thorough. Intellectually, I realize there's no cause for alarm, but I wish someone would tell my adrenal system. Right now my heart feels like it's going to fly clean out of my chest and I can barely catch a breath. My dark thoughts return with a vengeance.

Coming face-to-face with my own mortality was not on the agenda for today. I'd hoped to go to the grocery store, maybe do some light yarn shopping. The last thing I expected was to sit in a moodily lit room and wonder what Fletch might do without me. Who'd make sure he never runs out of milk for his cereal? Who'd cook him a pork roast whenever he had a bad day? Who'd double-check the electronic bill pay records to guarantee *Magic Mike* would be available on demand? Who'd hold Edina by the scruff while Fletch put the Prozac in her mouth? These are important jobs, and I need to be here to fulfill them.

I don't want to be sick.

I don't want to go through treatment.

I don't want my life to change.

Hell, I finally found a decent suburban colorist; I don't want to lose my stupid hair.

I feel like working on uncovering the Tao of Martha has helped me crack the code on how to make myself and those around me happy. That's important. That has meaning. I'm in no way ready to give that up. I've come too far already.

The ultrasound technician enters and explains the process. She asks if I've ever had an ultrasound.

I reply, "I had one scheduled twenty-five years ago for possible fibroids, but the lab was running late on the morning of my test and I couldn't hold all the water I was required to drink. Right before my test I had to pee, so they couldn't do a reading with an empty bladder. I was supposed to come back, but then I got busy. For twenty-five years, apparently."

"So, no?"

I nod.

The ultrasound tech squeezes some of the gel on old Rightie and I'm pleasantly surprised it's not shockingly cold. "I thought the gel was always freezing," I say. "Or is every medical procedure I've ever seen on TV a lie?"

Oh, good. I haven't yet lost that certain *jackass sais quoi* that makes me who I am.

"We use a warmer," she says. "Why make anyone more uncomfortable than they already are, right?"

Yes, I think to myself. *That's* my *job*.

The ultrasound tech runs the wand over my trouble area and explains, "What we saw is a bright point that wasn't there before. Generally, these spots are nothing more than a little tissue thickening, but it's cause for a second look." She moves the wand back and forth, her eyes fixed on the screen back behind my head. She nods to herself and then tells me, "I'm going to have the radiologist see you, but honestly? Right now, I'm not encountering anything problematic."

YES!

THANK YOU, JESUS!

THANK YOU, MARTHA STEWART!

THANK YOU, ALPACA YARN CO!

But right as I begin to plan my one hundredth birthday party, the technician clucks her tongue and begins to concentrate on a previously unchecked section that's low on my right rib cage, about six inches southwest of my armpit.

"Huh," she says.

Huh?!

There is no *huh*! There is only "Looks floppy, but great; see you next year!"

She presses the wand down more firmly and takes steady, measured breaths. Then she tells me she's going to get the radiologist and I'm welcome to sit up if I'd like.

"Sure, that'd be terrific. It'll be easier for me to throw up that way," I reply. I'm pretty sure I'm not joking.

The doctor comes in and introduces herself. She has me lie back and begins her scan. The ultrasound tech taps on the screen and says, "That's the spot I was telling you about." The doctor repositions the wand and begins to press.

Okay, I say to myself. *This is fine. She's going to look at this area for ten seconds and I'll be fine. I'll be able to put my pants on, roll on some Secret, and I'll be good to go. Perhaps we'll go out for sub sandwiches, since Fletch has been waiting so long.*

I count to ten, and when she doesn't finish pressing, I up my count to twenty. She'll be done here in twenty seconds; I just know it.

Correction. Thirty seconds.

Fifty seconds.

Okay. Let's be done at sixty seconds.

By sixty, I meant seventy.

Shit.

Eighty seconds?

Please?

After almost one hundred and twenty excruciating seconds the doctor is finished. Finally.

The ultrasound technician hands me a towel. "Here, you can use this to wipe off."

"That's what she said," I reply.

Holy crap, I hate me sometimes.

Or maybe I don't?

Maybe these one-liners are the little bits of happiness trying to manifest themselves?

"You're set," the doctor says, and I cover myself. "Now, here's what I found—there's a lymph node that we're only now seeing because we took so many shots of the bright spot. Most likely it's been there your whole life and it's no more worrisome than, say, a blood vessel. What I'd suggest—"

I interrupt. "Is this bad or am I okay? If I'm okay, then I'm not telling you how to do your job, but maybe you want to lead with the good news."

The ultrasound tech lets out a tiny snort in the darkness.

I'm instantly mortified by my fat, uncontrollable mouth, but that's when it occurs to me that my humor is a self-defense mechanism. Even though I may come off like a stark raving asshat, being funny is the most important tool I have to stay sane. The ability to say what I think is the key to allowing me to feel in control.

So my perpetual inappropriate quips have value in keeping me happy . . . even though they might also cause me to have to knit the radiologist an "I'm Sorry I'm Such an Asshole" ascot.

Fortunately the doctor has a sense of humor, or at least a decent bedside manner. "Yes, you're okay. We're going to keep an eye on the spot and we'll have you back in six months for a recheck. But you're fine. Although there's no way to prevent breast cancer . . ."

I interject, "Dr. Oz and his superfoods beg to differ. Related note? My friend Lisa appeared on Dr. Oz after she went public with her weight loss from having the gastric sleeve. I was all, 'Did he ask you about your bowel movements?' That question is his home-run swing, to the point that I have to wonder if he's creepy in real life with the poop chat. I bet at dinner parties, people are like, 'Yo, Oprah—Dr. Doody asked me if my last dump was smooth or like marbles. Please don't seat me next to him ever again.'"

Yep. Still an asshole.

The doctor and tech exchange looks.

Yeah, I've seen those looks before.

"Ahem, yes. As I was about to say, early detection is key. Just be very cognizant of changes and be diligent on your self-exams. So, you're all done and you're free to go."

I nod, letting her information sink in. "Thank you so much. But let me ask you something. When I diagnose this on WebMD—and I will be diagnosing this on WebMD—what specifically do I need to look for? Do I type in 'breast lymph node' or what?"

"You don't have to Google anything. Just come back in six months."

Pfft. I did not earn my imaginary medical degree for nothing, lady.

I make a plan to follow up with my primary-care physician and then I pretty much fly back to the dressing room and into my clothes. I know I've been given the all-clear signal, yet part of me wants to make sure I'm gone before they change their mind. Also, poor Fletch has been waiting for two hours and he must be a wreck. I haven't e-mailed him any updates because I didn't know anything until right now. The last thing I wanted to do was commit my freakout to electronic paper, dredging up all that scared him ten years ago when we lost everything.

When I get to his waiting room, I give him a big thumbs-up. That seems easier than launching into an entire explanation on how I'm the Lake Forest Hospital Women's Center's answer to Jerry Seinfeld. So I simply tell him, "I'm never taking off my pearls again."

While we drive to the sub sandwich shop, Fletch explains that he didn't really grasp the gravity of the situation until a woman came out crying.

"Whoa, wait, which woman?" I ask.

"I think she had one of those bob haircuts?" he says.

I suddenly feel queasy all over again. "What happened?"

"Her doctor said she was cancer-free." I let out an enormous sigh of relief. So she and I are both okay—I hope the other six ladies who were waiting are just as lucky. "She was crying; her husband was crying. Now they're going out for a celebratory lunch. Say, should we be doing something more festive than sub sandwiches?"

I think about how excited Fletch was when we discovered the authentic *Jersey Shore*-looking shop in Deerfield earlier this week. That's what I love so much about having worked on this project. Not only do I understand what it takes to lift my spirits, but I've imparted that wisdom to Fletch, too. We're both so much better at taking the reins when it comes to acting on happiness increasers. With his bliss at the forefront of my mind, there's nowhere else I'd rather go right now.

"We're good," I tell him. Then I open my bag and straighten out the knitting I stashed in there. When I was called back the third time, I just shoved the whole lot in there haphazardly, and I want to untangle the yarn before it's too late.

But it's not too late. All is well. I'm okay.

We pick up our subs and bring them home to eat. We're at the table in the kitchen and Fletch does that thing I see only when he's really content—he smiles when he chews.

I'm okay; ergo, *we're* okay.

"Hey," I say. "I just discovered a new tenet in the Tao. Ready for it? '*Living* is a verb.'"

He chews and nods. "Profound. But what does that mean?"

"That means you never know what tomorrow brings. Today is a gift. You have to embrace the now."

"Seems more of an Oprah thing to say and less Martha," he comments.

Apparently I need to be clearer. "In terms of the tangible, that means you can have Twinkies for dessert."

"Cool." He takes another bite, chews meticulously, and then swallows. "What about the Ding Dongs?

"They're open for business, too."

He grins. "I love today."

I smile back at him. "I love today, too."

But I have no time to swim in the well of emotion.

For I have cookie recipes to ogle . . . and Apology Scarves to knit.

T·W·E·N·T·Y-T·H·R·E·E

AND THEN WE CAME
TO THE END

M̲y gratitude for getting back to the banalities of my life is immea-
surable, and I'm thrilled that my greatest worry at the moment is
treat-based.

Over the course of this year, one of my goals was to learn to cook the
kind of comfort foods that I normally buy premade. I've since mastered
brisket, pulled pork, buffalo chicken, corn pudding, apple pie, and
cheesecake, among other dishes. (Invite me to your next barbecue; you
shan't be sorry!)

None of the above was particularly difficult, either, once I had a few
tries under my belt. Cheesecake's crazy-simple; it's just that it requires a
special pan and a water bath, which always seemed daunting but wasn't.
Given the ease of preparation, I now feel like a huge sucker for paying
ten dollars for a half pound of all things pulled and smoked when I could
have made them at home for pennies on the dollar.

Therefore, when I ran across a recipe for easy toffee, I was all, "Oh, I *got* this." I love toffee like a fat kid loves cake. (I realize this statement is redundant given my present pant size, but humor me, okay?) Good toffee is like crack, which explains why vendors dole it out in tiny cellophane wrappers.

I searched through Martha's repertoire for toffee but I kept running into recipes that required a candy thermometer or were made with corn syrup. Neither of those options worked for me. I recently ruined a batch of cinnamon rolls because my candy thermometer reads a constant seventy degrees, regardless of being immersed in boiling buttermilk.

As for toffee made with corn syrup?

No.

The key to perfect toffee is butter. Each bite should be creamy and melt in your mouth. Corn syrup is too sweet in this instance.

Anyway, this recipe seems like a no-brainer, and I quickly assemble the four required ingredients. I mean, four ingredients? Come on! Easy toffee, indeed.

While I melt butter and brown sugar in a saucepan, I chop walnuts and sprinkle them over a buttered eight-by-eight Pyrex pan. Then I stir some more and admire my beautiful cooking vessel. A few years ago I took a cupcake boot-camp class and we used these amazing copper saucepans that were shaped like soup bowls. I was in awe of how consistently they heated, so when I found out I could order one, I did.

Fifteen phone calls, countless e-mails, and twelve months later, the pan finally arrived. Somewhere around month three, the clerk at the cooking school asked if I wanted to cancel my order, but at that point I was committed. I was going to get my pan, damn it, no matter how long it took.

Really didn't see it taking a year.

Around the sixth month, I figured this was an elaborate ruse to scam my credit card information, and at nine months, I contemplated giving up. But that's when the clerk told me that the French workers were back in the factory and my pan would arrive any day. Ninety days, any day—same diff. Yet the pan was worth the wait.

So, my mixture boils and it already smells heavenly. The sweet tang of the butter makes my mouth water. It's all I can do not to stick my tongue in the middle of it . . . and give myself second-degree burns.

I reduce the heat and stir vigorously. I considered using a wire whisk here, but was afraid if the whole mix became sticky, that would be the wrong tool. So I'd grabbed a white silicone spoon for stirring.

I'm supposed to keep mixing for seven minutes. Around minute five, the toffee bubbles up and then reduces down, turning the most gorgeous caramel color. I want to wear this color, I want to paint my walls this color, and I want to pour this color directly into my maw all shot-girl style. This color is tantamount to *perfection*.

That's when I notice a blob, so I figure the candy's starting to congeal. I must be getting close to being done. Huh. Looks like there's a chunk of unmelted butter in there, which is odd, considering the mix has been boiling for a while now. Weird.

I pull out my spoon to inspect, but all I'm left with is the stem. The bowl of my spoon has completely disintegrated into the toffee. Um . . . apparently I wasn't using silicone. I immediately grab the pan and dump the contents in the garbage disposal, but not before calculating exactly how much melted plastic might be "dangerous" to consume.

Okay, Easy Toffee, that was not your fault.

Let's try this again.

After washing my awesome pan, I reload all the ingredients and begin the boiling/simmering process again. The instructions are very clear that I have to heat and stir for seven minutes. I imagine the timed element is the trade-off for not using a candy thermometer or having to mess around with the "soft ball" stage, which always sounded less like a treat to me and more like a medical condition.

So I boil and then I reduce. Around the four-minute mark, the contents bubble up like they did before, and again my kitchen fills with a heady aroma. This time I'm definitely using a silicone spatula, so all should be well.

Around five minutes, the mix turns dark and begins to swell again. (No soft balls here, amirite?) I reduce the heat a bit more and I continue to stir. Personally, I'd have taken this off the stove at the four-minute mark, but the recipe was really clear about the time constraints, so I keep going.

At minute six, the toffee begins to blacken and smolder. Yeah, I think we're done. The smoke pouring from the pan seems ominous, but maybe this is one of those instances like when roasting marshmallows—the crusty blackness looks horrible, but inside it's an obscenely gooey treat. So I pour the mix onto the walnuts and sprinkle the chocolate chips on top.

As soon as the toffee comes into contact with the nuts and chocolate, it begins to bubble and smoke in earnest and the Pyrex's contents morph into a bowl of molten lava. I quickly reread the recipe and at no point does it mention this should look like Mount St. Helens.

Yet the proof of the pudding is in the eating, so I tentatively dip the end of the spatula in and I blow on it until the candy hardens. Mind you,

I've never *seen* black toffee before, but perhaps that's a thing now.

Black toffee is not a thing now.

This toffee tastes like war or Lucifer's tears. This toffee is a molten pool of broken Christmas promises. If sadness had a flavor, it would be the contents of the Pyrex. Actually, I snagged a tiny bite of the portion with melted spoon in it and it was WAY better than this roiling mass of roofing tar.

Um, listen, Easy Toffee . . . I don't mean to tell you how to do your job, but this is unacceptable. I'm marking you down as Does Not Meet Minimum Standards of Performance. You're on notice. The first batch was clearly my fault, but this time, it's all you.

Because I am not someone who has her ass handed to her by a four-ingredient recipe, I try again.

Apparently, I am someone who has her ass handed to her by a four-ingredient recipe.

Once the smoke dissipates, I take another stab at the toffee.

Five and a half minutes later, I'm ready to stab the toffee.

EASY TOFFEE, YOUR NAME IS A LIE. I CURSE YOUR VERY EXISTENCE.

"Smells like a tire fire in there," Fletch comments from the other room.

Pfft. You should taste it.

I'm determined to not be beaten by this stupid recipe. This time I turn down the heat far lower than recommended. I bet the cook who wrote this recipe doesn't have my miracle pan; ergo, her toffee took longer.

No dice.

Okay, let me revise my previous statement.

Whoever posted this recipe on the Internet is a dangerous person who is responsible for murdering stick after stick after stick of my delicious European butter. He or she is a psychopath intent on ruining the holidays for people who are new to making candy. That person lures you in all friendly-like, all, "Hey! Want some toffee! It's easy! So easy that 'easy' is its middle name!" Then you try it his way, again and again and again and a-goddamned-gain, and you end up with a kitchen that smells like two-for-one day at the crematorium.

Why? Why does someone want to ruin toffee for me? What's the end game? Who are you and what do you have to gain by messing with me? Does the warden know you're posting recipes from the computer in the prison library? Listen, I'M SORRY YOU WEREN'T HUGGED ENOUGH AS A CHILD, OKAY? But don't ruin toffee for innocent bystanders. That's not going to make your daddy love you.

Defeated and redolent of charcoal, I'm down to my last stick of butter. It's do-or-die-or-be-stuck-using-corn-syrup time. I'm going to do this, but I'm going to do it my way. I'm not going to follow the directions; I'm going to follow my instincts. The minute I think everything looks ready, then it will be ready. Seven minutes is for suckers; boil and be done.

Then I melt and stir and reduce, and four minutes into the process, I determine I've reached a stopping point. Gingerly, I remove the pan from the stove and pour the mix over the walnuts. Then I carefully tap out the half cup of chocolate chips and cover the pan with a cookie sheet and place it in the oven—not to bake, just to retain heat—while everything melts together.

Ten minutes later, I inspect the contents. The chocolate's soft enough to spread, so I do so with a clean spatula. Then, per the instructions, I slice the toffee into small portions now before it hardens.

I wait until the concoction's fully cooled before taking an extraordinarily small bite, and I'm immediately struck by how buttery this confection is. Holy cats, this was worth sacrificing almost two pounds of Plugrá. This is amazing! This is delicious! The combination of walnuts, semisweet chocolate, and sweetly caramelized butter is transcendent! These little toffee bites are going to be the star of the show on my holiday cookie platters!

Then? When people ask me how I made it? I'm going to tell them, "I have the best recipe. It's so easy!"

And I will laugh and laugh and laugh.

Christmas is not going to sneak up on me like that asshole Thanksgiving did. I plan to be ready. So, in the next week, I need to prepare a spot for the tree, decorate the mantels, and handcraft some ornaments. I wasn't kidding about glittering the shit out of this Christmas.

I also want to get a jump start on my holiday baking. Unfortunately (for my pants) all the toffee is gone, so I've got to relive that goat rodeo as well as figure out what else I want to bake.

I've finally been able to transition all my baking supplies to the butler's pantry and the ingredients are fairly organized. The last step in this arduous journey is making it pretty. Are aesthetics necessary? Of course not. But putting everything in matching, hermetically sealed jars is so in Martha's wheelhouse that I can't not do this.

I ballpark exactly how many containers I'm going to need and then I head to the Container Store. Honestly, I haven't been in one of these places for years. I always thought their merchandise was overpriced and superfluous. Of course, the last time I was here, I thought dressers and silverware racks were superfluous, so it's definitely been a while.

As I stroll the aisles, I find a million useful items, such as attractive yet sturdy boxes in which to ship my hand-knitted scarves, and adorable gingham waxed paper for lining holiday treat containers. Everything I pass suddenly seems useful to living a more orderly life, and my cart quickly fills. I keep saying to myself, "Do people know about this place?"

I find a whole bunch of simple jars with rubber seals and I pick out sizes that range from sixteen ounces to five quarts. I make sure to grab a few extras, because I suspect once I start putting ingredients in jars, I'm not going to want to stop.

I'm in such a state of excitement when I get to the cash register that I accost the clerk. "I found the best stuff!" I squeal. "Tell me, do people know how awesome this place is?"

She points to the fifteen people who've stacked up in line behind me. "I suspect so."

My total's less than I'd even budgeted, as some of the smaller jars are only two dollars. Plus, when the rubber seals on these things fall apart, they're easily replaced, so I anticipate keeping them indefinitely.

Once home, I wash and dry the jars. Then I systematically transfer the contents from bags and boxes to matching jars. I immediately apply the labels, because there's no way I could determine which is the self-rising flour and which is all-purpose just by sight.

As I fill and organize, I also get a good idea for what my cabinet is missing. For example, I have white, semisweet, and milk-chocolate chips, but no dark chocolate. I keep track of new needs as I continue.

I have to laugh when I come to my container of milk powder. When I made pies to bring to Joanna's house for Thanksgiving, I discovered I required said ingredient, but I had no clue as to what it was. The last thing I wanted to do was to hit the grocery store in search of an esoteric item the night before Thanksgiving. Then I Googled it and found that's just the foodie way to say powdered milk. I've never been more

pleased with myself when I realized I had a whole storehouse of milk powder in my prepping basement. Ha!

Jen—1

Apocalypse—0

From start to finish, I complete my project in just under two hours. Unless you count the six months it took to get everything to this state.

But overall? I'd say this was time well spent.

I live in mortal fear of a Christmas tree fire, so I'm never going to be one of those people strapping a fir to the top of the station wagon on the day after Thanksgiving. In the Big Book of What-if that is my thought process, the optimum day to buy a tree is December 10. It's not so late in the season that only Charlie Brown trees are left, but it's close enough to Christmas that retailers are on their second and third shipments; ergo, the trees are more freshly cut.

I'd originally bookmarked a place in the Chicago area where we could chop down our own Christmas tree, but since they wouldn't let Fletch bring his own chain saw, he wanted no part. Instead, we head to Pasquesi's.

"How tall are our ceilings?" Fletch asks. I grab a cart at the entrance because I want to pick up some potpourri and dog food while we're here.

"You don't remember this conversation from two years ago?" I ask as we walk past the ornaments display.

"Nope."

"Then let me remind you—you guesstimated they were twelve feet high and it turns out we were off by a yard. Don't you recall how we had to hack off a good two feet, and the top branch was all bent over where it touched the ceiling because it was still too tall?"

"That doesn't sound like something I'd do." He zips up his coat as we approach the greenhouse where the trees are displayed.

"I know! You measure everything! So when you said twelve feet, I was all, 'Twelve feet must be shorter than I thought.' I didn't second-guess you at all because you're always so precise. And for once, the person bringing inappropriately sized stuff into the house was you. *That* was satisfying."

"I don't recall."

"Well, it was traumatic for you, so I'm sure you blocked it from your memory. Okay, we're here; how do we do this?" The way Pasquesi's has the trees on display is so smart. Instead of having them all netted and stacked up, each tree is hanging from a line connected to the ceiling. So buyers can not only visualize how full or sparse the whole tree may be—they can see how straight the trunk is.

I quickly locate a staffer. "Hi, excuse me, can you please tell me where the eight-foot trees are?"

"Of course," the friendly clerk replies. "All the eight-footers are in this row, over here are the seven, and beyond that are the six. The ones above eight feet are outside."

"Thank you!"

In terms of selecting the perfect tree, my standards are fairly low. As long as it's not too flammable and it's relatively symmetrical, I'm all set. I cruise down the row of hanging eight-footers, spin a couple of them around, and determine that any one of them would be perfect.

"Here, Fletch, this one's a keeper." I gesture toward a stout green Fraser fir. "Smells really fresh, too."

Fletch casts a discerning eye. "No, not this one. I don't like the trunk. It lists to the right."

"Oh. Didn't notice. Then how about this guy next to it."

He gives it a thorough once-over. "Nope. This isn't it. I don't care for this bare spot."

"But the hole is tiny and the rest of it's so lush. Couldn't this part face the wall?"

"No. It's just not right."

I shrug. "Whatever." I peruse for a couple of minutes and then say, "Here's a nice, full one on the end."

"Hmm." He paces around the tree and then gives it a spin. "I get the feeling everyone's touched this one."

"I have no idea what that means."

"It's on the end. Everyone who's gone by has touched it. It's been *handled*." He scrunches up his face and wriggles his fingers when he says this.

I nod. "So you know, you sound like a crazy person. For the record. Just putting it out there."

We go on like this as we inspect every tree in the row, all of which leave Fletch wanting. At this point, I've had enough. "Here's what's going to happen, Fletch. I'm cold, so I'm going to humor you for the next five minutes, and then I'm going inside to shop for potpourri. If you want my input in the next five minutes, I'm here for you. After that, this is all on you, because I lost the ability to care once my fingers went numb."

After eighteen years, I should remember I'm married to the King of Overcomplication. Right before we got married, I wanted to register for new bedding, as the dogs had pretty much destroyed what we'd been using. We went to a dozen stores and Fletch took issue with every single comforter I liked. Exasperated, I finally said, "Please tell me what's so awesome about the one we have so I can replace it with something identical," to which he replied, "I can't really remember what it looks like." So I picked the one I liked in the first place and he never noticed the difference.

"I just don't *connect* with anything in this row. None of these are the appropriate vehicle for our Christmas."

"But they're all perfect! And they're all the same damn thing!"

"I'll know it when I see it."

I tap my watch with a gloved, yet still-frozen digit. "Tick, tick, tick, four minutes."

We peruse some more and finally Fletch says, "Hey, I think I found one!" He's now a row over from where we were looking.

"Those are seven feet," I remind him. "If that's the size you want, fine, but they're seven feet."

"Yeah, but they seem taller than the eight-foot trees."

"No, they don't. They seem like they're seven feet. They seem like they're a foot shorter than the eight-footers; hence the placement in the seven-foot row."

He's resolute. "I'm pretty sure this is taller."

"Going to buy potpourri now. Lemme know how this all works out for you."

Twenty minutes later, Fletch finds me sniffing diffusers. "Here," I say. "Smell these." I stick a bamboo-scented bottle under his nose, followed by orange verbena.

"I like the first one," he says, gesturing to the bamboo bottle.

"Orange verbena it is. You find us a tree?"

"Yep, and it's perfect. They're giving it a fresh cut and wrapping it up. Once we check out, we pull around to the side and they'll tie it to the car."

"Excellent."

Transaction complete, we head home. Even though we live only a couple of miles from the nursery, that's a long enough ride for us to completely forget the eight-foot fir on the top of the roof, which we discover only once we try to pull into the garage.

If shame had a sound, it would be the scrape of branches against an unyielding garage door, followed by the unremitting braying of a jackass.

After I finish laughing myself into an asthma attack, I say, "Maybe this is one of those bad-luck trees, like the one that split a couple of years ago. Or, oh, remember the one in Bucktown that got so wide we couldn't even walk past it?"

"That won't happen, because I bought the very best tree on the lot."

"You finally found an eight-footer you liked?"

His face is lit by the dashboard when he turns to look at me. "No, I went with one of the seven-foot ones because they were taller."

"Okay, your call. I abdicated from the decision-making process and I'm fine with that. But if at any point you decide this tree is too short, I'm allowed to do the I Was Right dance."

"Deal." Fletch takes my gloved hand and we shake on it.

On Sunday evening, after doing my I Was Right dance, we're at Home Depot looking for another tree. Apparently seven feet *is* shorter than eight feet, regardless of any sort of row-based optical illusion. However, getting a second tree works out well, because I can put the seven-footer in the living room and do that one up with all my handmade decorations. The bigger tree can go in the great room, where we'll deck it with our non–potentially craptacular ornaments.

"This one is fantastic!" Fletch exclaims, knocking the trunk against the ground to dislodge any stray needles. Few fall. "We have a winner."

I peer at the tag. "Sweetie, says here it's ten feet."

"With a fresh cut, it'll work, no problem."

Yeah . . . if you believe in Christmas miracles.

But I don't argue. Instead, I give him a side hug. "If this tree makes you happy, then I'm happy."

With a cheeky grin, he turns to the clerk. "Sold!"

I think we all know how this is going to end.

Everything I hoped to accomplish in this year of *Living* begins to coalesce as we approach Christmas. For example, I have a rollicking good time with Laurie making glittered ornaments and pinecones.

And Joanna and I laugh our butts off decorating sugar cookies while discussing what our eighteen-year-old selves would think of us twenty-seven years later. (Consensus: nerds. Old nerds. I wouldn't have it any other way.)

I'm overwhelmingly proud when everyone genuinely appreciates what I knitted for them.

Using ribbon I had custom-made for the occasion on Martha-recommended Name-Maker.com that read Ho, Ho, Ho, Motherfucker, I had a ridiculously good time putting together Christmas cookie jars for everyone. And is it really the holidays without cookies made to match my first book cover?

Normally when I wrap Christmas presents, I'm in a rush and do so as quickly and sloppily as possible. But this year, having become or-

ganized, I blocked off a whole evening so I could wrap while watching the Christmas episode of *Downton Abbey*, followed by *The Sound of Music*. I believe my happiness is self-evident in the wrap jobs.

In crafting my own swags and greenery displays, I not only save money, but also create something beautiful and festive and welcoming.

Even though it's temporarily hidden by the second tree, I love the vintage dog wall I've started over Maisy's old favorite sitting spot. Although technically, I use English bulldog photos, I feel they perfectly capture Maisy's essence. As I find other items that remind me of her, I'll add them. And if I could somehow make the portraits fart on command, then it would almost be like she was here.

For now, Hambone's doing her best to fulfill that portion of Maisy's legacy.

I still miss Maisy every single day, yet I carry her Tao

with me. I want to be awesome, give awesome, and get awesome, so tonight we've amended our holiday party from last year. Instead of the massive event we threw in 2011, tonight will be a lot more low-key. Mostly it's going to be a bunch of good friends sitting around playing Apples to Apples and Catch Phrase and drinking wine.

The menu's simple, and I cooked all the dishes in the past couple of days, so there's no need to scramble before the gathering. Everything's in a CorningWare pan, ready to be popped in the oven when the time comes. Julia and Finch are already here, and we have enough time before the party that I get to teach her how to make my dipped peppermint pops.

Will tonight be the spectacle that it was last year?

No . . . because it doesn't need to be.

I don't have to host a big party to give 2012 the finger, because in the scheme of things and despite a significant loss, it's been the best year of my life.

By spending the

year in the pursuit of the Tao of Martha, I've indeed gotten my groove back. I feel like me again. I'm substantially happier than I was when I started this year, for reasons great and small. I mean, I like knowing where my shoes are and I don't miss the Drawer of Shame. Having a consistent way of storing everything makes my life so much easier. And if I want to whip up a batch of peppermint pops with my buddy, it's so gratifying to have ingredients in stock and in place so that's possible. I have great appreciation for the fact that Attempted Feline Homicides are down a hundred percent around here.

More important, I'm proud that I've done my part to make this a better year for those I care about. I'm pleased that Fletch (and his beard) have flourished in what's now a more stable, peaceful household. I love that we've honored Maisy's life by rescuing another pit bull. And maybe this sounds weird, but I've had such fun not only discovering my limitations, but finding creative ways to work around them.

As we rapidly approach the end of the year, I'm sorry to see 2012 go,

but I'm excited for a new year as well, as I've finally discovered and come to embrace the ultimate piece of the Tao of Martha:

The only way to fail is not to try.

ACKNOWLEDGMENTS

First, I'd be nowhere without the decades of effort Martha Stewart put in to establish herself as the one true domestic diva. Every time I give a thoughtful and appropriate handmade gift or create a fantastic dinner out of random ingredients, I'm in your debt. Sorry for getting a bit shouty back in the July chapter, but as a dog lover yourself, you likely understand my stress. Anyway, thank you for making me TEAM MARTHA. (And for your buttercream recipe. Always your buttercream recipe.)

Although change is scary, I have to extend major gratitude to super agent, Scott Miller. Having you on board has made all the difference . . . even though it affords Fletch the opportunity to be smug and say, "I told you so." (Pfft, like he doesn't do that anyway.) Seriously, though, cheers to new beginnings!

As always, I'm so appreciative of the gang at New American Library—Kara Welsh, for your continued faith in me; Tracy Bernstein, for your guidance and for pushing me; and Claire Zion, Craig Burke, Melissa Broder, sales and marketing, art, and the production copy editors who are forced to let me slip words like "stabby" into my books. Thank you for everything thing you do.

For Tiffany Ward, Brian Grazer, and my new BFF, Austin Winsberg—wow. You guys are my Dream Team . . . and didn't we almost have it all?

ACKNOWLEDGMENTS

For my girls who helped me with this year's endeavors, I'm the luckiest person in the world to have you in my life. Joanna Schiferl, Julia Pawlik-Fincher, Stacey Ballis, Gina Barge, Tracey Stone, Wendy Hainey, Becca Foster-Goodman, and Angie Felton, I so appreciate you participating in all my schemes, even if you did sometimes mock me. (Not that I didn't deserve it.) I'll totally make room for you in my bunker.

For Laurie Dolan, who was next to me for so much of this project, you rock/you are my rock. (Your choice.) I'm sorry I took years off your life with my ninja watering skills. Please note that Fletch has since confiscated that particular hose nozzle. (And coming up, this is your year.)

Thanks to Caprice Crane and Karyn Bosnak, who participated in spirit (and FaceTime.) And sincere thanks to Lisa Lampanelli, with two caveats: A) Tell Stacey I absolutely WAS bitten by a crab, and B) I'm still waiting for my Best Guest crown and scepter. Please make it happen, or I shall be forced to explain what an estuary is yet again.

I will always be grateful to Drs. Thornhill, Feinmehl, and the rest of the Buffalo Grove Vet Specialty Clinic. Thank you for three bonus years. You are miracle workers.

Even though they can't read this book (or wouldn't care to, given thumbs and an adequate attention span), I have to recognize the pets in my life, particularly my sweet, sweet Maisy. I'm a better me because of you. To the rest of the crew, every time I have to clean up your "deposits" on the living room rug, you help to keep me humble. Actually, that's not really a selling point. It's called housebreaking because you're *breaking my house*. Stop. Seriously. Please, stop.

As always, the cupcake to my buttercream is Fletch. You're the reason for everything, and I'm so happy that I finally engaged in a project that's actively made your life better, too. But isn't it nice that after eighteen years of banana hoarding, drawer stuffing, and sneaking burritos in your car, I finally have it together? You're welcome!

And finally, to my readers . . . to express the depths of my gratitude, I'd like to send Fletch to each of your houses to paint some furniture for you. (Note: Each piece takes six to eight weeks.) Seriously, you're the best, and I couldn't be more grateful. Thank you!!

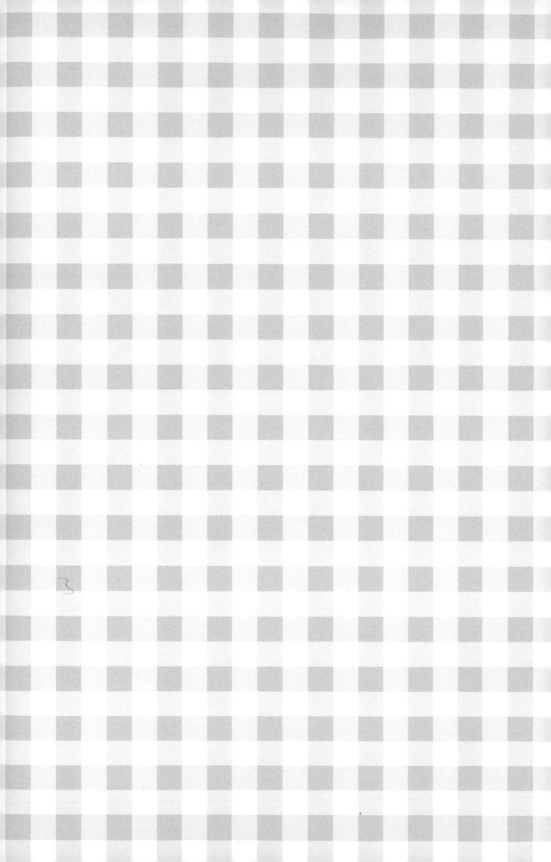